Praise for *21 Great Leaders*

"What a unique combination this book provides! You will discover an intriguing view of twenty-one world-class leaders followed by leadership lessons that will help you grow as an influencer. My friend Pat Williams has written a leadership classic."

John C. Maxwell
New York Times bestselling author

"More and more I am convinced that one of the best ways to teach leadership is through the use of stories. When it comes to storytelling, no one does it better than Pat Williams. His newest book, *21 Great Leaders*, is a tour de force that integrates leadership stories and lessons that will help anyone with the practical insights they can put into practice."

John Baldoni
Internationally recognized leadership educator and executive coach
Author of *MOXIE: The Secret to Bold and Gutsy Leadership* and *Lead with Purpose.*

"Pat Williams' new book *21 Great Leaders* is magnificent. The stories are fascinating and the leadership lessons at the end of each chapter will prove invaluable to leaders at every level."

Frances Hesselbein
President and CEO of the Frances Hesselbein Leadership Institute
Recipient of the Presidential Medal of Freedom

"Leadership may be an elusive commodity these days, but this highly useful collection will serve to remind leaders and would-be leaders alike that they need only look again to proven leaders of the past for the lessons and inspiration they need to face modern challenges. This primer should be read by everyone who aspires to manage and influence others."

Harold Holzer
Chairman of the Lincoln Bicentennial Foundation

"All Americans who love their country can benefit from this important book. Although most political dogs in government are probably too old to learn new tricks, the nation might return to its former glory if they emulated the great leaders Pat Williams describes so brilliantly."

Harlow Giles Unger
Author of *John Marshall, The Chief Justice Who Saved the Nation*

"Wow! What a compelling collection of leaders who personify leadership excellence at the highest level."

John Swofford
Atlantic Coast Conference Commissioner

"In these difficult times, we all need to step up and lead. Pat Williams uses *21 Great Leaders* to show us how."

Dr. Larry J. Sabato
Director, UVA Center for Politics
Author of *The Kennedy Half Century*

"Plutarch, who wrote the biographies of every great man in the ancient world, said their virtues were like a 'looking-glass, in which I may see how to adjust. . .my own life.' Pat Williams holds up twenty-one great men and women from George Washington to Bill Gates as mirrors for our time. Look at them, and learn."

Richard Brookhiser
Author of *Founders' Son: A Life of Abraham Lincoln*

"Pat Williams asks us to join him in observing excellent leadership in twenty-one men and women from across the political spectrum. He has an eye for the revealing anecdote, an ear for different voices, and a knack for storytelling."

Joseph J. Ellis
Author of *Founding Brothers*

"Whether you are involved as a leader in sports, business, or your family, you will find immense value in Pat Williams' book, *21 Great Leaders*. It's a great read full of fantastic stories and practical advice that will increase your influence. You will not be disappointed in this investment into your leadership library."

Mike Slive
Southeastern Conference Commissioner

"*21 Great Leaders* is a thoughtful and insightful reflection on the lives and lessons of leaders—recent and distant—who've made a meaningful difference. Pat's near encyclopedic knowledge of history and leadership, and his extraordinary personal experience as a leader and coach, give this book an authenticity that is incomparable. *21 Great Leaders* is at once a deep meditation and a practical guidebook that you will find useful in becoming the best leader you can be."

Jim Kouzes and Barry Posner
Coauthors of the bestselling *The Leadership Challenge*

21
GREAT LEADERS

Learn Their Lessons, Improve Your Influence

PAT WILLIAMS

WITH JIM DENNEY

SHILOH RUN  PRESS
An Imprint of Barbour Publishing, Inc.

Published by Shiloh Run Press, an imprint of Barbour Publishing, Inc., P.O. Box 719, Uhrichsville, Ohio 44683, www.shilohrunpress.com

Our mission is to publish and distribute inspirational products offering exceptional value and biblical encouragement to the masses.

Member of the
Evangelical Christian
Publishers Association

Printed in the United States of America.

Dedication

This book is dedicated
to my friend John Maxwell,
a great teacher, mentor, and
role model of leadership

Contents

Introduction: *The Seven Sides of Leadership* 9

The First Side of Leadership: VISION 13
1. Walt Disney: *Dream, Believe, Dare, Do!* 15
2. Nelson Mandela: *A Rainbow Vision* 25
3. Steve Jobs: *A Dent in the Universe* 37

The Second Side of Leadership: COMMUNICATION 49
4. Winston Churchill: *Sending Language into Battle* 51
5. Martin Luther King Jr.: *"I Have a Dream"* 60
6. Ronald Reagan: *The Great Communicator* 69

The Third Side of Leadership: PEOPLE SKILLS 79
7. Sam Walton: *The Ten-Foot Rule* 81
8. Franklin D. Roosevelt: *Stricken and Strengthened* 89
9. Pope John Paul II: *The Force of Forgiveness* 98

The Fourth Side of Leadership: CHARACTER 107
10. George Washington: *When the Summons Comes* 109
11. Billy Graham: *Moral Firewalls* 119
12. Theodore Roosevelt: *The Man in the Arena* 128

The Fifth Side of Leadership: COMPETENCE 137
13. Thomas Jefferson: *The Competent Polymath* 139
14. Bill Gates: *Compute—and Compete* 149
15. Dwight D. Eisenhower: *Competent to Decide* 158

The Sixth Side of Leadership: BOLDNESS 167
16. Rosa Parks: *Tired of Giving In* 169
17. Harry S. Truman: *The Buck Stops Here* 178
18. Margaret Thatcher: *The Lady's Not for Turning* 186

The Seventh Side of Leadership: A SERVING HEART 197
19. Gandhi: *The Great Soul* 199
20. Mother Teresa: *In Service to God's Holy Poor* 209
21. Abraham Lincoln: *The Great Emancipator* 219

Notes 233
Acknowledgments 253
Contact Information 255

Introduction

The Seven Sides of Leadership

A leader is one who knows the way,
goes the way, and shows the way.
JOHN C. MAXWELL

My most memorable year as a father was the year we had sixteen teenagers living under the same roof. Every morning at seven, those sixteen teens would gather around our long dining room table for breakfast. I would sit at the head and look down the row of glazed eyes and uncomprehending expressions. I would step into my leadership role and try to get their minds engaged.

We had a daily routine called "The Question of the Morning." Every morning I came up with a new question—something to ignite a spark of cognition in the sleepy recesses of their brains. One morning my question was "Twenty years from now, what are you going to remember about your dad?"

They whispered among themselves—then, David (a future marine) stood up as their spokesman. "Dad," he said, "the thing we'll all remember most is that you were always motivating us."

I had to laugh. My kids had found me out. They knew exactly what I'd been doing: motivating and inspiring them to function together as a team, to work hard in school, to play hard in sports, to keep their rooms neat, to stay out of trouble, to get real with God, and to set high goals for their lives.

In short, I had been practicing leadership in the home.

The point is this: we all are leaders in some arena of our lives—on a national stage, in the workplace, on the campus, or in the home. So we had better give some thought to our leadership roles. We had better find out what leadership demands of us and how to become more effective and influential as leaders.

That's why I wrote this book—and I believe that's why you're reading it.

What Is Leadership?

If you're like most people, you have leadership responsibilities in dozens of arenas in your life—in your home, your profession, your community, your religious life, and your neighborhood. You have a leadership role to play in your blogging and social media, your advocacy for political and social causes, and your service on committees, boards, and juries.

I define leadership as "the ability to achieve difficult, challenging goals through other people." Leadership is an attractive quality that people recognize in an individual who has developed a certain set of traits and skills. Leadership is not bossing people around or manipulating people. Rather, leadership is inspiring people to achieve what they *want* to achieve but could never achieve without the influence of an inspiring, guiding individual.

There are very few "born leaders," people who are genetically gifted with leadership ability. Most leaders are made, not born—and that's good news for you and me. This means leadership can be learned. Leadership ability, including that elusive quality known as "charisma," can be studied and practiced.

Our world is crying out for leaders. Who should the next leader be? The person next to you? The person behind you? Nope, you're it. You're the next business leader, community leader, youth leader, or civic leader our world is looking for.

After decades of study and experience, I've concluded that the essence of leadership comes down to seven key ingredients—the Seven Sides of Leadership:

1. *Vision.* The first task of leadership is envisioning a clear idea of what you want to achieve then inspiring your people to transform your vision into reality.

2. *Communication skills.* Next, the leader must be able to communicate the vision to the team or organization. Communication skills are essential to leadership.

3. *People skills.* Great leaders have the people skills to help people feel confident, energized, and motivated to achieve great things. People skills are vital tools of influence that can be learned and improved with practice.

4. *Character.* Good character is essential to trust. People decide whether or not to follow you based on whether or not they perceive you to be a person of good moral character.

5. *Competence.* People are willing to be led by those with proven competence as leaders. The word *competence* encompasses the word *compete*. Competent leaders make organizations competitive.

6. *Boldness.* Boldness is a form of courage, the willingness to take reasonable risks in order to achieve worthwhile goals. Boldness is not recklessness or throwing caution to the wind. A bold leader seizes timely opportunities, acts firmly and decisively, and avoids second-guessing. The confidence of a bold leader inspires optimism throughout the organization.

7. *A serving heart.* An authentic leader is not a boss but a servant. Followers don't exist to serve the leader; the leader exists to serve, empower, equip, motivate, and inspire the followers. Serve them well, and they will turn your leadership vision into a reality.

Some people are naturally gifted with some of these traits, but I've never known anyone who was born with all seven. Fortunately, the Seven Sides of Leadership are learnable skills. We can acquire them and improve them with practice. The more complete we become in all seven of these traits, the more effective we will be in every leadership arena of our lives.

How to Use This Book

This book consists of twenty-one leadership biographies. Almost every one of these leaders has had a powerful impact on the way we live our lives today. If George Washington or Abraham Lincoln had never lived, if Walt Disney or Steve Jobs had not persevered through setbacks and failures, if Rosa Parks had surrendered to injustice, or if Pope John Paul II or Ronald Reagan had not survived their 1981 assassination attempts, we would be living in a very different world today.

Almost every one of these twenty-one leaders exemplifies all Seven Sides of Leadership (I say "almost," because I see Steve Jobs as a fascinating exception). I could have easily placed Walt Disney in the boldness category, yet I think he best exemplifies a leader of vision. Ronald Reagan foresaw a world beyond Soviet Communism, and that marks him as a man of vision—yet he is justly known as the Great Communicator, so I have placed him in the communication category. Franklin D. Roosevelt was certainly a bold leader, a man of visionary ideas, and a leader who communicated brilliantly through his "fireside chats," yet a close inspection of his career shows that he led largely through his people skills.

None of these leaders was perfect as either a leader or a human being (though two have been beatified as saints). I don't hesitate to show their flaws, because we can learn as much from mistakes and failures as we can from successes. Here are twenty-one flesh-and-blood human beings like you and me. We can emulate their virtues, learn from their flaws, identify with their struggles, and take away lessons that will transform our leadership lives. If you want to lead a team, a company, an industry, or a nation, why not learn from the best?

At the end of each chapter, you'll find a list of leadership lessons I've drawn from the life of each leader. As you read, you may discover some additional insights of your own (if so, please write and share them with me!). The twenty-one leaders in this book are the best the leadership world has to offer. The lessons of their lives and the genius of their words are here to be plucked and savored straight from the vine.

Discover these rich lessons, apply these insights to your leadership life—then go make some leadership history of your own!

Pat Williams
Orlando, Florida
January 15, 2015

The First Side of Leadership

VISION

1

WALT DISNEY

Dream, Believe, Dare, Do!

If you can dream it, you can do it.
WALT DISNEY

In 1986, I moved my family to Orlando, Florida, on a quest to achieve the impossible. I was possessed by a vision to build a new NBA franchise in a city that had no pro sports tradition. My partners and I would have to build a fan base from scratch, create a team out of thin air, and build a world-class sports arena before the NBA would even listen to us.

Many experts told me I was crazy; it would never happen. Miami, maybe. But Orlando? Forget it! But I couldn't forget it. The vision would not let go. So I turned for insight to another dreamer who had come to Orlando and achieved the impossible: Walt Disney. I knew he had also heard throughout his career, "It can't be done!" Yet he had proven the naysayers wrong every time. He had built his Magic Kingdom out of dreams and pixie dust.

I had to know his secrets. So I began an intense study of the life and leadership traits of Walt Disney. Out of that study came a wealth of leadership insight and two of my most popular, bestselling books, *Go for the Magic* and *How to Be Like Walt*.

Though Walt Disney never lived in Orlando (he only visited central Florida a few times before his death), the city bears the imprint of his personality. His vision for Walt Disney World transformed Orlando into a city like no other. The soul of Walt Disney lives in this place.

In those early days, I had many conversations with longtime Disney executives Bob Matheison, Dick Nunis, and Bob Allen. All were personally mentored by Walt. I learned so much about Walt Disney that I felt I knew him personally. Thanks to the lessons I learned from Walt's life, we ultimately achieved our "impossible" dream of the team we call the Orlando Magic.

One summer evening in 1989, I had dinner with Dick Nunis, who started as a Disneyland ride operator in 1955 and ultimately became head of Disney Attractions. Dick told me story after story of Walt's leadership life. I asked him to sum up the success secrets of Walt Disney, and I wrote down his insights on a paper napkin.

"First," Dick said, "Walt had integrity—you could trust him. Second, he could see the future—he was a visionary. Third, he had great people skills and knew how to get the best out of everyone. Fourth, he was a great motivator and coach. Fifth, he was a bold risk taker—but he only took calculated risks. Six, he was eager to learn from everyone. Seventh, he invited people to challenge his ideas so he could continually improve them. Eighth, he looked at every project and problem from all angles. Ninth, he was fanatically committed to excellence."

There were many insights compressed into that brief description of Walt Disney. One that jumped out at me was Dick's statement that Walt "could see the future—he was a visionary." Over the years, I continually encountered similar observations from people who knew Walt.

Imagineer Bob Gurr, who designed many of the vehicles still used at Disneyland, told me, "Walt always saw the entire picture. He was the grand master of the vision." According to film critic Leonard Maltin, "Walt was a futurist. Walt was a visionary. There was no single more forward-thinking person than Walt Disney." And Disney historian Paul Anderson said, "Vision—that was Walt's special gift. He could envision Disneyland in every detail, and he pursued it relentlessly when everyone else predicted failure."

World magazine editor Marvin Olasky described how Walt's vision transcended the times in which he lived: "Walt Disney built his vision in the 1950s and early 1960s when the Cold War was at its height and the likelihood of nuclear disaster seemed high. He wanted Disneyland to be not just a theme park but a portal to a better time and a different world."[1]

Bob Matheison told me about working with Walt during the planning of his Florida project. "Walt was always thinking far out into the future," he said. "He'd become irritated and impatient with our limited thinking. 'You aren't thinking far enough ahead,' he'd say. 'We haven't even begun to think big!'"

Walt died five years before Walt Disney World opened in Florida in 1971. Mike Vance, the creative director of Walt Disney Studios, was there for the opening ceremonies. Someone said to him, "Isn't it too bad Walt Disney didn't live to see this?"

"He did see it," Vance replied. "That's why it's here."[2]

Vision is the First Side of Leadership. Walt Disney set the standard for visionary leaders.

A Good, Hard Failure

Walt Disney was born in Chicago on December 5, 1901. He spent his happiest, most formative years on a farm outside of Marceline, Missouri. There he developed an interest in drawing animals. The Santa Fe railroad passed near the farm, and Walt loved to climb a hill and watch the trains pass by.

When Walt was nine, his family was forced to sell the farm and move to Kansas City, Missouri. There Walt met his boyhood friend Walter Pfeiffer, who introduced him to the world of theater and motion pictures. Those were tough times, and

Walt had to help his father, Elias, deliver newspapers to more than seven hundred customers. Walt arose at 4:30 a.m. and had to finish his route before school. It was exhausting work, and Walt's schoolwork suffered. Throughout his life, Walt had nightmares about delivering newspapers in the snow.

In 1917, Elias Disney moved his family to Chicago. There fifteen-year-old Walt took night courses at the Chicago Academy of Fine Arts. Patriotic to the core, he dropped out of high school at age sixteen to join the army but was turned down for being underage. He joined the Red Cross as an ambulance driver, but by the time he got to France, World War I was over.

In 1919, Walt moved to Kansas City, where his older brother Roy (his future business partner) worked in a bank. Walt took an advertising job at the Pesmen-Rubin Art Studio, where he met animator Ub Iwerks, who later helped Disney create Mickey Mouse. Iwerks was still working at Walt's side forty years later, designing the special effects for *Mary Poppins*.

Walt founded the Laugh-O-Gram Studio in 1922, which produced animated cartoons for theaters in Kansas City. Though his Laugh-O-Gram cartoons and Alice Comedies (combining animation with live action) were wildly popular, the proceeds didn't cover the generous salaries Walt paid to his growing stable of employees. His financial woes grew, and he was evicted from his studio building. In July 1923, he filed for bankruptcy.

Despite having failed, Walt remained optimistic. Though he had only forty dollars in his wallet, he bought a first-class train ticket (he was going in style) and set off for Hollywood.

"It was a big day," Walt later recalled, "the day I got on that Santa Fe California Limited. I was just free and happy."[3] But, he added, "I'd failed. I think it's important to have a good, hard failure when you're young. I learned a lot out of that."[4]

In October 1923, twenty-one-year-old Walt Disney and his brother Roy started the Disney Brothers' Studio, located on Hyperion Avenue in Silver Lake, near Hollywood. Walt convinced Ub Iwerks to join him in California. In 1925, Disney hired Lillian Bounds as an animation cel inker—and after a brief courtship, they wed.

Walt and Ub created a popular cartoon character, Oswald the Lucky Rabbit, only to have the character stolen from them by an unscrupulous distributor, Charles Mintz. (Nearly eighty years later, the Walt Disney Company would trade ABC sports commentator Al Michaels to NBC for the rights to Oswald.) After losing Oswald, Walt and Ub created a new character, Mickey Mouse, inspired by a mouse Walt had tamed at his Kansas City studio.

Other Disney characters followed—the Three Little Pigs, Donald Duck, Goofy, and Mickey's pal Pluto. Walt could have amassed a fortune by churning out an endless supply of animated short features. But a visionary is not content to rest on his or her leadership laurels.

So Walt envisioned a project that was completely unprecedented—a full-length animated feature based on the Brothers Grimm tale *Snow White and the Seven Dwarfs*. Skeptics dubbed the project "Disney's Folly." Walt's wife, Lillian, and brother Roy tried to dissuade him, but Walt's vision possessed him and wouldn't let go. He hired an instructor from the Chouinard Art Institute to teach his animators new techniques for drawing animals and human beings in a realistic way. His technicians invented new special-effects processes.

Snow White began production in 1934—and by mid-1937, the studio was out of money. Walt had mortgaged the studio and his own home. He had nothing left to hock. The scheduled release was a few months away. If Walt couldn't borrow more money and complete the film, the Disney Studio was doomed.

At Roy's insistence, Walt screened a rough cut for Joe Rosenberg, head of studio loans at the Bank of America. They met in the screening room of Walt's Hyperion Avenue studio. The film contained patches of crude pencil animation; some sequences were spliced out of order. After an hour, the film came to an abrupt halt—the ending hadn't been drawn yet. Walt acted out the ending—then he waited for Rosenberg's answer.

"Well, Walt," Rosenberg said, rising, "thank you for showing this to me."

Walt searched Rosenberg's eyes for a positive sign. He found none. He accompanied the banker to the parking lot. Rosenberg got into his car then leaned out the window and said, "Walt, that picture is going to make a hatful of money. You'll get your loan." Those words saved the Disney Studio.

As Joe Rosenberg predicted, *Snow White and the Seven Dwarfs* made a hatful of money—enough for Walt to build a huge new studio complex in Burbank. More full-length features followed—*Pinocchio, Fantasia, Dumbo, Bambi*—creating a pantheon of Disney characters, generating enormous wealth through merchandising, theme parks, and television.

WALT'S "SCREWBALL IDEA"

Walt's vision of Disneyland goes back to his boyhood and a place called Electric Park—an amusement park at 46th Street and the Paseo in Kansas City. Walt and his younger sister, Ruth, often rode the trolley to Electric Park. Like Disneyland, the place featured thrill rides, band concerts, shooting galleries, penny arcades, ice-cream shops, boat rides, nightly fireworks, and a scenic railroad around the park. Walt treasured the memory of sitting beside the train engineer, pulling the cord that blew the steam whistle. Electric Park opened in 1907, at the dawn of the electric age, and featured a hundred thousand electric lightbulbs that transformed it into a fairyland at night.[5]

By the time Walt was in his early thirties, he envisioned building an even greater park of his own. In a news story before Disneyland's grand opening, the *Long Beach Independent-Press-Telegram* (Friday, July 15, 1955) reported, "Plans for this wonderland first began to go on paper as far back as 1932 when Walt's magnificent dream began to take form. In cleaning files at the Burbank studio recently, original Disneyland sketches, bearing the 1932 date, were found."[6] The dream of Disneyland grew stronger after he became a father. Walt recalled:

> Well, it came about when my daughters were very young and Saturday was always Daddy's day with the two daughters. . . . I'd take them to the merry-go-round. . .and as I'd sit while they rode the merry-go-round and did all these things—sit on a bench, you know, eating peanuts—I felt that there should be something built, some kind of amusement enterprise built, where the parents and the children could have fun together. So that's how Disneyland started.[7]

In the summer of 1948, Walt took a train ride that put his Disneyland vision on a fast track. Accompanied by animator and fellow railroad enthusiast, Ward Kimball, Walt boarded the Santa Fe Super Chief, bound for the Railroad Fair in Chicago. There Walt and Ward toured vintage railroad locomotives and cars and talked to old-time railroad men. Each night, the fair put on a dazzling fireworks display over Lake Michigan. Walt was especially impressed by a replica of President Lincoln's funeral train. Lincoln was one of Walt's heroes, and boarding the black-draped train as a band played "The Battle Hymn of the Republic" moved him to tears.

After the fair, Walt and Ward took the Wabash Railway to Dearborn, Michigan, where they visited the Henry Ford Museum and Greenfield Village. Exhibits included historical buildings that Ford had moved to Dearborn from their original sites, including Noah Webster's Connecticut home, the Ohio bicycle shop where the Wright Brothers build the first airplane, and some of the original structures of Thomas Edison's New Jersey laboratory complex. An 1870s steam train circled the grounds.

Walt returned to California with a vision for a project he called Mickey Mouse Park, which he planned to build adjacent to his Burbank studio. Walt's brother Roy dismissed the plan as a "screwball idea." It would be the height of irresponsibility, he said, to risk studio money on Mickey Mouse Park. Walt agreed he wouldn't spend studio money on the park. Out of his own pocket (and without Roy's knowledge), Walt paid Disney artists to draw up plans for his Disney-themed amusement park.

It didn't take long for his vision to outgrow the little patch of land across Riverside Drive. Walt no longer dreamed of a park. He dreamed of a kingdom—a magic kingdom. And circling Walt's enchanted domain like a fire-breathing dragon was a steam-powered train.

Selling the Vision

Harriet Burns was a set painter for Disney's *Mickey Mouse Club* when Walt recruited her to design attractions for his theme park. She told me, "Walt was a simple, honest, basic person with midwestern values. An ethical man. Nothing he did was about money. It was always about the project." It's true. Walt had almost no interest in money, except as a means to finance his expensive visions. Money was his brother Roy's problem. The only currency Walt cared about was imagination. "I plow back everything I make into the company," he said. "I look at it this way: If I can't use the money now, if I can't have fun with it, I'm not going to be able to take it with me."[8]

Walt always dreamed beyond his means. Disneyland was a dream so vast, so expensive, that it was absurd to think he could ever afford it. Yet it exists—because Walt dreamed it.

There was a mule-headed obstinacy to Walt's visionary genius. He once said, "If management likes my projects, I seriously question proceeding. If they disdain them totally, I proceed immediately."[9] Walt believed that if Roy and the board of directors approved his ideas, his vision wasn't big enough. He was satisfied only when his dreams drew active opposition.

In 1952, Roy earmarked $10,000 of studio money for the Disneyland project. It was a tiny sum, but it signaled a huge shift in Roy's thinking. Walt knew that once Roy was in for ten grand, he was in to stay.

Walt created a separate company, WED Enterprises, to design his park, and he recruited top Disney artists and technologists to lend their imagination to the project. Walt invented a concept now called "cross-functional" or "interdisciplinary" teams, drawing people from different fields of expertise to work toward a common goal. His handpicked teams of artists, sculptors, engineers, and machinists combined their creativity to build structures, transportation systems, and thrill rides that had never existed before. Because his WED Enterprises innovators combined functions of imagination and engineering, Walt called them Imagineers.

Harriet Burns told me, "I worked in the art department at WED. Walt would sit on a stool and relax with us because we were so informal. He was always positive, always encouraging us, always contributing his own ideas."

Construction costs for Disneyland far exceeded Walt's original projections. Roy would have to come up with ever more creative sources of funding before the park could open, so he met with executives at all three networks to pitch a *Disneyland* TV show. He came away with an offer from ABC worth $5 million. In exchange, ABC got a sure-fire hit TV show and one-third ownership of Disneyland. The *Disneyland* series convinced powerful financiers that the project was on a firm footing. Soon investors were lining up to lend Walt money.

Disney quietly bought up a patchwork of orange groves in Anaheim, California.

As workers began removing trees and excavating land, Walt took his close friend, TV personality Art Linkletter, to the Anaheim site. Linkletter told me about that visit.

"We drove for miles," he said. "When we got there, I couldn't believe what I saw. There was nothing but orange groves and bare dirt. We were miles from any big population center. I thought Walt had lost his mind. Why would anyone want to put a bunch of roller coasters out in the middle of those orange groves? Why would anyone drive for miles to get there?"

Walt took Art on a tour, describing all the lands of his Magic Kingdom: Main Street U.S.A., Adventureland, Frontierland, Fantasyland, and Tomorrowland. "You've got to get in on this, Art," he said. "Buy up all the property around the park, and just hold it for a few years. Once Disneyland is up and running, you'll be able to sell it to developers for a hundred times what you paid for it."

"I just couldn't see what Walt saw," Art Linkletter told me. "I should have listened to him, but I couldn't grasp his vision. Years later I did a calculation. Every step I took that day was worth about $3 million—or would have been had I taken Walt's advice, I would have been a billionaire. I let it slip through my fingers."

Walt wanted Art to buy property around Disneyland to control the environment around Disneyland. Walt wanted clean, family-friendly surroundings—not the cluster of seedy motels and miniature golf parks that eventually sprang up. As former Disneyland President Jack Lindquist put it, the park was surrounded by "ugly urban sprawl at its worst."[10]

On Sunday, July 17, 1955, Walt hosted a live TV preview of Disneyland. The hour-long TV special was cohosted by Walt's friends Art Linkletter, Robert Cummings, and Ronald Reagan. It was the fulfillment of a vision Walt first glimpsed when he beheld the wonders of Electric Park.

THE CITY OF TOMORROW

At first, Walt said he'd never build another park. But by the late 1950s, he was dreaming even bigger dreams—a Community of Tomorrow in Florida. In 1963, after commissioning numerous studies, Walt was leaning toward Orlando, a sleepy little citrus town in central Florida, as the site of his new project. In November 1963, Walt and his associates flew cross-country in a private plane and viewed the property from the air. "This is it," he said.

Within two years, the land acquisition for the Florida project was nearly complete. The Disney Company had assembled nearly 27,400 acres of Florida real estate—about 43 square miles (for comparison, Manhattan is less than 34 square miles). In October 1965, the Orlando *Sentinel* published speculation that the mysterious Orlando land buyer was Disney. The price of Central Florida real estate skyrocketed—but by that time, the land acquisition was 99 percent complete.

I have studied the plans for Walt's grandest vision. He envisioned nothing less than a futuristic planned community in which thousands of people would live, work, play, and dream. His gift to the human race would be a clean, healthy, utopian community—an Experimental Prototype Community of Tomorrow, or EPCOT. Science-fiction writers have envisioned such a future, but only Walt Disney dared to build it.

Walt's City of Tomorrow would have consisted of fifty well-planned acres, a climate-controlled city beneath a glass dome, with walkways laid out in concentric circles and monorails circling the city. The gentle whoosh of Disney's mass-transit system would eliminate noise and smog. The city hub would feature gleaming high-rise office buildings and entertainment complexes, and one of the outer circles would consist of tree-lined neighborhoods with schools, churches, shopping districts, and parks.

Corporations would test new products in Walt's City of Tomorrow, and their sponsorship would underwrite the city's expenses. Walt devoured every book on urban planning he could find, becoming a self-taught expert on everything from infrastructure to emergency services.

Ralph Kent of the Disney Design Group told me, "Walt Disney was a humanitarian and a utopian. That's what his dream of EPCOT was all about. He was always thinking about how to make life better for the people of the world. He was promoting peace, understanding, and human progress. We'd tell him, 'No one will be interested in that stuff.' Walt said, 'I'll teach by entertaining people.' And he did."

In October 1966, Walt made a promotional film in which he laid out his vision for EPCOT, the City of Tomorrow. In that film, Walt introduced a scale model of his utopian community. He spoke excitedly about his vision for his signature achievement—but just two months after he made that film, Walt Disney died.

After his death, Walt's successors scaled back his dream. His City of Tomorrow was downsized to a theme park. The EPCOT Park opened in 1982; it was a futuristic place, dominated by a 180-foot-tall geodesic dome called Spaceship Earth. It was impressive—but it was not Walt's EPCOT. Without Walt at the helm, his successors didn't know how to build Walt's dream, so they settled for a theme park.

As Walt's grandson, Walter Disney Miller, told me, "EPCOT was my grandfather's biggest dream—the city of the future that would point the way to a better world. His dream remains unbuilt. When he died, the company lost the driving personality that focused the organization's energies on a single goal."

Let's not be too hard on Walt's successors. It may have been wise to downsize his dreams. Without Walt himself at the helm, building his dream might have proved impossible. It's a tragedy for us all that the life of this visionary leader was shortened by cigarette smoking.

Leadership Lessons from Walt Disney

Some say that vision is the ability to see the future. I disagree. No one can see the future. Vision is the ability to *make the future happen*. Vision is a form of creativity. When you see something no one else can see, and *you believe you can make it real* even though everyone says you're crazy, that's vision. Vision is imagination plus action. Without action, a vision is nothing more than a daydream.

A vision must be visual, and it must also be describable in words. A vision is a word picture you can transfer from your imagination to the imagination of others through the art of communication. If you can't communicate your vision, how will you make it real?

The world divides people into "dreamers" and "doers." According to this view, dreamers supposedly have their heads in the clouds. Doers have their feet on the ground. Dreamers deal with what might be; doers deal with what is.

Visionaries don't see the world that way. Visionaries don't distinguish between dreamers and doers. Visionaries *combine* both functions. Visionary leaders have their heads in the clouds and their feet on the ground. They are realistic dreamers. They don't just daydream. They strategize and set goals; they recruit talent and build teams; they communicate their vision; they delegate tasks; they invest endless hours of hard work. They take risks and solve problems. They overcome obstacles and opposition. Visionaries make the impossible possible.

Walt's nephew Roy E. Disney told me, "If Walt had one great gift, it was that he kept his head down and kept trying. Over the years, he was told that his ideas were impractical, impossible, and would never work: 'Walt, you'll lose your shirt on *Snow White*,' or 'Walt, give up this crazy obsession with an amusement park!' Walt knew his ideas were good and the naysayers were wrong. Walt proved that the only way to get things done is by sticking to your ideas and your beliefs."

Visionaries don't foresee the future. They *build* it. You and I are living in the future Walt envisioned and built.

Someone asked Walt how he achieved so much in one lifetime. He replied, "I dream, I test my dreams against my beliefs, I dare to take risks, and I execute my vision to make those dreams come true."[11] That's a concise formulation of visionary leadership. Walt's success formula consists of four parts, which can be summarized in four words: *dream, believe, dare,* and *do*. Let's take a closer look at Walt's success formula:

1. *Dream.* Walt said, "I dream." He begins with a vision of a better future.

2. *Believe.* Walt said, "I test my dreams against my beliefs." Walt made sure that his vision of the future was consistent with his core values. He also made sure he had the confidence, the belief in himself, to accept this bold challenge.

3. *Dare.* Walt said, "I dare to take risks." Walt took counsel of his confidence, not his fears. He wasn't reckless, but he believed in himself, and he bet on himself to win.

4. *Do.* Walt said, "I execute my vision to make those dreams come true." Walt wasn't just a dreamer; he was a doer as well. He focused all his energies on his dreams, he motivated his people to build his dreams, and he turned his dreams into a reality.

Don't worry that you can't see the future. Nobody can. Your vision doesn't exist out there in the future. Your vision exists *within you.* If you can envision it, if you believe in yourself, if you can sacrifice and take risks for your dream, if you can work tirelessly to build it, then you are a visionary leader.

> *Everybody can make their dreams come true. It takes a dream,*
> *faith in it, and hard work. Yet the work isn't all that hard*
> *because it is so much fun you hardly think of it as work.*
> WALT DISNEY

2

NELSON MANDELA

A Rainbow Vision

---

*There are times when a leader must move out
ahead of the flock, go off in a new direction,
confident that he is leading his people the right way.*

NELSON MANDELA

Nelson Mandela was a prince who could never be king. He grew to become something greater than a king. He became a visionary leader.

He was born July 18, 1918, in the village of Mvezo, in South Africa's Cape Province. His clan name was Madiba, and his parents named him Rolihlahla, a Xhosa word that meant literally "tree shaker," someone who shakes things up.

Mandela's patrilineal great-grandfather was Ngubengcuka, a ruler of the Thembu people from 1809 to 1832. Nelson's grandfather was one of Ngubengcuka's many sons. It was a polygamist culture, and Nelson Mandela's lineage was traced through a "lesser" wife, so he was a descendant of the "left-handed house"—of royal blood, but disqualified from the throne.

Nelson's father, Gadla Henry Mphakanyiswa, was a local chief and an adviser to the tribal king. In 1926, when Nelson was eight years old, a white government official accused Gadla of corruption—likely a trumped-up charge. Gadla was a proud man with a stubborn integrity, and he sometimes angered white officials by defying their unjust decrees. The accusation was a devastating blow to Gadla's reputation and self-esteem.

Gadla was a follower of the tribal god Qamata, but Nelson's mother, Gadla's third wife, Nosekeni Fanny, was a Christian. She sent him to a Methodist missionary school when he was seven where he took the English name Nelson. "I defined myself through my father," Nelson recalled, adding that he especially identified with his father's qualities of "a proud rebelliousness, a stubborn sense of fairness."[1]

In 1927, Gadla came down with a lung disease. Nine-year-old Nelson stood at his father's deathbed and watched Gadla draw his last breath. Though Nelson admired his father, he was never close to him. He didn't recall feeling grief, but rather a sense of being "cut adrift."[2]

Learning Leadership at the Great Place

After Nelson's father died, his mother took him to the Great Place, the Thembu royal palace at Mqhekezweni, to live as a ward of Chief Jongintaba Dalindyebo. Nelson didn't see his mother again for years. Chief Jongintaba and his wife, Noengland, raised him as their own child. Nelson became friends with the chief's son, Justice. Like Nelson's mother, Chief Jongintaba was a Christian, and he and his wife took Nelson to church every Sunday. Nelson was educated in a Methodist mission school next to the palace, and the Christian faith became an important part of Nelson's life.[3]

As the foster son of the chief, young Nelson attended the tribal meetings at the Great Place. Meetings dealt with civic affairs, agricultural issues, and problems caused by the white apartheid government. All Thembu tribesmen were free to speak before the chief and his councillors. The meetings were held in the outdoor courtyard of the chief's house. Chief Jongintaba would convene the meeting—then say nothing until the end.

Though women were not permitted to attend, there was no class discrimination among those who spoke. "Everyone was heard," Mandela recalled, "chief and subject, warrior and medicine man, shopkeeper and farmer, landowner and laborer." No one was interrupted or given a time limit. Meetings lasted many hours. Young Nelson was impressed that all men were valued as equals.[4]

Nelson observed the communication styles of those who spoke. Some argued succinctly, some used dramatic oratory and tugged at the emotions, some relied on logical argument, and some droned on and on, never getting to the point.

Nelson's foster father, Chief Jongintaba, was often the target of criticism—yet the chief never interrupted, never defended himself, never showed emotion. In the end, he would often make changes in response to the complaint. Chief Jongintaba was a leader who used his authority to solve people's problems, not to serve himself.

Tribal meetings lasted until a consensus was reached (though some matters were held over and resolved at a later meeting). In contrast to Western democracies, the tribal democracy of Chief Jongintaba did not make decisions by majority rule. Under majority rule, the interests of the minority is often crushed by the majority, causing feelings of alienation and disenfranchisement. A consensus democracy permits the majority opinion to prevail but includes compromises that address the concerns of the minority.

The meetings would draw to a close at sunset, and the chief would speak. He would summarize all that had been said (Nelson was amazed that his foster father kept every argument and counterargument in his head). Then he would render a conclusion. Dissenters were not forced to accept the chief's conclusion. If those present did not agree, they scheduled another meeting and agreed to settle it later. The chief's conclusion was usually accepted by consensus.

Nelson learned that an authentic leader is a humble servant, not a self-important boss. He often recited an axiom he learned from Chief Jongintaba: "A leader is like a shepherd. He stays behind the flock, letting the most nimble go out ahead, whereupon the others follow, not realizing that all along they are being directed from behind."[5]

Nelson studied African history and learned about such heroes as the Marota warrior-king Sekhukhune and the Basotho diplomat-king Moshoeshoe. "My imagination was fired," he said, "by the glory of these African warriors."[6]

Chief Jongintaba wanted Nelson to become a counselor for the Thembu royal house. He sent Nelson to Clarkebury Boarding Institute, a Western-style school for black Africans in Thembuland. There Nelson made friends, played sports (including boxing and long-distance running), and discovered the joys of gardening. Though Nelson endured indoctrination in the superiority of English government, he maintained his passion for African history and culture.

Nelson went on to the University of Fort Hare, a small, elite institution of higher learning for black Africans in Alice, Eastern Cape. He studied English, anthropology, political science, and law. He joined the drama society and performed in a play about Abraham Lincoln. That play helped shape his thinking about leadership. Nelson played John Wilkes Booth. "I was the engine of the play's moral," he later recalled, "which was that men who take great risks often suffer great consequences."[7]

BECOMING RADICALIZED

Though Mandela had friends involved in the African National Congress (ANC), he avoided the radical organization. World War II broke out while Mandela was at the university. Though no fan of colonialism, he vocally supported Great Britain's cause. After becoming involved with a campus food boycott, he was suspended by the university. He left without a degree.

Mandela went to Johannesburg in 1941 and found work as a law clerk. There he met people of many races—black Africans, Europeans, Indians, Jews, and people of mixed race—and they all got along as equals. Some were involved with the Communist Party. Nelson rejected Communism because its doctrinaire atheism violated his Christian beliefs. But he was becoming politicized and was increasingly attracted to radical activism.

Nelson Mandela studied law at the University of Witwatersrand. As the only native African student, he was often subjected to racism. Mandela was deeply influenced by a friend, Anton Lembede, who advocated African nationalism, and under Lembede's influence, he joined the ANC. In 1944, he helped create the ANC Youth League (ANCYL). That same year, he married fellow ANC activist Evelyn Mase; their first child, a boy, was born in 1945.

Mandela's radical activities caused his studies to suffer. He failed his final year at Witwatersrand three times, and the school expelled him in 1949. By 1950, the

ANC and the Communists were stepping up their activism and strikes. The white apartheid government responded with increased repression and the Suppression of Communism Act, which radicalized Mandela even more. He began reading Marx, Engels, and Lenin—and his mistrust of Communism began to erode. Yet Mandela was also influenced by Mahatma Gandhi and his path of nonviolent resistance, which ran counter to the violence advocated by the Communists.

In 1952, Nelson Mandela was elected ANC Transvaal president and deputy national president, and the government arrested him, along with twenty other activists, under the Suppression of Communism Act. Mandela was banned from ANC meetings and talking to more than one other ANC member at a time—effectively barring him from leadership.

A Vision of Reconciliation

In May 1954, Mandela's wife, Evelyn, gave birth to a daughter. Their marriage was crumbling (Evelyn suspected him of adultery). She joined the Jehovah's Witnesses religion, which rejects political involvement. When Nelson tried to convince her to join the struggle, she tried to convert him to her religion. He insisted he was serving the people; she said serving God was a higher calling.

In December 1956, Mandela and 155 other resistance leaders were arrested and charged with high treason. The government placed the arrestees in large communal holding cells in Johannesburg Prison. Mandela could not have been happier. He recalled, "Many of us had been living under severe restrictions, making it illegal for us to meet and talk. Now, our enemy had gathered us all together under one roof."[8] While awaiting trial, the activists made plans and exchanged ideas.

After two weeks in prison, Mandela returned home. Evelyn and the children were gone, the house had been emptied to the walls, and his marriage was over. The divorce was finalized in March 1958. In the midst of the divorce proceedings, Mandela courted a social worker, Winnie Madikizela, and they were married in June.

The Treason Trial began in August 1958 before a three-judge panel in Pretoria. The trial lasted until 1961, when Mandela and his codefendants were acquitted. The verdict vindicated Nelson Mandela. It also humiliated and enraged the apartheid government.

At this point, Mandela was fully radicalized. He studied Fidel Castro's violent takeover of Cuba and the guerrilla tactics of Mao and Che Guevara. Though Mandela denied ever being a member of the Communist Party, he cooperated with party leaders. The Communists were violent people, yet Mandela remained committed to avoiding violence.

As a young man in his thirties, Mandela had a vision of South Africa's future in mind. He did not want a bloody civil war between the races. He envisioned reconciliation between whites and blacks in a future South Africa—a South Africa at peace with itself. He did not oppose sabotage, since the cutting of power lines could be forgiven. But he feared that the loss of even one life might ignite an unending blood feud.[9]

The ANC named Nelson Mandela to be a secret delegate to the Pan-African Freedom Movement for East, Central, and Southern Africa, which met in Ethiopia in February 1962. He met with Emperor Haile Selassie and also visited Egypt, Morocco, and other African nations.

In August 1962, after he returned to Durban, South Africa, police raided his home and took him into custody. Mandela was pleased with his arrest. He believed his trial would give him a platform to make his case for equality in South Africa. The government later moved him to Pretoria, where his wife, Winnie, could visit him.

"I AM PREPARED TO DIE"

Mandela's trial, known as the Rivonia Trial, began November 26, 1963. Mandela showed up in his traditional African kaross. The charges included sabotage and collaborating with Communists to overthrow the government. Mandela represented himself and called no witnesses in his own defense. On April 20, 1964, Mandela was given time for a "plea of mitigation," a speech asking the court for mercy. Mandela delivered, instead, a political speech, his famous "I Am Prepared to Die" speech.

He explained how he and the ANC engaged in sabotage against property—but carefully avoided any risk of injury or death. These acts of sabotage were, he said, acts of nonviolent opposition to the state in the spirit of Mahatma Gandhi. The ANC, he said, had exhausted all other nonviolent means, and the white government had only increased its oppression of black African people. "Each disturbance," he said, "pointed clearly to the inevitable growth amongst Africans of the belief that violence was the only way out—it showed that a government which uses force to maintain its rule teaches the oppressed to use force to oppose it."

Sabotage, he asserted, was a last resort. "It was only when all else had failed," he said, "when all channels of peaceful protest had been barred to us, that the decision was made to embark on violent forms of struggle. . . . We did so not because we desired such a course, but solely because the government had left us with no other choice."

As to the charge that he and the ANC had collaborated with Communists, Mandela recalled the alliance between Britain and the Soviet Union during World War II. The two nations had joined forces to defeat Hitler. In the same way, he said, the ANC and the Communists had joined forces to end apartheid. The Communists, he added, "were the only political group in South Africa who were prepared to treat Africans as human beings and as their equals."

Then Mandela looked the judge square in the eyes and stated his vision for South Africa's future: "I have dedicated my life to this struggle of the African people. I have fought against white domination, and I have fought against black domination. I have cherished the ideal of a democratic and free society in which all persons will live together in harmony and with equal opportunities. . . . If it needs be, it is an ideal for which I am prepared to die."

Mandela's words echoed in the stunned courtroom for several seconds. Then, from the black African side of the room, came a collective sigh of relief. Unmoved, the judge called the next witness.

Mandela's speech was never supposed to be heard outside the courtroom. The South African government imposed official censorship on the press. But excerpts of the speech soon appeared in newspapers around the world. A clamor arose in the United Nations and the World Peace Council, demanding Mandela's release. The South African government turned a deaf ear to the world.

Years later, Mandela said he believed the judge was prepared to condemn him to death. Because Mandela had essentially dared the court to impose death, the judge was practically forced to impose a lesser sentence. When the trial ended on June 12, 1964, Mandela was found guilty on all charges and sentenced to life in prison at hard labor.

The Prison Years

Mandela was shipped to South Africa's harshest prison, Robben Island, where he remained for the next eighteen years. His cell measured eight feet by seven feet, and he slept on a straw mat. He broke rocks into gravel and worked in the limestone quarry, where the glare from the white stone permanently damaged his eyesight. His mother died in 1968, and his firstborn son was killed in a car accident in 1969; Mandela was barred from attending either funeral.

Though the world was aware of Nelson Mandela at the time of his trial, the man and his plight faded from public consciousness. Then, in the late 1970s and early 1980s, a global resurgence of interest in South Africa brought Mandela's name to the fore. An international "Free Mandela!" campaign prompted the United Nations to press for his release. Again, the white government turned a deaf ear to the world.

Because of the Cold War, the United States took a convoluted approach to South Africa and Nelson Mandela. President Ronald Reagan wanted to send a strong antiapartheid message to South Africa, so he sent Edward Perkins, a politically independent black American diplomat, as ambassador to South Africa. The Reagan administration wanted to tilt South Africa toward equality and freedom, but without shoving South Africa into the arms of the Communists. The ANC had received direct support from the Soviet Union, so the Reagan administration didn't feel the United States could openly press for the release of Mandela.

Through Edward Perkins, Reagan quietly pushed for Mandela's release. Reagan gave Perkins full authority to make policy in Reagan's name. Perkins, in his memoir

Mr. Ambassador: Warrior for Peace, wrote, "I do not think either [Secretary of State George] Shultz or the president [Reagan] has been given the credit they deserve for the decision to turn around the apartheid policy. Against the advice of his political advisers in the White House, the president said, 'Go to it.'"[10]

In 1982, the government moved Nelson Mandela to Pollsmoor Prison in Tokai, Cape Town. South Africa was changing. International sanctions were working and fears of a potential civil war were increasing. British prime minister Margaret Thatcher also called for Mandela's release. Under growing pressure, South African foreign minister Roelof Frederik "Pik" Botha offered to release Nelson Mandela. But Mandela refused to walk free while the ANC was still banned.

Mandela was troubled by word that his wife, Winnie, had been involved in the torture and murder of political opponents in Soweto. In 1986—one year after Winnie Mandela received the Robert F. Kennedy Human Rights Award—she gave a notorious speech in Munsieville Township, encouraging the practice of "necklacing," hanging gasoline-filled tires around victims' necks and burning the victims alive. She said, "We shall liberate this country" with "our boxes of matches and our necklaces."[11] Political violence damaged the reputation of the antiapartheid movement in the mid-1980s.

In August 1989, F. W. de Klerk became president of South Africa. Unlike his predecessors, de Klerk believed apartheid could not be sustained. Either the government would grant equality to black Africans—or the nation risked a race war. In November 1989, the Berlin Wall fell, signaling a new hunger for freedom around the world. F. W. de Klerk met with his cabinet to discuss change in South Africa, including the legalization of the ANC.

The government freed Nelson Mandela in February 1990. The event was broadcast around the world. Mandela delivered a stirring speech at Cape Town's City Hall, asking all people to join him in a commitment to peace and reconciliation between the black African majority and the white minority. He stayed for a while in the home of his friend Archbishop Desmond Tutu and later gave a speech before a crowd of one hundred thousand people at Johannesburg's Soccer City.

Free at last, Mandela went on a worldwide speaking tour, meeting with Prime Minister Margaret Thatcher of England, Cuban president Fidel Castro, Pope John Paul II, President George H. W. Bush of the United States, and many others. His old prison cell on Robben Island is now a United Nations World Heritage Site.

Mandela's marriage to Winnie was shattered by her violent activities and her infidelity. Mandela separated from Winnie in April 1992; the divorce was finalized in 1996.

PRESIDENT MANDELA

Nelson Mandela and F. W. de Klerk met together to negotiate South Africa's future. They knew they had to avert civil war—or the blood of countless people, black and white, would be on their souls. They hammered out an interim constitution that included an American-style bill of rights.

In July 1993, Mandela and de Klerk went to the White House, where President Bill Clinton awarded each man the Liberty Medal. Soon afterward, they were jointly awarded the Nobel Peace Prize in recognition of their achievements for peace—and as an incentive to continue their quest.

The election of April 1994 ended apartheid and transformed South Africa into a multiracial democracy. F. W. de Klerk represented the National Party; Nelson Mandela represented the ANC. The two men debated on South African TV, and the debate ended with Mandela reaching out to shake de Klerk's hand—a symbol of Mandela's vision for South Africa.

The ANC swept into the National Assembly with 62 percent of the vote, and the National Assembly elected Nelson Mandela as the nation's first black African president. He was inaugurated in Pretoria on May 10, 1994, and the ceremony was televised globally.

It was a stunning triumph. The black African majority of South Africa had achieved political power without bloodshed. Nelson Mandela headed an ANC-led government of national unity. Former president F. W. de Klerk became the nation's first deputy president and a top adviser to President Mandela.

During his presidency, Mandela visited his boyhood village, Qunu. He walked around, greeted the townspeople, and even helped settle some tribal disputes. He was a leader who enjoyed (as Tom Peters put it) "leading by walking around." He lived simply and donated a third of his income to the Nelson Mandela Children's Fund.

Did Nelson Mandela have his political blind spots? Absolutely. After spending most of his life either fighting for human rights or being unjustly imprisoned, Mandela made friends with some of the worst dictators and human rights violators in the world: Muammar Qaddafi of Libya, Akbar Hashemi Rafsanjani of Iran, Suharto of Indonesia, and Fidel Castro of Cuba (he praised Castro as "a source of inspiration to all freedom-loving people").[12] These errors in judgment do not, in my view, take anything away from his remarkable achievement in liberating South Africa from apartheid—and doing so without a bloody civil war.

NELSON MANDELA'S RAINBOW VISION

Nelson Mandela's personal trademark was the array of colorful batik shirts he wore, which came to be known as Madiba shirts (Madiba was Mandela's Xhosa clan name). He would change his shirts four or five times a day, wearing every hue of the rainbow. It was fitting, because the rainbow symbolized his vision for the country.

In Mandela's inaugural address on May 10, 1994, he said, "We shall build a society in which all South Africans, both black and white, will be able to walk tall, without any fear in their hearts, assured of their inalienable right to human dignity, a Rainbow Nation at peace with itself and the world."[13]

South Africa is a nation of many colors and many cultures. Mandela had dreamed of bringing them all together, unified and strong, free and equal. The rainbow metaphor resonated deeply in Nelson Mandela's soul. The rainbow, after all, was the metaphor God used to symbolize a covenant of peace in the biblical story of the flood of Noah. This appealed to the Christian soul of Nelson Mandela. The rainbow was also important in Mandela's Xhosa culture, where it was identified with a vision of hope for the future.

Nelson Mandela wanted everyone to be represented in the new Rainbow Nation. He wanted black South Africans to know their time had come. He wanted white South Africans to embrace the coming change.

One year into Mandela's presidency, in May–June 1995, South Africa hosted the Rugby World Cup Tournament in Johannesburg. The tournament inflamed a national debate. Most black South Africans considered rugby a "white man's game" and demanded the removal of the South African team emblem, the springbok gazelle. The springbok, said blacks, symbolized apartheid. But white South Africans were proud of the springbok. The South African rugby team had been known as the Springboks since 1906. The controversy heightened racial tensions at the beginning of Mandela's presidency.

Prior to democratic rule, black South Africans had supported anyone playing against the Springboks. To them, the all-white Springboks were part of the oppressive system of apartheid. But Nelson Mandela saw an opportunity to use sports to realize his dream of South Africa as a Rainbow Nation.

Before the tournament, Mandela visited the team and chatted with the players. He wore a Springboks cap and said that the nation would support the team throughout the tournament. The Springbok's slogan fused the aspirations of the team with Mandela's vision: "One Team, One Country."

The opening match against Australia was a handy victory for South Africa. Two days after that win, at the urging of team manager Morné du Plessis, the team made a pilgrimage to Robben Island. Du Plessis wanted the team to understand who Nelson Mandela was and what he had suffered for his vision of a Rainbow Nation. "There was a cause-and-effect connection between the Mandela factor and our performance in the field," du Plessis said. "It was cause-and-effect on a thousand fronts. . . . It all came perfectly together. Our willingness to be the nation's team and Mandela's desire to make the team the national team."[14]

On Robben Island, the players examined the cell where Nelson Mandela had spent eighteen of his twenty-seven years in prison. They imagined what it must have been like for Mandela—a tall, athletic man like themselves—to be confined in that cramped space. Some players wept.

The underdog Springboks stunned the world, defeating Western Samoa in the quarterfinals and France in the semifinals. The final was held at Ellis Park in Johannesburg on June 24. The Springboks faced "unbeatable" New Zealand, the best team in the world. From the stands, clad in Springboks jersey and cap, President Mandela cheered them on.

The Springboks led 9–6 at halftime, but New Zealand evened the score with a drop goal in the second half. The score was still tied at full-time. South Africa and New Zealand both scored penalty goals in the first half of extra time, but a Springbok drop goal capped the game with a storybook ending.

The stadium erupted in celebration. The game had become a metaphor of the hopes and dreams of millions of people—and of the leadership vision of one extraordinary man. Nelson Mandela presented the William Webb Ellis Cup to Springboks captain François Pienaar. That scene stands as one of the most iconic moments in sports history.

That night, the people of the Rainbow Nation poured into the streets of South Africa. They danced and celebrated—as one.

LEADERSHIP LESSONS FROM NELSON MANDELA

Nelson Mandela served one term as president of South Africa then retired from politics—but not from leadership. He continued to play a vital role on the world stage throughout the closing years of his life.

On December 5, 2013, Nelson Mandela died at his home in Johannesburg, surrounded by his family. He had suffered from a long respiratory illness and died at the age of ninety-five. His body lay in state from December 11 through 13 at the Union Buildings in Pretoria. It rained on and off throughout those days—and the rain produced some beautiful rainbows.

Today South Africa is defined by its peaceful elections and peaceful race relations. But South Africa is also defined by crime, poverty, inadequate education, ineffective health care, and government corruption. South African leaders who followed Nelson Mandela have not always followed his example of selflessness, integrity, and vision. Mandela's vision has lapsed into disrepair.

Nelson Mandela did more than anyone thought one man could do. Now the nation needs leaders who will learn from Mandela's example, check their selfish impulses at the door, and become visionary leaders in their own right.

Here are some leadership lessons that we can learn from the amazing life of Nelson Mandela:

1. *Let your vision power your leadership life.* Nelson Mandela had many great

leadership qualities, but I believe his vision was the engine that powered his other leadership skills.

When people talk about the qualities that made Nelson Mandela great, they usually think of his *forgiveness*. Instead of holding grudges or seeking revenge, Mandela reached out to enemies and converted them into friends. Or people think of his *perseverance*. Though sentenced to life in prison, he refused to give up his vision for South Africa's future.

But Mandela's vision of a unified South Africa came first. His vision of a unified South Africa gave him a reason to forgive. And his vision of a unified South Africa sustained him as he persevered through the long years of isolation.

2. *Let your vision be your road map to keep you focused on your goals.* In *10 Simple Secrets of the World's Greatest Business Communicators*, leadership expert Carmine Gallo writes:

> Few visions have had as profound an impact as Nelson Mandela's "dream of an Africa which is in peace with itself." . . . His vision saw him through those years [in prison] and inspired hundreds of millions of people in South Africa and around the world. Your vision might not be as grand as a world in which race and color don't matter, but it proves that a big and bold vision cannot be underestimated. Mandela had a road map; he knew where he wanted to lead his people and how to get there. What's your road map?[15]

What is your dream? What is your vision for the future? No matter how challenging and intimidating your dream may be, it probably doesn't compare to the challenges that Nelson Mandela faced. Write down your vision. Post it on the wall. Read it every day. Then go make your leadership dream come true.

3. *Don't confuse your vision with your viewpoint.* Stay true to your vision. Be obsessed with your vision, be possessed by your vision—but hold your viewpoint loosely. In the realm of ideas, always be willing to flex, learn, change, and grow.

Nelson Mandela demonstrated a remarkable ability to revise his views while maintaining his vision for South Africa. Mandela was a socialist at heart. In January 1992, he flew to Davos, Switzerland, for the five-day World Economic Forum. Before that trip, Mandela was committed to a socialist agenda, including nationalizing South African corporations.

Ironically, delegates from two Communist nations, China and Vietnam, urged Mandela to adopt free-market capitalism instead. A member of the South African delegation recalled that Mandela had some "interesting meetings with the leaders of the Communist Parties of China and Vietnam. They told him frankly as follows:

'We are currently striving to privatize state enterprises and invite private enterprise into our economies. We are Communist Party governments, and you are a leader of a national liberation movement. Why are you talking about nationalization?'"

The Chinese and Vietnamese economies were thriving. Their advice forced Mandela to rethink South Africa's future. "They changed my views altogether," Mandela told his biographer, Anthony Sampson. Mandela dropped his nationalization plans, and pushed South Africa to open its markets to global investment. The nation soon had the fastest-growing economy on the African continent.[16] It happened because Nelson Mandela had the wisdom to revise his economic beliefs while holding fast to his vision for South Africa's future. Wise leaders adapt their belief systems in order to stay true to their vision.

4. *To communicate effectively and persuasively, communicate your vision.* During Mandela's Rivonia Trial, he was literally on trial for his life. In April 1964, he delivered his famous "I Am Prepared to Die" speech, saying, "I have cherished the ideal of a democratic and free society in which all persons will live together in harmony and with equal opportunities." The judge was not impressed by Mandela's vision—but his words rallied the world to his cause. It took years of sanctions and diplomatic pressure to win Mandela's freedom and dismantle apartheid, but Mandela's vision prevailed.

What is your vision for the future? What is the cherished ideal you would bet your life on? If you want to make a difference, if you want to make some history, then learn from Nelson Mandela. Communicate your leadership vision.

It always seems impossible until it's done.
NELSON MANDELA

3

STEVE JOBS

A Dent in the Universe

There's an old Wayne Gretzky quote that I love: "I skate to where
the puck is going to be, not where it has been." And we've always tried
to do that at Apple. Since the very beginning. And we always will.

STEVE JOBS

Steve Jobs didn't set out to be a visionary. He once said that when he and Steve Wozniak cofounded Apple, "we were out to build computers for our friends. That was all. No idea of a company."[1]

The first Apple computer, the Apple I, was hand-built by Wozniak in 1976. The introverted Wozniak (nicknamed "Woz"—rhymes with Oz) was the technical wizard. Jobs had a background in programming, but his real assets were extreme self-confidence, tons of ambition, and a charismatic personality.

Jobs and Wozniak demonstrated their first computer at the Homebrew Computer Club in Palo Alto in July 1976. The Apple I would not be recognizable as a computer today. It was a naked circuit board—the computer buyer had to purchase a power supply, keyboard, video display, and case in order to turn the Apple I into a working computer.

Steve Jobs came up with a "creative financing" scheme to get the company off the ground. He approached a local computer store chain, the Byte Shop, and talked the owner into ordering fifty Apple computers at $500 each, cash on delivery. Then he took the Byte Shop's purchase order to an electronics supplier and talked the credit manager into selling him the parts on net-thirty-day terms, using the purchase order as proof of Apple's ability to pay. Woz delivered the computers to the Byte Shop. Jobs collected the check, paid the parts supplier, and deposited a tidy profit in Apple's bank account.

While Jobs and Wozniak were building their company, Steve Jobs's visionary traits began to emerge. Jobs envisioned a true desktop computer for the masses, with the circuitry hidden inside a sleek plastic case—the Apple II. While seeking venture capital, Jobs met entrepreneur Mike Markkula, who invested $250,000 and became a one-third owner of Apple. Markkula helped Jobs and Wozniak take Apple from a partnership to a corporation.

Jobs unveiled the Apple II in April 1977—and the Apple II series would go on to a phenomenal seventeen-year run. The Apple II was so successful that, by the summer of 1979, copier behemoth Xerox offered to invest $1 million in Apple.

Jobs wanted Xerox's money, but he wanted something else even more. Connecticut-based Xerox maintained a West Coast R&D division called Palo Alto Research Center, or PARC. Jobs wanted a peek behind the curtain at PARC. Xerox agreed to give Jobs a tour of the top-secret facility in return for an opportunity to buy 100,000 shares of Apple at ten dollars per share (a year later, those shares were worth eighteen times what Xerox paid).

At PARC, Steve Jobs witnessed a demonstration of a new programming language. The computer screen was arranged in boxes called "windows." A point-and-click device called a "mouse" opened various "windows" and performed tasks on the screen. The PARC programmers called the system a "graphical user interface" or GUI (pronounced "gooey").

The tech wizards at PARC saw no commercial application for the GUI. They just thought it was a cool gimmick. Jobs recalled, "It was like a veil being lifted from my eyes. I could see what the future of computing was destined to be."[2]

Steve Jobs had just had a vision of the future—and his vision revolved around the graphical user interface. He realized that the next step in computing was not about keystrokes but mouse clicks.

And he was about to reinvent the future.

AN AIMLESS, UNMOTIVATED HIPPIE

Steve Jobs was born in San Francisco in February 1955. His birth father, Syrian-born Abdulfattah "John" Jandali, and his birth mother, Joanne Carole Schieble, met as students. They put baby Steven up for adoption because Schieble's parents opposed their relationship. Steven was adopted by Paul and Clara Jobs. Years later, Steve bristled if anyone referred to the parents who raised him as his "adoptive parents." He said (and rightly so), "They were my parents one thousand percent."

Clara taught Steve to read before he started school. Steve learned to tinker with electronics from his father, who was a carpenter by trade. Exceptionally bright, Steve had little patience for conventional schooling. Even after skipping a grade, he found school boring and unchallenging.

After graduating from high school in 1972, Jobs persuaded his parents to pay his way to Reed College, an expensive private liberal arts college in Portland, Oregon. Paul and Clara Jobs invested a big chunk of their life savings in Steve's college education, only to see him drop out during his second semester. He continued to hang around campus, couch-surfing in dorm rooms and cadging free meals at the Hare Krishna temple.

At Reed, he befriended Robert Friedland, an eccentric who operated a 220-acre apple farm and hippie commune near Portland. Jobs spent a lot of time at the commune, where (in exchange for room and board) he pruned trees and crushed apples for the commune's organic cider business. Friedland was heavily into Eastern mysticism, and Jobs looked up to him as the older brother he never had.

During his apple orchard days, Steve Jobs seemed like just another aimless, unmotivated hippie. He had no vision for his own life, much less the future of computing. By early 1974, Jobs was disillusioned with commune life—and with Robert Friedland. "It started to get very materialistic," Jobs told writer Michael Moritz. "Everybody got the idea they were working very hard for Robert's farm. . . . I got pretty sick of it and left."[3]

Jobs moved back home with his parents and scoured the "help wanted" ads. The headline HAVE FUN, MAKE MONEY intrigued him. It turned out the ad was placed by Atari, the electronic game company. Jobs strode into the lobby and announced that he wouldn't leave until Atari gave him a job. Atari founder Nolan Bushnell admired Jobs's brashness and hired him.

Steve Jobs had a theory that if he ate an all-fruit diet, plus a few vegetables, he would never have body odor and would not have to bathe regularly. When coworkers complained about his personal hygiene, Bushnell moved him to the night shift.

In mid-1974, Jobs went to India to seek enlightenment from Neem Karoli Baba (also called Maharaj-ji). Much of the 1960s hippie movement had already beaten a path to Neem Karoli's ashram door. Jobs arrived late. Reaching the town of Vrindavan, he learned that the guru had died the previous year. Jobs joined up with Daniel Kottke, and they kicked around India for seven months. Jobs returned home in traditional Indian garb, with his head shaved. When his parents came to pick him up at the airport, his own mother didn't recognize him.

Jobs returned to Atari, and Nolan Bushnell gave him a challenge: design a streamlined circuit board for the Atari arcade game *Breakout*, using fewer integrated circuits to save costs. Bushnell didn't know that Jobs had no expertise in circuit design. Jobs accepted—but neglected to mention that Steve Wozniak would do the actual work.

Jobs gave the assignment to Wozniak, and Woz crafted a circuit board that reduced the number of integrated circuits (ICs) by fifty. Jobs presented the streamlined board to Bushnell as his own work, and Bushnell paid him $100 per eliminated IC—a $5,000 bonus. Jobs told Wozniak that Bushnell had paid him $750, and that Woz's share was $375. Wozniak didn't learn of Jobs's deception until a decade later.[4]

Wozniak later reflected: "I think that Steve needed the money, and he just didn't tell me the truth. . . . If he had told me he needed the money, he should have known I would have just given it to him. He was a friend. You help your friends. . . . I would rather let it pass. It's not something I want to judge Steve by."[5]

During 1975 and 1976, Jobs and Wozniak regularly attended meetings of the Homebrew Computer Club in Palo Alto. There they got to know the target audience for the Apple I computer, which they unveiled in July 1976.

Around that same time, Jobs approached his old Atari boss, Nolan Bushnell, offering him a one-third stake in Apple in exchange for a $50,000 investment. Bushnell said no. Had he said yes, his one-third ownership would be worth more than $40 billion today. Bushnell gave Jobs some names and phone numbers that ultimately led him to Mike Markkula, whose $250,000 investment funded the Apple II—the computer that changed the world.

Departure and Return

Jobs and Wozniak produced about two hundred Apple I computers in the garage of Jobs's parents' home. To build Apple II, the company needed a headquarters, warehouses, a production line, and employees. The Apple II featured an "open architecture" that made it easy for computer users to customize their computers. The open architecture feature prompted VisiCorp, in 1979, to select Apple II as the standard desktop computer for its spreadsheet program VisiCalc. Apple II sales exploded.

In 1984, Apple launched the GUI-based Macintosh computer, announcing the product with a $1.5 million commercial during Super Bowl XVIII—the now-legendary "1984" commercial directed by Ridley Scott. With the introduction of the Mac, Apple came of age.

By 1985, Steve Jobs realized he was losing control of the company. Though Jobs had a charming public persona, behind the scenes he could be abrasive. His personality clashed with the leadership style of Apple CEO John Sculley, whom Jobs had recruited from PepsiCo in 1983. Sculley's forte was managing product lines; Jobs's forte was visionary innovation. Inventing the future is expensive, and Sculley (with the blessing of Apple's board of directors) continually blocked Jobs's expensive ideas.

In April 1985, the board authorized Sculley to strip Jobs of executive authority. Jobs responded by trying to oust Sculley, but the board sided with the more buttoned-down approach of John Sculley. Jobs was technically chairman of the company, but he had no duties. Frustrated, Jobs resigned and founded a new company called NeXT, Inc. The first NeXT computer went on sale in 1988, aimed at users in business and academia. Though sales of NeXT computers proved disappointing, the NeXTSTEP operating system would have a major impact on Apple.

After Jobs's departure, Apple entered a decade-long period of decline. Bill Gates and Microsoft introduced a GUI-based operating system called Windows, which chomped hard into Apple's market share. By the early 1990s, Apple clearly lacked the visionary leadership to launch a new wave of innovation.

In 1996, Apple acquired Steve Jobs's NeXT Corporation—and with it, Steve Jobs himself. In 1997, the board made Jobs interim CEO. Instantly, Apple began innovating once more. In 2000, the board dropped "interim" from Jobs's title, making him CEO of Apple Inc.

A Shadow on the Scan

Steve Jobs went to his doctor in October 2003, complaining of symptoms he attributed to kidney stones. He underwent a CT scan, and doctors noticed a suspicious shadow on his pancreas. They diagnosed it as a gastroenteropancreatic neuroendocrine tumor (GEP-NET)—one of the rarest and least aggressive cancers known to science. If you must have cancer, this is a good one to get.

The good news: the cancer was at an early stage. In most cases, a simple surgical procedure called enucleation (removing the tumor plus a safe margin of surrounding tissue) eliminates the cancer.

The bad news: Jobs wouldn't consent to surgery. Instead, he spent nine months pursuing "alternative therapies," including a special diet consisting largely of fruit and fruit juices.[6] Against the strenuous pleadings of his wife, doctors, and friends, Jobs delayed the surgery that probably would have saved his life. He said, "I didn't want my body to be opened. . . . I didn't want to be violated in that way."[7]

Ever since his teen years, Jobs had been a fruitarian vegan, fanatically committed to a diet consisting primarily (at times, entirely) of fruit. Jobs's biographer Walter Isaacson describes Jobs's relationship with food as an eating disorder.[8] From his teen years on, Jobs often went to unhealthy extremes, including bingeing, purging, fasting, and eating just one or two foods (typically apples or carrots or fruit juices) for weeks at a time.[9] In Jobs's youth, Isaacson said, he discovered "he could induce euphoria and ecstasy by fasting."[10] He achieved a drug-like endorphin high through malnutrition.

After Jobs was diagnosed with cancer, his eating disorder worsened, and he often subsisted on nothing but fruit smoothies.[11] Fruits are healthful, rich in vitamins, minerals, and cancer-fighting antioxidants. Most of us don't get enough of them. But Steve Jobs had an unhealthy obsession with fruit. In fact, his zeal to stay healthy and live longer may have significantly shortened his life.

Fruit contains fructose (fruit sugar), which the liver processes into a number of products, including artery-clogging triglycerides. Fructose in moderation is a healthy nutrient, but megadoses of fructose can be hazardous to your health in a number of ways, increasing your risk of diabetes and endocrine-related cancers—*such as a pancreatic neuroendocrine tumor.*

Steve Jobs's fructose-intensive diet may well have caused his cancer. Jobs continued bingeing on fruit even *after* his diagnosis. Research has shown that pancreatic tumor cells actually utilize fructose for cell division, so Jobs was probably *feeding* his cancer cells and *speeding up* the spread of his cancer. It's a tragic irony that sweet, wholesome fruit may have been as deadly to Steve Jobs as cigarettes were to Walt Disney.

Walter Isaacson theorized that the reason Jobs rejected surgery was not fear of the knife, but a lifelong habit of "magical thinking." He had always been able to charm people and alter circumstances with what he called his "reality distortion field."

Isaacson said, "I think that he kind of felt that if you ignore something, if you don't want something to exist, you can have magical thinking. And it had worked for him in the past."[12]

Jobs's years of studying Eastern religion had convinced him that reality is an illusion you can alter with your mind. If he didn't want the cancer to exist, he could make it magically disappear.

But the cancer refused to disappear. In fact, it spread. Nine months after his diagnosis, Jobs agreed to surgery. During his later interviews with Walter Isaacson, as his health was declining, Jobs talked about his hope for an afterlife. He wanted to believe that "when you die, it doesn't just all disappear. The wisdom you've accumulated. Somehow it lives on. . . . But sometimes I think. . .[life is] just like an on-off switch. Click and you're gone. And that's why I don't like putting on-off switches on Apple devices."[13]

By 2009, it was clear that Steve Jobs was getting worse, not better. He went to Memphis for a liver transplant. He went to Switzerland for experimental treatments. Nothing worked. He was dying.

But even as Steve Jobs was dying, Apple was thriving. In July 2011, CNN reported that the company Steve Jobs cofounded in his parents' garage had more cash on hand ($76.2 billion) than the US government ($73.8 billion).[14] In August 2011, Steve Jobs resigned as CEO, having spent most of the year on medical leave.

On October 5, 2011, Jobs was at home, surrounded by family members. At one point, he seemed to look past his wife and children. Once again, he was seeing something only he could see. Then he said, "Oh wow. Oh wow. Oh wow."[15]

Minutes later, at about two in the afternoon, his heart beat one final time then went still.

Lessons from a Flawed Visionary

Steven Jobs was one of the great visionary leaders of our time. He said his goal was to "make a dent in the universe."[16] He built, lost control of, then rebuilt the most successful company in history. Our world has been shaped by his vision and inventions. His vision has shaped not only the way we use computers, but the way we talk on the phone, take pictures, listen to music, read books, watch movies, and more. He created products that people didn't even know they wanted until they saw them. That's visionary leadership.

As a young man, Steve Jobs had no vision for his life. He had no formal training in engineering, industrial design, management, business administration, or leadership of any kind. Yet he became one of the great visionary leaders of the twentieth and twenty-first centuries. Let me suggest some lessons we can learn from this leader of vision:

1. *To sharpen your vision, absorb the lessons of failure.* Before Steve Jobs could

achieve heights of unprecedented success, he had to pass through a time of exile and failure. He had to hit the reset button on his career. He had to spend a dozen years in the wilderness of NeXT before he could make his triumphant return to Apple.

Jobs once reflected, "I didn't see it then, but it turned out that getting fired from Apple was the best thing that could have ever happened to me. The heaviness of being successful was replaced by the lightness of being a beginner again, less sure about everything. It freed me to enter one of the most creative periods of my life."[17]

That statement is amazingly similar to one Walt Disney made after the 1923 bankruptcy of his Laugh-O-Gram studio in Kansas City. Disney recalled setting off for Hollywood feeling "free and happy" in spite of being broke. Disney added, "I had failed. I think it's important to have a good hard failure when you're young."[18] Steve Jobs suffered his "good hard failure" when he was booted out of Apple at age thirty.

During his NeXT years, Jobs lost sight of what it means to be a visionary leader. He became obsessed with petty details while neglecting strategic priorities. On one occasion, he kept a delegation of visiting retail executives waiting on the sidewalk for twenty minutes while he gave meticulous instructions about sprinkler heads to a landscaping crew.

Jobs's senior advisers tried to get him to pay attention to big-picture issues of corporate vision and strategy, but he refused to listen. He became like Captain Queeg in Herman Wouk's *The Caine Mutiny*, a sea captain who obsessed over a quart of strawberries while his ship was on a deadly collision course. *New York Times* business writer Randall Stross wrote of Jobs's strangely unvisionary performance during the NeXT era:

> Mr. Jobs's lieutenants tried to warn him away from certain disaster, but he was not receptive. In 1992–93, seven of nine NeXT vice presidents were shown the door or left on their own.
>
> In this period, Mr. Jobs did not do much delegating. Almost every aspect of the machine—including the finish on interior screws—was his domain. The interior furnishings of NeXT's offices, a stunning design showplace, were Mr. Jobs's concern, too. While the company's strategy begged to be re-examined, Mr. Jobs attended to other matters.[19]

The failure of NeXT forced Steve Jobs to reexamine his leadership priorities. He learned that his top priority was to be the steward of the corporate vision, not the steward of the sprinkler heads. Kevin Compton, a senior executive at Businessland, contrasted the Steve Jobs who returned to Apple with the vision-impaired Steve Jobs who ran NeXT into the ground. "He's the same Steve in his passion for excellence," Compton said, "but a new Steve in his understanding of how to empower a large company to realize his vision."[20]

2. To be a leader of vision, avoid the character flaws of Steve Jobs. Emulate his visionary strengths without adopting his failings and flaws. Make every effort to become a complete seven-sided leader.

Steve Jobs was *not* a complete leader by any means. We can give him high marks as a leader of vision, communication skills, competence, and boldness, but he was almost completely lacking in people skills and a serving heart, and a bit sketchy in the character department (remember how he deceived his partner, Steve Wozniak). Why do I say that Steve Jobs lacked people skills and a serving heart? Let me introduce you to the dark side of Steve Jobs:

Ryan Tate observed in Gawker: "Jobs regularly belittled people, swore at them, and pressured them until they reached their breaking point. In the pursuit of greatness he cast aside politeness and empathy. His verbal abuse never stopped."[21] And Malcolm Gladwell, writing in the *New Yorker*, called Steve Jobs "a bully," and based that assessment on these facts:

> Jobs gets his girlfriend pregnant, and then denies that the child is his. He parks in handicapped spaces. He screams at subordinates. He cries like a small child when he does not get his way. He gets stopped for driving a hundred miles an hour, honks angrily at the officer for taking too long to write up the ticket, and then resumes his journey at a hundred miles an hour. He sits in a restaurant and sends his food back three times. He arrives at his hotel suite in New York for press interviews and decides, at 10 p.m., that the piano needs to be repositioned, the strawberries are inadequate, and the flowers are all wrong: he wanted calla lilies. (When his public-relations assistant returns, at midnight, with the right flowers, he tells her that her suit is "disgusting.")[22]

Adam Lashinsky of *Fortune* tells another revealing story. In 2008, Apple debuted MobileMe, an e-mail system for its iPhone. But MobileMe performed poorly, resulting in user complaints and poor reviews. Steve Jobs called a meeting with the MobileMe team. He opened the meeting with a question: "Can anyone tell me what MobileMe is supposed to do?"

One member of the team explained MobileMe's function.

"So," Jobs continued, "why the [expletive] doesn't it do that?" Then, in an obscenity-laced tirade, he blistered his team for the next half hour. "You've tarnished Apple's reputation," he said. "You should hate each other for having let each other down." Then, in front of the whole group, he demoted the team leader and named a new executive to head the team.

This incident, Lashinsky concluded, was no aberration. It's a glimpse into "Apple's ruthless corporate culture" under Steve Jobs—a culture that could often be "brutal and unforgiving."[23]

Steve Jobs had only himself to blame for the disastrous rollout of MobileMe. He had created a culture of fear in which no one dared to bring him bad news. The MobileMe team worked feverishly, day and night, hoping to perfect the software in time for the rollout. When they failed to meet their goal, no one dared give Steve Jobs the bad news. Leaders need to hear bad news long before it becomes a public humiliation. Jobs's dysfunctional leadership style guaranteed that bad news would not reach his ears until it was too late.

Great leaders don't have to be bullies. George Washington, Abraham Lincoln, Martin Luther King Jr., Nelson Mandela, and Ronald Reagan transformed nations while maintaining gracious, even courtly manners. They demonstrated respect for the people they led. The late UCLA head basketball coach John Wooden won ten NCAA national championships (seven in a row) and never once yelled or swore at his players. Tony Dungy coached the Indianapolis Colts to an NFL championship in Super Bowl XLI—and he never screamed or cussed.

Steve Jobs's abusive leadership style earned him many enemies and cost his company a lot of top talent. Yet Apple continues to thrive. How do we explain the contradiction? How did a leader who displayed only four of the Seven Sides of Leadership become one of the most successful business leaders in history? Relly Nadler, author of *Leading with Emotional Intelligence*, offers an explanation: The power of Steve Jobs's vision was so strong and compelling that it compensated for Jobs's leadership deficits. Nadler explains:

> Jobs' vision. . .overpowered what can be considered his coercive leadership style. . . . Did his employees just tolerate his style for the sake of being a part of changing the world? Did they accept his "emotional towel snapping" and humiliation in front of peers for the exhilaration and pride of being. . .[part of the] coolest company on the planet? I think so. The power of his vision. . .seemed to mute the negativity of his management.[24]

Dr. Nadler asks, could Steve Jobs have achieved the same heights without being a tyrant? His answer: absolutely. "His prickly, demanding personality was not the critical factor for his success," Nadler concludes. "Jobs often stated, 'This is just me,' without the awareness that he could or would benefit from changing."[25]

My advice: Study the visionary brilliance of Steve Jobs, harness the power of leadership vision. Then make sure you build *all the other sides of leadership* into your leadership life for good measure.

3. *To be a visionary leader, learn to focus.* In an interview with *Fortune*, Steve Jobs talked about a leadership lesson he learned while pruning trees in the apple orchards of Robert Friedland's hippie commune. Just as pruning branches makes apple trees more productive, pruning away extraneous ideas makes a company more productive. He explained:

> People think focus means saying yes to the thing you've got to focus on. But that's not what it means at all. It means saying no to the hundred other good ideas that there are. You have to pick carefully. I'm actually as proud of many of the things we haven't done as the things we have done.[26]

Great visionary leaders don't confuse their followers with an array of visions. They focus their followers' attention and energies on one compelling vision. Great visionary leaders have mastered the art of "pruning" ideas. They say yes to the best and no to the rest.

4. *To become a leader of vision, don't look around you—look within.* Once Steve Jobs got his priorities straight, it wasn't hard for him to be a visionary. He didn't need to study historical trends or read books by futurists in order to determine his vision of the future. He simply had to look within. He asked himself, "What should computers do that they don't already do? If I could build the perfect phone, what features would it have?" Then he gathered a team of engineers to design it and build it.

True visionaries don't study trends—they set trends. True visionaries don't try to anticipate change—they drive change. True visionaries don't need focus groups to tell them what the public wants—their instinct, intuition, and experience tell them what people will want the moment they see it.

The mature, visionary Steve Jobs peered into the future by looking within himself. He *imagined* the future; then he *committed* himself to building the future he saw within. Anyone can imagine possible futures. That's called daydreaming. But Steve Jobs committed time, energy, personnel, and resources to his dreams, and that's called visionary leadership.

Whatever his flaws—and they were huge—Steve Jobs envisioned and invented the future. Yes, he treated people badly. Some people walked away—but many stayed. Why did they stay? Because Steve Jobs showed them such an exciting vision of a future that, in spite of Steve Jobs's toxic personality and wretched people skills, they wanted to help build it.

Steve Jobs talked about changing the world, about making a dent in the universe. When you give people a vision of making a difference in the world, you give them a sense of *meaning*. For most people, being employed at Apple was more than a career. At his best, Steve Jobs made people believe their work had meaning.

That's our mission as visionary leaders: look within, discover our vision, then communicate that vision to our followers with power and a sense of meaning. When you and your followers truly believe that together you are making a dent in the universe, there's no limit to what you can achieve.

I think if you do something and it turns out pretty good,
then you should go do something else wonderful,
not dwell on it for too long. Just figure out what's next.
STEVE JOBS

The Second Side of Leadership

COMMUNICATION

4

WINSTON CHURCHILL

Sending Language into Battle

If you have an important point to make, don't try to be subtle or clever.
Use a pile driver. Hit the point once. Then come back and hit it again.
Then hit it a third time—a tremendous whack.

WINSTON CHURCHILL

In 2013, the British national morning newspaper *The Independent on Sunday* conducted a poll of readers to find the most inspiring public speaker of the past fifty years. John F. Kennedy placed third in the poll. Dr. Martin Luther King Jr. placed second. And in first place, with 39 percent of the vote, was Sir Winston Churchill.[1]

The speeches of Winston Churchill during World War II did more than merely inspire the British people. His speeches may well have saved Western civilization from destruction by Nazi Germany. For a seventeen-month period, from the beginning of the Battle of Britain, July 1940, until the entrance of the United States into World War II, December 1941, the British Isles were on the ropes. Hitler's Luftwaffe pounded Britain's shipping and military installations then turned to terror-bombing civilians.

Hitler was eager to launch Operation Sea Lion, a massive air and sea invasion across the English Channel. Only the stubborn resolve of the British people stood between Hitler and his goal of conquering Great Britain. Germany had already conquered France with astonishing speed, and Britain was next in line to fall. But the British people would not falter, would not fail. They were sustained by the thundering words of Winston Churchill.

On April 9, 1963, President John F. Kennedy officiated a White House ceremony proclaiming Sir Winston Churchill an honorary citizen of the United States. Though Churchill was in poor health and could not attend the ceremony, he and his wife watched a live transatlantic television broadcast and heard President Kennedy say, "In the dark days and darker nights when Britain stood alone—and most men save Englishmen despaired of England's life—he mobilized the English language and sent it into battle. The incandescent quality of his words illuminated the courage of his countrymen."[2]

That's a fitting description of the way Churchill waged a war of words against

Hitler's planes and bombs. Churchill's granddaughter, Celia Sandys, once observed that both Churchill and his wartime nemesis Adolf Hitler were known for their ability to reach the emotions of the masses—but there was a huge difference between Hitler and Churchill. "Hitler could persuade you that *he* could do anything," said Sandys, "but. . .Churchill could persuade you that *you* could do anything." Her grandfather, she added, never used speechwriters but wrote all of his speeches himself.[3]

The first of the Seven Sides of Leadership is vision. But the most compelling vision ever conceived is useless if you, the leader, cannot communicate your vision to your people. The ability to communicate effectively and persuasively is essential to leadership. Churchill was a great leader because he was an inspiring speaker. He mobilized the English language and sent it into battle.

OVERCOMING IMPEDIMENTS

Churchill's reputation as an inspiring speaker is all the more amazing when you realize what he overcame. Churchill was afflicted by a speech impediment. It's well known that Churchill had a lisp. He worked hard to overcome it, so it's scarcely noticeable in the recorded speeches of his later years.

But there are indications that Churchill, in his early life, battled a far more serious speech impediment—a pronounced stutter. An article published online by the Churchill Centre and Churchill Museum dismisses the suggestion that Churchill stuttered, calling it a "myth."[4] Yet early accounts refer to his serious speech impediment. Journalist Harold Begbie knew Churchill in his early career and wrote about his speech impediment in 1921. Though Begbie didn't specifically refer to a stutter, his description sounds like more than a lisp:

> Ever since I first met him, when he was still in the twenties, Mr. Churchill has seemed to me one of the most pathetic and misunderstood figures in public life. . . .
>
> Mr. Churchill is one of the most sensitive of prominent politicians, and it is only by the exercise of his remarkable courage that he has mastered this element of nervousness. Ambition has driven him onward, and courage has carried him through, but more often than the public thinks he has suffered sharply in his progress. The impediment of speech, which in his very nervous moments would almost make one think his mouth was roofless, would have prevented many men from even attempting to enter public life; it has always been a handicap to Mr. Churchill, but he has never allowed it to stop his way. . . .
>
> Mr. Churchill is more often fighting himself than his enemies.[5]

That assessment from 1921 was confirmed twenty years later in an article by Louis J. Alber and Charles J. Rolo in the *Kansas City Star*, February 6, 1941. In a story headlined, "Churchill Has Mastered a Stutter and a Lisp to Become an Orator," Alber and Rolo write:

> Winston Churchill grew up with a lisp and a stutter, the result of a defect in his palate. It is characteristic of the man's perseverance that, despite this handicap, he has made himself one of the greatest orators of all time.
>
> Churchill has never cured the lisp. And the stutter still breaks out when he gets excited—which is often.[6]

Churchill was born into the aristocracy. His father was Lord Randolph Churchill, chancellor of the exchequer and a gifted public speaker; his mother was an American socialite, Jennie Jerome. Placed in the care of a nanny, Elizabeth Ann Everest, young Winston had little contact with his parents. His father rarely spoke to him.

After Lord Randolph died at age forty-five, Winston thought that he, too, would die young. So he made up his mind to make his mark on the world before his time was up.

Though extremely intelligent, Churchill earned mediocre marks in school because of a rebellious streak. He was educated at several boarding schools, including Harrow School. He often wrote to his mother, begging her to visit him, but his parents maintained a distant, even cold relationship with him. We have to wonder if Winston's sense of abandonment might have played a role in his stuttering.

Churchill met his future wife, Clementine, at a party and proposed to her on August 10, 1908. They were married one month later on September 12.

As a young cavalry officer, Churchill experienced both the adventures and the horrors of war, seeing action in India, the Sudan, and the Second Boer War in South Africa. He gained fame as a war correspondent and author. Despite his early accomplishments, Churchill felt he lived in the shadow of his father. Winston Churchill's grandson, Nicholas Soames, offered this comparison between Lord Randolph and Sir Winston:

> Unlike his father, Churchill was not a natural speaker. Lord Randolph Churchill, in his very brief prime between 1880 and 1887, was the most brilliant platform speaker and parliamentary debater of the day. Lord Randolph was that relative rarity, a natural spontaneous debater in the Commons, quick to invoke the deadly weapons of mockery and irony, and acutely sensitive to the mood of the House.

But his son Winston had not inherited these gifts. For him, every speech, however brief, had to be carefully prepared. . . . There was much truth in the jibe of his greatest friend, F. E. Smith, that "Winston has spent the best years of his life composing his impromptu speeches."[7]

Though we remember Churchill for his wartime accomplishments as prime minister, he held numerous political and cabinet positions over a career that spanned half a century. Prior to World War I, while still in his thirties, Churchill held a succession of high positions in the government, including First Lord of the Admiralty (a position similar to Secretary of the Navy in the United States government).

Churchill was in command of the Gallipoli campaign, a joint British-French assault at the Dardanelles, with the goal of capturing the Ottoman Empire's capital of Constantinople (now Istanbul). The Ottomans defeated the allies, resulting in thousands of deaths on both sides. The disastrous end of the Gallipoli campaign forced Churchill out of the government.

But he would return.

A WAR OF WORDS

During the 1930s, Churchill accurately predicted the rising threat of Hitler and Nazi Germany at a time when the British government viewed Hitler as someone to be appeased. As the world stood by, Hitler annexed Austria and parts of Czechoslovakia. In September 1939, when Germany invaded Poland, Churchill warned of grim days ahead but also shared his vision of a peaceful world to follow. On January 20, 1940, less than four months before becoming prime minister, Churchill delivered a radio speech called "House of Many Mansions," predicting freedom for the nations Hitler had conquered. He said:

> Their liberation is sure. The day will come when the joybells will ring again throughout Europe, and when victorious nations, masters not only of their foes but of themselves, will plan and build in justice, in tradition, and in freedom a house of many mansions where there will be room for all.[8]

Churchill understood the power of an optimistic vision, even in dark times.

By the spring of 1940, it was clear that the government of Prime Minister Neville Chamberlain had failed to grasp the enormity of the Nazi threat. On May 7, debate raged in Parliament over war in Europe. On May 10, Chamberlain resigned.

As the German war machine smashed through France, Holland, Belgium, and Luxembourg, King George VI commissioned Winston Churchill to form a new government. Churchill became the wartime prime minister. Years earlier, diplomat Harold Nicolson had written prophetically that Churchill "is a man who leads forlorn hopes, and when the hopes of England become forlorn, he will once again be summoned to leadership."[9]

On May 13, 1940, Churchill delivered his first speech as prime minister before the House of Commons. Many in Parliament were skeptical of his leadership and still associated him with the disastrous Gallipoli campaign in World War I. As he rose to address the House of Commons, the reception was chilly—but as he delivered his thundering conclusion, the room was electrified:

> I have nothing to offer but blood, toil, tears and sweat. . . .
>
> You ask, what is our aim? I can answer in one word: It is victory, victory at all costs, victory in spite of all terror, victory, however long and hard the road may be. . . .
>
> I take up my task with buoyancy and hope. I feel sure that our cause will not be suffered to fail among men. At this time I feel entitled to claim the aid of all, and I say, come then, let us go forward together with our united strength.[10]

With that speech, Winston Churchill gained the support of Parliament. Soon he would summon the resolve of the British people.

On June 4, 1940, after supervising an effort to evacuate a third of a million Allied troops from Nazi-occupied France, Churchill returned to the House of Commons and reported on the successful rescue. He acknowledged that the road ahead would be hard, but he concluded with these stirring words:

> We shall go on to the end, we shall fight in France, we shall fight on the seas and oceans, we shall fight with growing confidence and growing strength in the air, we shall defend our Island, whatever the cost may be, we shall fight on the beaches, we shall fight on the landing grounds, we shall fight in the fields and in the streets, we shall fight in the hills; we shall never surrender, and even if, which I do not for a moment believe, this Island or a large part of it were subjugated and starving, then our Empire beyond the seas, armed and guarded by the British Fleet, would carry on the struggle, until, in God's good time, the New World, with all its power and might, steps forth to the rescue and the liberation of the old.[11]

Even reading silently, you can feel the cadences, the rolling rhythms like ocean waves in a gathering storm, growing more and more powerful. Churchill knew how to infuse words with the power of stirring music.

On June 18, 1940, Churchill gave another address before the House of Commons that has come to be known as "Their Finest Hour." Paris had fallen four days earlier. It was a dispiriting moment, and Churchill wanted to lift the fighting spirit of the British people. In this address, Churchill closed by calling on the courage of his countrymen:

> The Battle of France is over. I expect that the Battle of Britain is about to begin. Upon this battle depends the survival of Christian civilization. Upon it depends our own British life, and the long continuity of our institutions and our Empire. The whole fury and might of the enemy must very soon be turned on us. Hitler knows that he will have to break us in this Island or lose the war. If we can stand up to him, all Europe may be free and the life of the world may move forward into broad, sunlit uplands. But if we fail, then the whole world, including the United States, including all that we have known and cared for, will sink into the abyss of a new Dark Age. . . .
>
> Let us therefore brace ourselves to our duties, and so bear ourselves that, if the British Empire and its Commonwealth last for a thousand years, men will still say, "This was their finest hour."[12]

Churchill delivered many more inspiring speeches throughout the war: "The Few," honoring British airmen in the midst of the Battle of Britain ("Never in the field of human conflict was so much owed by so many to so few"); "Give Us the Tools," an urgent appeal to the people of America, February 9, 1941 ("We shall not fail or falter. . . . Give us the tools, and we will finish the job"); and "Do Your Worst," a radio address on July 14, 1941, a message of gratitude to all the emergency workers who served during the Battle of Britain—and a message of defiance to Hitler ("We will have no truce or parley with you, or the grisly gang who work your wicked will. You do your worst—and we will do our best").

One of Churchill's speeches has become the subject of myth. The speech is called "Never Give In," delivered at Harrow School, October 29, 1941. It's often said that Churchill spoke just ten words: "Never give in, never give in, never, never, never, never!" Well, those ten words were *included* in the speech, but Churchill said a good deal more than that. He spoke about the difficult first year of Great Britain's war against Nazi Germany. He encouraged the students to face the "overwhelming might of the enemy" with perseverance.

He closed with words of hope: "These are not dark days; these are great days—the greatest days our country has ever lived; and we must all thank God that we have been allowed, each of us according to our stations, to play a part in making these days memorable in the history of our race."[13]

Though Churchill's speech was longer than ten words (it was 750), he was careful not to overtax his young listeners. Churchill understood that less is often more.

Churchill delivered another brief yet emotional address on May 8, 1945, following the end of the war in Europe. Vast crowds celebrated in the streets. Churchill came out on the balcony of the Ministry of Health and raised the V sign. The crowd cheered.

"God bless you all," he said, his amplified words echoing. "This is your victory!" The crowd shouted back, "No, it is yours!"

"It is the victory of the cause of freedom in every land," he continued. "In all our long history we have never seen a greater day than this. Everyone, man or woman, has done their bit. Everyone has tried, none has flinched. Neither the long years, nor the dangers, nor the fierce attacks of the enemy, have in any way weakened the unbending resolve of the British nation. God bless you all."[14]

World War II was over in Europe. Winston Churchill had waged a war of words against airplanes and bombs—and words had prevailed.

THE CURTAIN FALLS

The crowds that cheered Winston Churchill at the end of the war rejected him in the 1945 election. Out of office, Churchill became the leader of the loyal opposition. In his new role, Churchill continued to make his influence felt.

In 1946, he came to the United States to deliver a speech in Missouri. On the train ride to Missouri, Churchill lost $250 in a poker game with President Truman and his aides but otherwise had a good time.[15]

Churchill delivered one of his greatest speeches at Westminster College in Fulton, Missouri, on March 5, 1946. He called it "The Sinews of Peace." It was, in some ways, similar to Ronald Reagan's "Evil Empire" speech of March 8, 1983. Churchill warned that the Soviet Union had not kept its wartime agreements, and that Soviet-style Communism had spread like a shadow across Eastern Europe:

> From Stettin in the Baltic to Trieste in the Adriatic, an Iron Curtain has descended across the Continent. Behind that line lie all the capitals of the ancient states of Central and Eastern Europe. . . . This is certainly not the Liberated Europe we fought to build up. Nor is it one which contains the essentials of permanent peace.[16]

Churchill coined a vivid metaphor—"Iron Curtain"—to describe the growing Soviet sphere of domination in Eastern Europe. Many were alarmed at Churchill's bluntness—yet Churchill's words were prophetic. Leaders are called to speak unpleasant truths that often provoke an angry reaction. The truth about the "Iron Curtain" needed to be spoken. Some have said that this speech began the Cold War—but Churchill didn't start the Cold War. He simply called our attention to it.

In 1951, Churchill was called back as prime minister of Great Britain. Perhaps the people of Great Britain, having watched the Iron Curtain descending across Europe, felt they needed a warrior to lead them. Churchill suffered a series of mild strokes during those years, and he knew his health was declining. He resigned as prime minister in April 1955 and tried to remain active in public life.

On January 15, 1965, Churchill suffered a severe stroke. He lingered for nine days; then, on the morning of Sunday, January 24, he passed away at the age of ninety. A grateful world mourned.

LESSONS FROM THE LIFE OF A WARRIOR OF WORDS

Winston Churchill towered as a role model of the Second Side of Leadership, communication skills. His career is rich in lessons for our leadership lives today. Some examples:

1. *Always communicate hope and optimism.* As prime minister, Churchill was often the bearer of bad tidings. Yet he never delivered bad news without surrounding it in hope. Even as Hitler's armies rolled through Europe, Churchill envisioned a coming day when "the joybells will ring again." Even when Churchill had nothing to offer the British people but "blood, toil, tears and sweat," he inspired them with a promise of "victory, victory at all costs."

In your leadership life, you will sometimes be called to deliver bad news. Make sure you treat every "bad news day" as an opportunity to inspire and motivate your followers with the promise of ultimate victory.

2. *Repeat, repeat, repeat.* Churchill wanted to make sure the boys at Harrow School did not miss his meaning. So he said, "Never give in, never give in, never, never, never, never!" Sometimes it helps to repeat a statement multiple times in one speech. Sometimes it helps to repeat the same message again and again, week after week. People learn by repetition.

Great leaders don't hesitate to communicate the vision then communicate it again and again and again. Don't assume that communicating it once is sufficient. By about the tenth time you've delivered the same basic message, you'll be sick of it— but that's when people are beginning to grasp what you're telling them. Be relentless in communicating your vision.

3. *Be witty.* A gentle sense of humor is an enormous asset to a communicator. During a parliamentary debate, Churchill appeared to be nodding off as a political opponent spoke. The speaker was offended and distracted by Churchill's apparent slumber. Glowering at Churchill, he said, "Must you sleep while I'm speaking?"

"No," Churchill replied, "it is purely voluntary."[17]

Avoid using humor to attack others—but a quick wit can be extremely helpful in deflecting other people's attacks on you.

4. *Be visual.* Churchill understood the power of visual symbols—even something as simple as his two-fingered V for "victory." Churchill began using that sign in July 1941 when the BBC launched its "V for Victory" campaign, encouraging listeners in Nazi-occupied Europe to scrawl the letter V to show support for the Allies. After Churchill adopted that symbol, the V for Victory sign went viral around the world.

When you speak, make your message memorable by making it visual. Use symbols, pictures, props, PowerPoint, and any other medium you can think of to reach not only the ears of your listeners, but their eyes as well.

5. *Be succinct.* As a speaker, don't wear out your welcome. Often, the less you say, the more they'll remember. Churchill's speech to the students at Harrow School was just 750 words long. Even more concise, Abraham Lincoln's Gettysburg Address was 272 words long, and his second inaugural address was only 700 words. As King Solomon observed in Ecclesiastes: "The more the words, the less the meaning, and how does that profit anyone?"[18]

There is a maxim that is often attributed to Winston Churchill: "A good speech should be like a woman's skirt; long enough to cover the subject and short enough to create interest."

I don't think he actually said it, but I'm pretty sure he would agree.

Of all the talents bestowed upon men, none is so precious as the gift of oratory.
He who enjoys it wields a power more durable than that of a great king.
He is an independent force in the world.
WINSTON CHURCHILL

5

MARTIN LUTHER KING JR.

"I Have a Dream"

---

*Ultimately a genuine leader is not a searcher for consensus
but a molder of consensus. . . . I would rather be a man
of conviction than a man of conformity.*
DR. MARTIN LUTHER KING JR.

Thanks to my mother, I am a witness to history.

In the summer of 1963, I was in Florida, planning to drive to Indiana University and complete my master's in physical education. I called my mother to tell her I was going to stop by Wilmington, Delaware, for a visit, but she said, "Don't come to Wilmington. Meet me in Washington, DC. I'm going to hear Dr. Martin Luther King Jr."

Mom idolized Dr. King. She had been involved in social causes for as long as I can remember. I had no idea what an important event the March on Washington would be.

On August 28, 1963, my mother, my sister Carol, and I were three faces in a crowd of 250,000 people thronging the National Mall. People tend to remember only Dr. King's speech, but there were many speakers and performers that day. I heard speeches by James Baldwin, Sidney Poitier, and Marlon Brando. Gospel singer Mahalia Jackson sang "How I Got Over"; Bob Dylan and Joan Baez sang "When the Ship Comes In"; and Peter, Paul, and Mary sang "Blowin' in the Wind."

Then came the main event—Dr. King himself.

I remember how Dr. King's words stirred my emotions. I was close enough to see the passion in his eyes as he said, "I have a dream that one day this nation will rise up and live out the true meaning of its creed: 'We hold these truths to be self-evident, that all men are created equal.'" There was power in those words—in their sound, their cadence, the refrains of "I have a dream!" and "Let freedom ring!"

There was power in the way Dr. King's speech echoed great words and great ideas from Lincoln's Emancipation Proclamation and the Gettysburg Address, the Declaration of Independence and the Constitution, great Negro spirituals and the Bible.

There was power in the metaphors Dr. King chose. America, he said, had "given the Negro people a bad check, a check which has come back marked 'insufficient funds.'" He spoke of transforming "the jangling discords of our nation into a beautiful symphony of brotherhood." He echoed the thundering Old Testament prophet Amos, saying, "we will not be satisfied until justice rolls down like waters and righteousness like a mighty stream."

I didn't realize at the time that Dr. King's closing words were not a part of his prepared text. There is a point, about twelve minutes into the speech, where Dr. King says, "Unearned suffering is redemptive" and "this situation can and will be changed."

I'm told that, as the applause roared, Mahalia Jackson said to Dr. King, "Tell them, Martin! Tell them about the dream!"

At that moment, Dr. King apparently made a split-second decision. He set his prepared text aside, and from then on he didn't use any notes. He spoke straight from his heart.

"I still have a dream," he said. "It is a dream deeply rooted in the American dream. . . ."

COMMITTED TO NONVIOLENT RESISTANCE

Martin Luther King Jr. was born in Atlanta on January 15, 1929. His father, "Daddy King," was a Baptist minister who taught young Martin to resist segregation.

Once, Reverend King Sr. took young Martin to a shoe store. They sat down in the front of the store. The young white shoe clerk said, "I'll be happy to wait on you if you'll just move to those seats in the rear."

"There's nothing wrong with these seats," Daddy King said. "We're comfortable here."

"I'm sorry," the clerk said, "but you'll have to move."

Daddy King took Martin by the hand and they walked out.

"This was the first time I had seen Dad so furious," Martin later recalled. "I still remember walking down the street beside him as he muttered, 'I don't care how long I have to live with this system, I will never accept it.'"[1]

In high school, Martin Luther King Jr. excelled in public speaking and debate. Once, while returning by bus from a speaking contest in a neighboring city, Martin and his speech teacher were ordered by the bus driver to give up their seats to a white passenger. Martin refused at first, but his teacher persuaded him to comply with the law. "That night will never leave my mind," he later said. "It was the angriest I have ever been in my life."[2]

An exceptional student, Martin skipped the ninth grade and went straight from the eleventh grade to Morehouse College without formally graduating from high school. He was a college freshman at age fifteen. He graduated from Morehouse in 1948 and went on to Crozer Theological Seminary in Chester, Pennsylvania. He earned a PhD in systematic theology at Boston University and became pastor of the Dexter Avenue Baptist Church in Montgomery, Alabama, at age twenty-five.

Dr. King was inspired by *The Kingdom of God Is within You*, a treatise on nonviolent resistance by Leo Tolstoy; Henry David Thoreau's essay "On Civil Disobedience"; theologians Paul Tillich and Reinhold Niebuhr; and the life of Gandhi, who employed nonviolent resistance to achieve India's independence.

Dr. King played a key role in the 385-day-long Montgomery Bus Boycott, December 1955 through December 1956. The boycott began when Rosa Parks, a secretary of the Montgomery NAACP, refused to obey a bus driver's order that she give her seat to a white passenger. During the boycott, Dr. King was arrested and his house was firebombed. His leadership during the boycott elevated him to national prominence.

COMMUNICATING THE DREAM

Dr. King's "I Have a Dream" speech is the purest example of the Second Side of Leadership ever spoken. It's a speech about a leadership vision—a vision in which we live out our creed that "all men are created equal," a vision in which people will be judged by the content of their character, not the color of their skin. It's a powerful dream, a transformative vision—but a dream accomplishes nothing until it's communicated. On that hot August day when Dr. King spoke those words, his vision spread to 250,000 souls on the National Mall and to the millions who were watching on TV.

An uncommunicated vision accomplishes nothing. But a vision expressed by a skilled communicator can change the world. When the First Side of Leadership is joined to the Second Side of Leadership, the river of history changes course.

Dr. Martin Luther King Jr. was a complete seven-sided leader. But if I had to pick one side of leadership that marked his life more than any other, it would be communication skills. There is much we can learn about the Second Side of Leadership by studying the words of Dr. Martin Luther King Jr. You can actually hear the rhythms and the inflection of his rich voice echoing in the words on the page. Let's listen:

In "Paul's Letter to American Christians," November 4, 1956, Dr. King imagined a letter the apostle Paul might write to the church in America. He delivered this message at Dexter Avenue Baptist Church, Montgomery, Alabama. Here's an excerpt:

> America, as I look at you from afar, I wonder whether your moral and spiritual progress has been commensurate with your scientific progress. It seems to me that your moral progress lags behind your scientific progress. . . . You have allowed the material means by which you live to outdistance the spiritual ends for which you live. You have allowed your mentality to outrun your morality. You have allowed your civilization to outdistance your culture.

Through your scientific genius you have made of the world a neighborhood, but. . .you have failed to make of it a brotherhood.[3]

Notice the counterpoint of ideas in this passage—the contrast of our mentality versus our morality, our civilization versus our culture. There are rhythms in these contrasts that make Dr. King's message even more powerful and convicting.

In "Loving Your Enemies," November 17, 1957, Dr. King expresses his views on nonviolence at the Dexter Avenue Baptist Church, Montgomery, Alabama:

This morning, as I look into your eyes, and into the eyes of all of my brothers in Alabama and all over America and over the world, I say to you, "I love you. I would rather die than hate you." And I'm foolish enough to believe that through the power of this love, somewhere, men of the most recalcitrant bent will be transformed. And then we will be in God's kingdom. We will be able to matriculate into the University of Eternal Life because we had the power to love our enemies, to bless those persons that cursed us, to even decide to be good to those persons who hated us, and we even prayed for those persons who despitefully used us.[4]

Loving our enemies is a constant theme in Dr. King's sermons. He weaves the timeless teachings of the Sermon on the Mount together with eye-opening original phrases such as "matriculate into the University of Eternal Life." The combination of old and new, familiar and startling, forces us to think deeply about what it means to love our enemies.

"Eulogy for the Martyred Children," September 18, 1963, is the message of comfort Dr. King delivered at the memorial service for three martyred girls. The girls—Addie Mae Collins, Carol Denise McNair, and Cynthia Diane Wesley—were killed in the bombing of the Sixteenth Street Baptist Church in Birmingham. A fourth girl, Carole Robertson, was memorialized in a separate service. The church was bombed on Sunday, September 15, 1963—less than three weeks after Dr. King's "I Have a Dream" speech. Dr. King's eulogy helped accelerate passage of the Civil Rights Act of 1964. Here's an excerpt:

God still has a way of wringing good out of evil. And history has proven over and over again that unmerited suffering is redemptive. The innocent blood of these little girls may well serve as a redemptive force that will bring new light to this dark city. . . .

Death is not the end. Death is not a period that ends the great sentence of life, but a comma that punctuates it to more lofty significance. Death is not a blind alley that leads the human race into a state of nothingness, but an open door which leads man into life eternal. Let this daring faith, this great invincible surmise, be your sustaining power during these trying days.[5]

In "How Long, Not Long," March 25, 1965, Dr. King again shares a vision from his heart. Standing on the steps of the state capitol in Montgomery, immediately after the Selma-to-Montgomery March, he says:

However difficult the moment, however frustrating the hour, it will not be long, because "truth crushed to earth will rise again."
How long? Not long, because "no lie can live forever."
How long? Not long, because "you shall reap what you sow." . . .
How long? Not long, because the arc of the moral universe is long, but it bends toward justice.
How long? Not long, because "His truth is marching on."[6]

The rhythm of the words lifts our hearts and makes us feel empowered and emboldened. In our public speaking, we need to choose not only our words but the cadence of our words. How our words sound is almost as important as what they mean.

On April 3, 1968, Dr. King delivered his last speech: "I've Been to the Mountaintop." He spoke at the Mason Temple in Memphis, Tennessee, the headquarters of the Church of God in Christ. He closed with these prophetic words:

Well, I don't know what will happen now. We've got some difficult days ahead. But it really doesn't matter with me now, because I've been to the mountaintop. And I don't mind.

Like anybody, I would like to live a long life. Longevity has its place. But I'm not concerned about that now. I just want to do God's will. And He's allowed me to go up to the mountain. And I've looked over. And I've seen the Promised Land. I may not get there with you. But I want you to know tonight, that we, as a people, will get to the promised land!

And so I'm happy tonight. I'm not worried about anything. I'm not fearing any man. Mine eyes have seen the glory of the coming of the Lord![7]

The following evening at about 6:00, Dr. King was on the balcony of his hotel room at the Lorraine Motel, along with other members of his entourage. He turned to musician Ben Branch. "Ben," he said, "make sure you play 'Take My Hand, Precious Lord' in the meeting tonight. Play it real pretty."[8]

Then a gunshot shattered the calm evening. Dr. King fell, mortally wounded.

The Second Side of a Seven-Sided Leader

Like Dr. King, you may have a dream you want to communicate. Great leaders are great communicators. That's why the Second Side of Leadership is communication. With these principles as our starting point, let me suggest some ways to become a more effective communicator of your leadership vision.

1. *Use humble words to communicate grand ideas.* The more you study Dr. King's life, the more you appreciate what a learned intellectual he was. He was extremely well read and well acquainted with great literature and great ideas. Yet he communicated his grand and sweeping thoughts in humble words. He never tried to impress his audiences with jargon or big words. He used language to serve God and people, not to serve his own ego.

Dr. King learned the beauty of simple words from his father, Daddy King. Whenever Martin began to "gain altitude" and become grandiose in his preaching, Daddy King (who always sat front and center) would lean forward and whisper, "Keep it simple, son, keep it simple."[9]

A number of years ago, an American president proposed a new policy of urban development. That policy, he said, would "strengthen linkages among macro-economic sectoral place-oriented economies." Translation: his new policy would enable cities to cooperate together for mutual economic benefit.[10] You have to wonder why he didn't just say so.

If you really want to impress people with your communication skills, always communicate clearly and concisely. When people understand you, they think you're brilliant!

2. *Throw away the script and speak from your heart.* What do people remember from the "I Have a Dream" speech? The conclusion—the final one-third of the speech. There's nothing wrong with the first two-thirds. During the first twelve minutes, Dr. King made a powerful case for human equality. But when Dr. King set aside his notes and talked about his dream, his words thundered. When Dr. King told us, "I have a dream," an electric thrill went down our collective spine. His dream of America's future gripped our hearts and captured our imaginations. He enabled us to see that dream through his eyes—and he made us want to take part in it.

How are the last five minutes of the speech different from the first twelve minutes? Answer: In the last five minutes, Dr. King spoke straight from his heart, no notes, no script.

You might say, "I can't give a speech without notes! And I can't memorize a speech word for word." I'm not suggesting you memorize a speech by rote. Your audience wants you to share your convictions, your ideas, with spontaneous passion. You won't find energy and enthusiasm in a stack of notes. You must communicate straight from your heart.

How did Dr. King deliver his "I Have a Dream" speech completely impromptu and unrehearsed? Actually, he didn't. Two months earlier, Dr. King had given a speech at the Detroit Walk to Freedom (June 23, 1963). The organizers of the Detroit event included Rev. C. L. Franklin (father of singer Aretha Franklin), Harry Belafonte, and Mahalia Jackson. Dr. King's Detroit speech contained many of the same phrases and ideas found in the last five minutes of the "I Have a Dream" speech. If you compare the two speeches side by side, you find many strong similarities—but they're not the same speech.

Dr. King had practiced the Detroit speech many times. Mahalia Jackson had heard him talk about the dream at the Walk to Freedom—and she wanted to hear those stirring words again. So she called out to Dr. King, "Tell them about the dream!" Dr. King simply had to reach into the depths of his soul and pull out the ideas and passion he had delivered in Detroit two months earlier.

You can communicate powerfully, without notes, straight from the heart, just as Dr. King did. The key to delivering a compelling, heartfelt speech is always to have ready what I call a "signature speech"—a presentation you have crafted and rehearsed hundreds of times and can tailor to the occasion. You can stretch it out by adding a few stories or condense it by mentally editing your speech on the fly.

The beauty of a signature speech is that you can deliver that speech a thousand times—*and it will never be the same speech twice*! You know the outline, themes, stories, and organization of the speech; you know exactly what you want to say at all times—but every time you give that speech, you compose a new and original version, sentence by sentence, as you speak. You deliver your speech the same way you would have a one-on-one conversation with a friend. You compose it as you go, while looking your audience in the eye.

And most important of all, you speak confidently, with passion and enthusiasm, in a compelling conversational style. If you want to communicate *your* dream, *your* leadership vision, in a way that persuades and inspires, throw away the script. Speak from your heart.

3. *Communicate passion, not just ideas and information.* Great communicators don't just dump information on their listeners—they fire up their listeners with excitement and enthusiasm. If you want to transmit information, send an e-mail. But if you want to motivate and persuade, you have to communicate your passion.

Dr. King communicated passion and enthusiasm every time he spoke. He used rolling phrases to stir the souls of his listeners. He employed a powerful rhetorical device called *anaphora*—repeating important phrases for emphasis: "Now is the time. . ."; "One hundred years later. . ."; "We can never be satisfied. . ."; "Let freedom ring. . ."; "Free at last. . ."; and above all, "I have a dream. . . ."

Dr. King didn't sugarcoat the obstacles his people would face on the way to the promised land of equality and brotherhood—but in the midst of the crisis, he communicated hope. As he spoke, he opened the floodgates of his emotions, and his listeners were carried away on that emotional flood.

Your message should be logically organized and supported by facts (as Dr. King's message was). You want to *reach* the emotions of your listeners, not manipulate them. But facts and logic alone are not enough. Your leadership vision deserves a powerful presentation. Tell them about your dream—and tell them with passion.

4. *Speak with authority.* Dr. King did not mince words. He spoke like a general issuing marching orders to his troops: "We shall always march ahead. We cannot turn back."

Avoid "weasel words" that suck the power and authority out of your message. People use weasel words to avoid taking responsibility for their thoughts. Qualifiers are weasel words that cloud your meaning. For example, avoid saying "basically"—it weakens your statement. "To be honest" makes people wonder if you were dishonest before. Replace the squishy-sounding phrase "I feel" with a strong declarative statement. Instead of qualifying your position with "in my opinion," get the facts that enable you to speak with authority. Speak with confidence and you'll inspire confidence in your listeners.

No one wants to follow an uncertain leader. As the apostle Paul wrote, "If the trumpet does not sound a clear call, who will get ready for battle?"[11]

5. *Don't soft-pedal bad news.* Dr. King stated the truth with unsparing clarity: "One hundred years later, the life of the Negro is still sadly crippled by the manacles of segregation and the chains of discrimination." He always paired bad news with his optimistic vision of the change that was coming.

If your organization is struggling, if your game plan is not working, candidly say so. Then, with confidence and enthusiasm, give your listeners an injection of hope and optimism. Motivate them, energize them—then lead them into your vision of the future.

6. *Communicate a sense of urgency.* Dr. King wanted the nation to know that the African-American community had reached the end of its patience. He said, "We have also come to this hallowed spot to remind America of the fierce urgency of Now. This is no time to engage in the luxury of cooling off or to take the tranquilizing drug of gradualism. Now is the time. . . !" Motivate your listeners to action with a sense of urgency.

7. *Identify with your listeners.* Let them know you're struggling alongside them, not talking "at" them. Tell them you understand their sacrifices. As Dr. King said, "I am not unmindful that some of you have come here out of great trials and tribulations." When you acknowledge their sacrifices, they'll know they can trust you

and follow where you lead.

8. *Finish strong!* Many good speeches have been ruined by weak endings. Don't let your presentation trail off. Drive your point home with a powerful statement or a heart-tugging story. End with a call to action. Your closing sentence should pull your audience out of their chairs for a standing ovation.

Learn from Dr. King. Lead like Dr. King. Tell them about the dream.

And so I say to you today, my friends, that you may be able to speak
with the tongues of men and angels; you may have the eloquence
of articulate speech; but if you have not love, it means nothing.
Dr. Martin Luther King Jr.

6

RONALD REAGAN

The Great Communicator

I suppose I became a kind of preacher. I'd preach in my speeches
about the problems we had and try to get people roused and to say
to their neighbors, "Hey, let's do something about this."
RONALD REAGAN

In 1976, former California governor Ronald Reagan waged a bruising primary battle against President Ford for the Republican nomination. Ford held a slight lead in the delegate count heading into the Republican National Convention in Kansas City—but he had failed to secure the nomination. If Reagan could persuade enough uncommitted delegates, he could wrest the nomination from the incumbent president.

The Reagan camp waged an epic behind-the-scenes battle for delegates, but Ford pulled out a narrow victory, winning 1,187 delegate votes to Reagan's 1,070. The convention fight came close to splitting the party. On the night of President Ford's acceptance speech, he invited Governor Reagan to the podium to address the delegates. As the band played "California, Here I Come," Ronald Reagan and his wife, Nancy, joined President Ford on the stage.

Amid the deafening celebration, Reagan turned to Nancy and said, "I don't know what to say!" Nancy's smile tightened.

Moments later, Reagan stepped to the microphone and began to speak. He talked about his vision for America—about restoring prosperity, eliminating the threat of nuclear war, and restoring constitutional liberties. Reagan spoke impromptu for five minutes—and when he finished, the hall interrupted in a thunderous ovation. Many delegates wept.

Reagan's biographer, Edmund Morris, recalled, "The power of that speech was extraordinary. . . . [There was a] palpable sense amongst the delegates that we've nominated the wrong guy."[1]

President Gerald Ford went on to lose the 1976 general election to Governor Jimmy Carter of Georgia. But millions remembered Reagan's impromptu remarks at the convention. That five-minute speech defined Ronald Reagan as a candidate with statesmanlike gravitas and political star power. In 1980, when Reagan ran again, he captured the White House.

Columnist George Will placed Ronald Reagan's convention speech in a historical context, concluding that those five minutes defined Reagan as a leader:

> Reagan's rise to the White House began from the ashes of the 1976 Republican convention in Kansas City. Truth be told, it began from the podium of that convention, with Reagan's gracious—but fighting—concession speech. No one who knew the man and listened to him carefully could have mistaken that speech for a valedictory statement by someone taking his leave from national politics. . . .
>
> As was the case with Winston Churchill, another politician spurned by his party and consigned to "wilderness years," the iron entered Reagan's soul after adversity. . . . The Carter presidency made the country hungry for strong leadership, and the Reagan of 1980 was stronger and more ready to lead than was the Reagan of 1976.[2]

Reagan quickly earned the title the Great Communicator. And the rest, as they say, is history.

THE MAKING OF A GREAT COMMUNICATOR

Born in 1911, Ronald Reagan spent most of his youth in Dixon, Illinois. He served as a lifeguard on the Rock River for six years and is credited with seventy-seven rescues. In 1932, he graduated with a degree in economics from Eureka College in Illinois. He worked as a radio broadcaster until 1937, when he moved to Hollywood.

As an actor in such films as *Santa Fe Trail* (with Errol Flynn), *Knute Rockne, All American* (playing George "The Gipper" Gipp), and *Kings Row*, Reagan honed his skills as a communicator. Between 1946 and 1959, he won seven one-year terms as president of the Screen Actors Guild, where he practiced his leadership skills. Reagan hosted TV's *General Electric Theater* and made countless personal appearances as the General Electric spokesman, sometimes delivering more than a dozen speeches per day.

In 1964, Reagan—a longtime FDR Democrat—endorsed Republican Barry Goldwater for president and gave a televised speech on Goldwater's behalf. Though Goldwater lost to Lyndon Johnson in 1964, Reagan's Goldwater speech vaulted him into the political arena. In 1966, he won the first of two terms as governor of California.

Another key Reagan speech was his address to the first Conservative Political Action Conference (CPAC) in 1974. There Reagan invoked the image of America as a "shining city upon a hill":

Standing on the tiny deck of the *Arabella* in 1630 off the Massachusetts coast, John Winthrop said, "We will be as a city upon a hill. The eyes of all people are upon us, so that if we deal falsely with our God in this work we have undertaken and so cause him to withdraw his present help from us, we shall be made a story and a byword throughout the world." Well, we have not dealt falsely with our God, even if he is temporarily suspended from the classroom.[3]

Reagan won the 1980 election in a landslide. On January 20, 1981, he delivered his first inaugural address—a speech he drafted in longhand on a yellow legal pad. There he hammered home one of the core themes of his career: "Government is not the solution to our problems; government *is* the problem."

On January 13, 1982, Air Florida Flight 90 took off from Washington National Airport then stalled due to icing on its wings. The plane clipped the 14th Street Bridge then plunged into the ice-encrusted Potomac River. Only four passengers and a flight attendant survived. Standing on the shore, a man named Lenny Skutnik saw passenger Priscilla Tirado in the freezing water by the tail of the plane, too weak to hold on. Skutnik dove in, swam to the plane, and pulled Tirado to safety.

Less than two weeks later, on January 26, 1982, Lenny Skutnik sat next to the First Lady as President Reagan delivered the State of the Union address. It was the first time a president recognized an American hero during the address, but it would soon become an annual tradition. It was a memorable object lesson in American values.

In a series of speeches in 1982 and 1983, Ronald Reagan spoke boldly about America's chief adversary, the Soviet Union. On June 8, 1982, Reagan became the first American president to address the British Parliament, where he denounced the Berlin Wall as a "dreadful gray gash across the city. . .the fitting signature of the regime that built it." He also shared his optimistic conviction that "the march of freedom and democracy" would "leave Marxism-Leninism on the ash-heap of history as it has left other tyrannies which stifle the freedom and muzzle the self-expression of the people."[4]

On March 8, 1983, Reagan delivered one of his most controversial speeches, his address to the Annual Convention of the National Association of Evangelicals in Orlando, Florida—the "Evil Empire" speech. He urged his listeners to beware the temptation to "ignore the facts of history and the aggressive impulses of an evil empire, to simply call the arms race a giant misunderstanding and thereby remove yourself from the struggle between right and wrong, and good and evil."[5]

Reagan's speech sent shock waves around the world. The Soviet news agency Tass denounced President Reagan's "pathological hatred of Socialism and

Communism," adding that Reagan could "think only in terms of confrontation and bellicose, lunatic anti-Communism."[6] Television journalist Lesley Stahl called the speech a "diatribe" and "the Darth Vader speech," reporting that even Reagan's wife, Nancy, had urged him not to give the "evil empire" speech.[7]

But deep inside the "evil empire," in a miserable gulag called Permanent Labor Camp 35, a Jewish-Russian dissident, Natan Sharansky, heard about the speech when a prison guard read a Soviet news account to him. "We dissidents were ecstatic," Sharansky later recalled. "Finally, the leader of the free world had spoken the truth."[8]

A COMMUNICATOR OF OPTIMISM

On March 23, 1983, Reagan addressed the nation on the subject of the Strategic Defense Initiative—or "Star Wars." Speaking from the Oval Office, he said, "What if free people could live secure in the knowledge that their security did not rest upon the threat of instant U.S. retaliation to deter a Soviet attack, that we could intercept and destroy strategic ballistic missiles before they reached our own soil or that of our allies?"[9] It was nothing less than a plan to make nuclear war impossible by making nuclear weapons obsolete.

Reagan's speech was greeted with howls of protest and derision. Soviet Premier Yuri Andropov declared that Reagan's plan would "open the floodgates to a runaway race of all types of strategic arms, both offensive and defensive." Senator Edward M. Kennedy said the speech was loaded with "misleading Red scare tactics and reckless 'Star Wars' schemes."[10]

President Reagan knew his most visionary idea would be controversial. In fact, every proposal he made was met with stiff resistance in the Congress and harsh criticism in the media. Yet Reagan got most of his agenda passed, from tax cuts to defense spending increases. How did he do it? By applying the Second Side of Leadership, communication skills.

He went over the heads of the news commentators and congressional leaders, taking his agenda directly to the American people. By creating support for his agenda among the voters, he put pressure on Congress to make compromises.

President Reagan continued to stir controversy throughout his presidency. On June 12, 1987, standing in front of Berlin's Brandenburg Gate and the Berlin Wall, he delivered a speech that *Time* magazine listed as one of the Ten Greatest Speeches of all time.[11] (Other speeches on that list included Socrates's "Apology," Frederick Douglass's "The Hypocrisy of American Slavery," Lincoln's "Gettysburg Address," and Churchill's "Blood, Toil, Tears, and Sweat.") In his Berlin Wall speech, Reagan said, "General Secretary Gorbachev, if you seek peace, if you seek prosperity for the Soviet Union and Eastern Europe, if you seek liberalization: Come here to this gate! Mr. Gorbachev, open this gate! Mr. Gorbachev, tear down this wall!"

It was not a polite request. It was an angry ultimatum—and the crowd of

Berliners loved it. They applauded those lines for nearly half a minute.

Eighteen months later, the Berlin Wall lay in rubble. The first hammer blow was delivered by Ronald Reagan himself.

David Gergen, Reagan's director of communications, explained in an interview with *Harvard Business Review* why his boss was such an effective communicator:

> Reagan recognized that to stir people, you must give voice to their own deep desires, inspiring them to believe they can climb mountains they always thought were too high. The leader and followers must unite around a shared vision. If there is a misalignment, a speech won't work. Jerry Ford could've spoken with Lincoln's eloquence and still wouldn't have won people over with his pardon of Nixon; he believed in his heart that it was the best way to move forward, but he failed to get buy-in in advance. . . .
>
> On the other hand, King's "I Have a Dream" speech. . .was the best of modern American speeches because he beautifully gave voice to people's own dreams.[12]

Huffington Post contributor James P. Farwell summed up the historic importance of Reagan's address to the nation following the Challenger space shuttle disaster in 1986:

> Beautifully written by Peggy Noonan, it captured the heartfelt anguish of a nation while celebrating the heroism of the fallen. He spoke *for* Americans, not *to* them. He expressed what Americans felt. It is a remarkable example of powerful strategic communication in that he was able to express compassion and strength as well as a firm resolution to stay focused on the future even in the face of tragedy. It was nothing less than a testament to the American identity.[13]

Ronald Reagan had great empathy and insight into the American psyche. He put into words the hopes, dreams, and innate optimism of the American people.

Lessons from the Great Communicator

Here are the lessons we can learn from Ronald Reagan, so that we can become "great communicators" in our own right:

1. *Use the power of communication to teach, inspire, and persuade.* When Michael Reagan appeared as a guest on my Orlando radio show in 2011, I asked him, "What was your dad's greatest strength as a leader?"

His unhesitating reply: "His ability to communicate. They called him the Great

Communicator, and it was absolutely true. Not only was he the commander in chief, but he saw himself as the communicator in chief. He used his communication skills to teach, to preach, and to get the American people on his side. Their support enabled him to plow right through the opposition. That's how he got things done."

You cannot lead effectively if you cannot communicate effectively. Some would say, "I'm the boss. I give orders; they comply. That's all I need to know about communication." But any dictator can demand compliance. Leaders inspire enthusiasm and motivate people to go beyond compliance. Only a real leader can cast a vision then energize followers to turn that vision into a reality.

Ronald Reagan changed the world through the power of communication. If you want to change your world and change your organization, you must become complete in the Second Side of Leadership.

2. *Communicate hope and optimism.* Ronald Reagan dared to believe that America could win the Cold War. History has validated his optimism. Michael Reagan describes how his father's optimism impacted the nation:

> My father communicated hope and optimism even in hard times. Long before the economy turned around, people felt good about America because Ronald Reagan was president. . . . In the wake of Vietnam, Watergate, the energy crisis, and stagflation, just changing the mood of America was an enormous achievement. Ronald Reagan always lifted America up. When he spoke about this land, you could see America through his eyes. He was like a child on Christmas morning—that's how he felt about his country, and he never tired of telling people how wonderful America is.[14]

Stephen F. Knott teaches national security affairs at the United States Naval War College. He contrasts Reagan's leadership style with that of his predecessor, Jimmy Carter:

> Ronald Reagan's. . .sunny optimism helped restore the people's faith in their nation and in the American presidency. Gone was the talk from the Carter years of a crippled presidency and the need to revamp the Constitution and import a parliamentary system to replace our system of checks and balances. Ronald Reagan's words will remain with us long after his policies are forgotten. . . .
>
> In the end, Reagan's words, like those of Thomas Jefferson, Abraham Lincoln, and Franklin Roosevelt, may prove to be his most durable legacy.[15]

If you are too young to remember the Carter years, take note of this excerpt from President Carter's Oval Office speech of July 15, 1979:

> The symptoms of this crisis of the American spirit are all around us. For the first time in the history of our country a majority of our people believe that the next five years will be worse than the past five years. Two-thirds of our people do not even vote. The productivity of American workers is actually dropping, and the willingness of Americans to save for the future has fallen below that of all other people in the Western world.
>
> This is not a message of happiness or reassurance, but it is the truth and it is a warning. . . .
>
> I'm asking you for your good and for your nation's security to take no unnecessary trips, to use carpools or public transportation whenever you can, to park your car one extra day per week, to obey the speed limit, and to set your thermostats to save fuel.[16]

President Carter thought he could lead the American people by scolding them and confronting them with a pessimistic vision of the future. When Reagan arrived, with his irrepressible charm and infectious optimism, the American people were eager to follow. As Warren Bennis observed in *On Becoming a Leader*, "The leader's world view is always contagious. Carter depressed us; Reagan, whatever his other flaws, gave us hope."[17]

Every day, you as a leader have a choice to make: "I am going to be a leader of optimism" or "I am going to be a leader of pessimism." As Colin Powell has said, "Perpetual optimism is a force multiplier."[18] A positive outlook can take all the resources you possess and multiply them exponentially. Here's why optimism wins:

- Optimists are more confident, so they accept challenging goals.
- Optimists believe setbacks and problems are temporary, so they don't give up.
- Optimists have confidence that their decisions will turn out right, so they are more decisive.
- Optimists don't take rejection personally, so they don't waste time on resentment.
- Optimists know that failure is never final, so they bounce back from adversity.
- Optimists enjoy life and love their work.

Where others see obstacles, look for opportunities. To lead successfully, become a communicator of optimism and hope.

3. *Communicate grand ideas in vivid, visual terms.* Ken Khachigian, Reagan's chief speechwriter, explained his boss's effectiveness this way:

> He "educated" America throughout his presidency. In an early

speech to a joint session of Congress, he made clear the dimensions of an approaching one trillion dollar national debt by saying: ". . .if you had a stack of thousand-dollar bills in your hand only four inches high, you'd be a millionaire. A trillion dollars would be a stack of thousand-dollar bills 67 miles high." (When I questioned where he came up with that number, he smiled and said: "by long division.") . . .

He told Mikhail Gorbachev to tear down the Berlin Wall—symbolism which spoke more loudly then the rest of his speech. He not only educated his country, he educated a world. . . . He was the Great Communicator because he was the great educator and great illustrator.[19]

In your leadership communication, be as vivid and visual as possible. Create word pictures. Use props and visual aids. Use motion and gestures, light and color, images and video to make your message come alive. At the same time, keep it simple. It's easy to overcomplicate your presentation but hard to oversimplify it. Become an educator and an illustrator.

4. *Always tell the truth.* People didn't always agree with Ronald Reagan, but even his enemies believed he was telling the truth as he saw it. In the foreword to his book *Speaking My Mind: Selected Speeches*, Reagan said:

Some of my critics over the years have said that I became president because I was an actor who knew how to give a good speech. I suppose that's not too far wrong. Because an actor knows two important things—to be honest in what he's doing and to be in touch with the audience. That's not bad advice for a politician either. My actor's instinct simply told me to speak the truth as I saw it and felt it.

I don't believe my speeches took me as far as they did merely because of my rhetoric or delivery, but because there were certain basic truths in them that the average American citizen recognized. When I first began speaking of political things, I could feel that people were as frustrated about the government as I was. What I said simply made sense to the guy on the street, and it's the guy on the street who elects presidents of the United States.[20]

As a leader, you must earn the trust of your followers. To earn that trust, always tell the truth.

5. *Become a storyteller.* Ronald Reagan's son Michael told me, "Judge William

Clark told me something about my father that I had never understood before. 'Michael,' he said, 'your dad was not just a storyteller. He spoke in parables. Even his jokes were parables. Whenever he wanted to teach an important truth, he would put it in the form of a story.'

"I had lived with Ronald Reagan all those years and had never seen that before. I had always thought of dad's stories as funny and entertaining. But Judge Clark was right—if you pondered what he was saying, you could always find a deeper truth beneath the surface.

"During the Cold War, Dad joked about life in the Soviet Union. One of his favorite stories went like this: In the Soviet Union, you had to wait ten years to buy a car. A Soviet citizen went to the government showroom and plunked down his savings for a car. The bureaucrat at the showroom said, 'Come back in ten years, comrade, and you can pick up your car.' The citizen said, 'Morning or afternoon?' And the bureaucrat said, 'Ten years from now, what difference does it make?' The citizen said, 'The plumber's coming in the morning.'

"Dad was giving us an insight into the harshness of the Communist system. It was a painless way of teaching us that people had to put up with shortages and red tape under Communism. Now, if all you got out of that story was a chuckle, that was fine with him. But if you listened closely, he'd always give you something to think about."

Dinesh D'Souza offers a similar insight, relating an encounter between President Reagan and former President Nixon:

> Nixon had visited Reagan in the White House and tried to engage him in a discussion of Marxist ideas and Soviet strategy, but Reagan simply wasn't interested; instead, he regaled Nixon with jokes about Soviet farmers who had no incentive to produce under the Communist system. Nixon was troubled to hear such flippancy from the leader of the Western world. He wrote books during the 1980s criticizing Reagan's lack of "realism" and warning that "the Soviet system will not collapse" so "the most we can do is learn to live with our differences" through a policy of "hard headed détente." Yet two and a half years after Reagan left office, Nixon admitted that he was wrong and Reagan was right.[21]

To be a great communicator, become a storyteller. History shows that great storytellers often make the best leaders.

6. *Trust your instincts and convictions.* In 1987, when Reagan was preparing to give his speech at the Berlin Wall, he circulated his speech to advisers in the State Department and the National Security Council. Dozens of advisers read the speech,

and almost without exception, they went apoplectic over one line: "Mr. Gorbachev, tear down this wall."

Secretary of State George Shultz opposed it, and so did National Security Adviser Colin Powell. One diplomat said that line was "in bad taste."[22] Every review copy of the speech came back with that sentence crossed out. But Ronald Reagan knew that it was the heart of the speech, the signature line.

Reagan called Deputy Chief of Staff Ken Duberstein, into the Oval Office and said, "I'm the president, right?"

"Yes, Mr. President," said Duberstein.

"So I decide whether the line about the wall stays in?"

"That's right, sir. It's your decision."

"Then it stays *in*."[23]

Even that conversation didn't settle the matter. While President Reagan was on Air Force One, flying to Berlin, both the State Department and the National Security Council faxed him new versions of the speech without the "tear down this wall" line. As historian Steven Hayward observed, many who opposed that line later tried to take credit for it.[24]

But that line was pure Reagan.

As a leader, you should solicit advice and consider it—then make your own decision. Have confidence in your instincts and convictions. Even if all your advisers say you're wrong, listen to that still, small voice within—and do what that voice tells you.

Then go out and give a speech for the ages.

I wasn't a great communicator, but I communicated great things,
and they didn't spring full bloom from my brow,
they came from the heart of a great nation.
RONALD REAGAN

The Third Side of Leadership

PEOPLE SKILLS

7

SAM WALTON

The Ten-Foot Rule

---

*Outstanding leaders go out of their way to boost the self-esteem
of their personnel. If people believe in themselves,
it's amazing what they can accomplish.*

SAM WALTON

On March 17, 1992, President George Herbert Walker Bush went to Bentonville, Arkansas, to award the Presidential Medal of Freedom to Sam Walton, the founder of Wal-Mart. "Mr. Sam," as Walton was known to his employees, was dying of cancer and not well enough to attend a White House ceremony, so the ceremony was held at Walmart headquarters before a crowd of senior Walmart officials, employees, family, and invited guests.

President Bush began by telling the story of Wal-Mart's rather inauspicious beginnings. "Back in 1962," he said, "Sam Walton started with one Walmart store in Rogers, Arkansas, just six miles from here. And I did hear a story about the opening of his second Walmart over in Harrison—"

The Walmart insiders in the crowd laughed.

President Bush grinned. "Obviously you've heard it, but I'm going to repeat it. For those of you in Washington, I will repeat it." The president nodded toward Sam Walton's successor as CEO, David Glass. "The way my esteemed friend David Glass tells it, Sam had watermelons for sale on the sidewalk and he offered donkey rides in the parking lot. The only problem was the heat, 110 degrees. Well, the watermelons popped, and the watermelon juice was everywhere. The donkeys did what donkeys do in a situation like that, tracking the stuff all over the place. And according to David, who had a nice successful business of his own, Sam's second Walmart store turned into the worst-looking store he'd ever seen. Dave went so far as to suggest to Sam that he ought to find some other line of work.

"Today, more people work for Sam's company than live in Tulsa, Oklahoma—380,000 at the last count. This includes the man with that sound career advice, David Glass."[1]

Sam Walton (known as "Mr. Sam" to his employees) was a people person. He loved the people who worked for him, and he loved the people who shopped at his stores. As former General Electric CEO Jack Welch observed, "Sam Walton understood people the way Thomas Edison understood innovation and Henry Ford, production. He brought out the very best in his employees, gave his very best to his customers, and taught something of value to everyone he touched."[2]

Michael Bergdahl worked alongside Sam Walton for years, serving as Walmart's Director of People at the Bentonville headquarters (Mr. Sam nicknamed him "Bird Dawg"). Bergdahl said, "Mr. Sam preached, emphasized, and taught the importance of having strong people skills. For the most part, the individuals Mr. Sam promoted into higher levels of responsibility were the leaders who had the proven ability to work with and motivate a large team of people."[3]

And Robert Slater, author of *The Wal-Mart Decade*, wrote that Mr. Sam "was chiefly concerned with assuring harmony among store managers, employees, and customers. . . . He worked at the people level, not the administrative one."[4]

As a business leader, Sam Walton was complete in the Seven Sides of Leadership. If there was one side of leadership that characterized him above all others, it was his commitment to the Third Side of Leadership, people skills. The company Sam Walton founded has grown considerably since President Bush awarded him the Medal of Freedom. Today Wal-Mart Stores Inc. employs 2.2 million people around the globe, including more than 1.3 million in the United States, and is the largest private employer in the United States and in Mexico.[5]

From the beginning, Sam Walton has said that he's not just in the retail business; he's in the people business. There's much we can learn about the Third Side of Leadership from the most successful retailer in history, Sam Walton.

The Story of Mr. Sam

Samuel Moore Walton was born in 1918 in Kingfisher, Oklahoma. Sam was ambitious even in his youth. As an eighth grader in Shelbina, Missouri, he achieved the distinction of becoming the youngest Eagle Scout in Missouri history. During the Great Depression, he worked at a variety of jobs, including delivering newspapers, delivering milk (produced by the family cow), and waiting tables (often paid only in tips and free meals).

Walton worked his way through the University of Missouri. His ambition in those days was virtually limitless. As he recalled in *Made in America*, "I even entertained thoughts of one day becoming president of the United States."[6] He recalled how he taught himself the art of meeting people and making friends:

> I had decided I wanted to be president of the university student body. I learned early on that one of the secrets to campus leadership was the simplest thing of all: speak to people coming down the sidewalk before they speak to you. I did that in college. I did it when I carried my papers. I would always look ahead and speak to

the person coming toward me. If I knew them, I would call them by name, but even if I didn't I would still speak to them. Before long, I probably knew more students than anybody in the university, and they recognized me and considered me their friend.[7]

Walton graduated in 1940 with a degree in economics. Three days after graduation, he started as a management trainee at a J. C. Penney store in Des Moines, Iowa. His career at Penney's was less than stellar. His handwriting was, by his own admission, completely illegible. Since sales receipts were written by hand in those days, this became a major problem when his receipts were audited. "Walton," his supervisor told him, "I'd fire you if you weren't such a good salesman. Maybe you're just not cut out for retail."[8]

He joined the army in 1942 and was assigned to the Army Intelligence Corps, eventually achieving the rank of captain. It was excellent on-the-job leadership training, and Walton's experience gave him confidence as a leader. While in the army, he began planning his postwar career as an entrepreneur. Assigned to an army post in Salt Lake City, he would visit the public library and check out every book on retailing. He also visited Zions Cooperative Mercantile Institution, the department store founded in 1868 by Brigham Young, looking for ideas.[9]

Sam Walton and his wife, Helen, were married in 1943. Their marriage lasted until Sam's death in 1992.

Walton set aside $5,000 from his army pay—a substantial nest egg for a twenty-six-year-old in 1945. He was eager to start a business, and with the help of a $20,000 loan from his father-in-law, he bought a Ben Franklin variety store in Newport, Arkansas. The franchise company put him through two weeks of retail management training, which gave him a good foundation in business basics—though Walton believed he learned more about retail by studying his competitor across the street.[10] Sam Walton succeeded in increasing the store's sales volume from $72,000 to $175,000 in the first three years—and his success was his undoing. The landlord decided to cancel the lease, take the store over (including franchise rights), and put his son in charge of the business. Though Sam was able to sell the inventory and fixtures to the landlord for $50,000, he had been forced out of business. He made up his mind that he would never again give a landlord veto power over the business he had worked so hard to build.[11]

Walton bought his next store in Bentonville, Arkansas, in May 1950. Before Walton arrived, that store was producing annual sales of $32,000; after one year, Walton had pushed it to $95,000.[12] With help from his brother Budd, a former fighter pilot, Sam scouted new store locations from the air in a secondhand airplane he had bought for $1,800.

As Walton expanded his operation, he learned the art of delegating. Whenever possible, he hired managers who were willing to invest their own money in exchange for a stake in the store. Because of their investment, these managers were highly motivated to run a successful store.

Walton opened the first store bearing the Wal-Mart name on July 2, 1962, in Rogers, Arkansas. He scrapped his original plan to call it "Walton's Five and Dime Store" when an employee pointed out that "Wal-Mart" would be only seven letters long, saving a lot of money in neon signage.

Most of Sam Walton's business strengths were related to his people skills. He was a great team builder, a great recruiter of talent, a great motivator, and a great listener. He got his best ideas from his people. When an employee suggested that Walmart might benefit from these newfangled machines called "computers," Walton pounced on the idea. In 1966, long before the advent of low-cost personal computers, Sam Walton attended an IBM school for retailers in Poughkeepsie, New York. Computers became an essential tool for maintaining control in his rapidly expanding operation.[13]

In 1982, Sam Walton was listed by *Forbes* as the richest man in America. He only began to slip from the top of the *Forbes* list in 1988, when he began distributing parts of his fortune to his heirs. On April 5, 1992, Mr. Sam passed away after a two-year battle with multiple myeloma.

(A personal note: As I discussed in my book *The Mission Is Remission*, I was diagnosed with multiple myeloma in 2011. Medical science is making enormous strides in treating multiple myeloma, and I wish Sam Walton could have had the benefit of the amazing medical advances that have kept my disease in remission for several years.)

The Soul of Leadership

I would define "people skills" as the ability to show people you care about them. When people know you care, they will adopt *your* vision as *their* vision, *your* success as *their* success, and they will work hard to make your shared vision a reality.

I could sum up my concept of people skills in a single word: *love*. By *love*, I don't mean an emotional feeling. I'm talking about the kind of love the ancient Greeks called *agape* (pronounced ah-GAH-pay)—love that is a deliberate decision. *Agape* love means that you, as a leader, continue cheering for your followers even when they mess up, cost you money, and break your heart. You choose to love your followers even when they disappoint you.

Loving your people and using good people skills doesn't mean you never apply discipline or enforce the rules. Sometimes the most loving thing you can do for your people is to hold them accountable for bad decisions. You do so because you want the best for them.

James Kouzes and Barry Posner, founders of The Leadership Challenge, write,

"Love is the soul of leadership. Love is what sustains people along the arduous journey to the summit of any mountain. Love is the source of the leader's courage. Leaders are in love: in love with leading, in love with their organizations' products and services, and in love with people."[14]

Love for people you lead is not an act, not a technique for manipulating people into staying later and working harder. Your leadership love must be sincere. Here are some people skills to help you authentically love your people:

People Skill No. 1: Be visible and available. In his 1982 bestseller *In Search of Excellence*, Tom Peters urges leaders to "manage by walking around" (MBWA). Sam Walton was an MBWA leader long before Peters coined the term. Peters observed that the most effective leaders spend considerable time simply "hanging out" with their people in the lunchroom or on the shop floor. Years before *In Search of Excellence* was published, Mr. Sam crisscrossed the country in his little two-seater plane, visiting every store in his empire, shaking hands and giving encouragement to the frontline staff while keeping his eyes and ears open at all times.

Mr. Sam was an iconic figure in his white cap with the blue Walmart logo on the front. He would teach and preach Walmart values, but he spent most of his time listening and learning. If he uncovered a potential problem, he would help people find solutions. Based on Sam Walton's example, here are some ways to improve your "walking around" skills:

1. Keep your visits spontaneous and unplanned. Make sure it's not all about business. Be genuine. Ask people about their families, the sports teams they follow, or the books they read.

2. Keep it friendly and nonthreatening. People should be thrilled, not terrified, when you appear unannounced on the floor.

3. Express a willingness to hear bad news. Reward candor, and you'll get more of it; punish candor, and you'll be left in the dark.

4. Ask for ways to improve the organization. Are there processes that aren't working? Can customer care be improved? Are there ways to improve products or services?

5. Avoid favoring one employee over another. Spend equal time and show equal interest in everyone.

6. Catch people in the act of doing things right. Praise people for their contribution to the organization.

7. Bring donuts. Or baked goods. Or pizza. Make your visit a time of fun and refreshment. Create a positive vibe, and you'll always have a positive impact.

Quality expert Neil Snyder observed, "Walton knew of no better way to scrutinize the stores than to talk to associates, shaking hands and meeting people, all the while keeping a sharp eye out for ideas, successes, and failures. . . . He was out on the floor with them, and that gave them pride."[15]

People Skill No. 2: Be a good listener. Many leaders are great talkers, but the greatest leaders are skilled listeners. Everyone in your organization needs to be heard. Be a leader who listens. Mr. Sam himself said, "Great ideas come from everywhere if you just listen and look for them."[16]

Sam Walton was committed to learning from everyone in his organization, regardless of position. Lee Scott was CEO from 2000 to 2009. He recalled, "For a long, long time, Sam would show up regularly in the drivers' break room at 4 a.m. with a bunch of donuts and just sit there for a couple of hours talking to them."[17]

People Skill No. 3: Delegate. The art of delegating is the essence of leadership. To accomplish goals through others, you must delegate tasks and authority. Early in my career as a sports executive, I did everything myself—and I had the angry stomach lining to prove it. But I quickly learned to delegate, and I eventually became very good at it. Today I have the cleanest desk in the state of Florida because I delegate so many tasks to my capable staff.

Though leaders *must* delegate authority, leaders *cannot* delegate responsibility. You should never say, "I take full responsibility—but my underlings are to blame." A leader is always responsible for the results. You are responsible to set benchmarks, maintain communication, and assess performance. When things go wrong on your watch, you are to blame, like it or not.

Give your people permission to make decisions—and mistakes. And count on it: they'll make some doozies. A wise leader will let them learn from mistakes. If you punish mistakes, you'll punish initiative and imagination. Unleash the talent of your people, and you'll be amazed at what they achieve.

People Skill No. 4: Be loyal. Always stand up for the people you lead. Critique their performance in private, but always defend them in public. You and your people rise or fall as a team. Be loyal to your people even when they let you down.

People Skill No. 5: Manage conflict. Great leaders face conflict squarely, resolve it fairly, and extract the lessons and benefits of it. Peter Drucker's first law of decision making states, "One does not make a decision without disagreements."[18] Let your people speak their mind and give them a chance to persuade you. Then you, the leader, must have the final say. Make sure everyone buys into your decision, agree or disagree. People have a right to their opinions, but they also have an obligation to implement your leadership decisions.

People Skill No. 6: Level with your people. One of "Sam's Rules for Building a Business" is "Communicate everything you possibly can to your partners. The more they know, the more they'll understand. The more they understand, the more they'll care. Once they care, there's no stopping them."[19] To lead people, you have to level with them. Great leaders speak the truth.

People Skill No. 7: Practice Sam Walton's Ten-Foot Rule. This is the rule he followed as a student at the University of Missouri. Whenever he was within ten feet of another person, he would speak to that person—calling them by name if he knew them. The

Ten-Foot Rule is one of the cornerstones of Walmart customer service: whenever you come within ten feet of the customer, make eye contact, greet the customer with a smile, and offer assistance. Today many businesses observe the Ten-Foot Rule, but it originated with Sam Walton.

MR. SAM'S CONFESSION

As the largest employer in the United States, Walmart has been continuously targeted by Big Labor for unionization. In 2009, the *American Prospect*, a pro-organized-labor publication, reported on Sam Walton's opposition to a minimum wage increase in the early 1960s:

> Around the time that the young Sam Walton opened his first stores, John Kennedy redeemed a presidential campaign promise by persuading Congress to extend the minimum wage to retail workers. . . . Congress granted an exclusion, however, to small businesses with annual sales beneath $1 million—a figure that in 1965 it lowered to $250,000.
>
> Walton was furious. . . . [He could hire employees] for a song, as little as 50 cents an hour. Now. . .he had to pay his workers the $1.15 hourly minimum. Walton's response was to divide up his stores into individual companies whose revenues didn't exceed the $250,000 threshold.[20]

It's true that Sam Walton opposed the federal minimum wage. But the claim that he responded with an illegal scheme to "divide his stores into individual companies" to avoid compliance is false. As Nelson Lichtenstein reports in *The Retail Revolution*, Sam Walton employed a business model in which each store was legally a stand-alone entity. He did so long before the change in the minimum wage law. This way each of his managers could invest in his own particular store and have a personal stake in the success of that store.

When the federal government more than doubled the minimum wage, Sam Walton used the *already-existing* structure of his business to avoid paying the higher wage. The courts ultimately ruled that Walmart's decentralized structure did not exempt the company from paying the higher minimum wage. The company issued checks for back pay and penalties.[21]

Sam Walton had sound fiscal reasons for resisting federal intrusion into his business. The federal minimum wage forces an employer to pay a store clerk in Bentonville, Arkansas, the same as a store clerk in New York City, where the cost of living is three or four times higher. Walton, who earned a degree in economics, believed market forces, not government fiat, should determine his labor costs. Still, he later regretted his opposition to the minimum wage. As he wrote in *Made in America*:

> In the beginning, I was so chintzy I really didn't pay my employees very well. . . . It wasn't that I was intentionally heartless. I wanted everybody to do well for themselves. It's just that in my very early days in the business, I was so doggoned competitive. . .that I was blinded to the most basic truth, really the principle that later became the foundation of Wal-Mart's success. . . . I ignored some of the basic needs of our people, and I feel bad about it.[22]

Long before he wrote those words, Walmart upgraded the compensation of its bottom-tier employees, offering profit-sharing plans and matching contributions to (401) k retirement funds. This incident was a "people skills" learning experience for Sam Walton.

AN OPEN-DOOR POLICY

Sam Walton maintained an open-door policy, which is still practiced today. He wanted everyone to know that they could take their ideas and concerns all the way to the CEO himself. Impractical? Maybe so. What if all 1.3 million Walmart employees in the United States decided to jam the CEO's office at once? Yet somehow it has always worked.

Mr. Sam's longtime associate, Michael Bergdahl, tells a story about Sam Walton's open-door policy. It was told to him by a man who started as an associate in a store and went on to work for the corporate office. In those days, the corporate headquarters in Bentonville had a hallway called "executive row," and all the executive offices literally had their doors open. "You could walk right into the executives' offices," this man told Bergdahl.

"I was taking a class one week at the corporate offices," he recalled. "I wanted to get a shirt signed by Sam Walton while I was there, so I walked over to executive row." He found that Mr. Sam was out visiting stores that day—but Sam's executive assistant offered to get the shirt autographed for him.

The next day, this man was in the classroom when the executive assistant walked in and gave him the shirt, boldly signed by Mr. Sam. The man's classmates ogled and envied his shirt.

"In all of my dealings with Mr. Sam," the man concluded, "he was always accessible."

When you are a complete leader with great people skills, your followers won't just want to work for you—they'll want to wear your name on their backs.

That's how Wal-Mart became Wal-Mart: ordinary people joined together
to accomplish extraordinary things.
SAM WALTON

8

FRANKLIN D. ROOSEVELT

Stricken and Strengthened

If you treat people right, they will treat you right—
ninety percent of the time.
FRANKLIN D. ROOSEVELT

Franklin Delano Roosevelt was born into wealth and privilege—yet he became a hero to the poor and the working class. FDR's years as president were turbulent years—the years of the Great Depression and the Second Great War. His policies defined American liberalism well into the twenty-first century. The world we live in today bears the imprint of his personality.

FDR was born on January 30, 1882, in Hyde Park, New York. Franklin's father, James Roosevelt, was a politically well-connected businessman. Young Franklin once accompanied his father to the White House, where he was introduced to President Grover Cleveland. The president shook hands with Franklin, who was four or five at the time, and said, "I have one wish for you, little man, that you will never be President of the United States."[1]

Roosevelt attended Groton, an Episcopal boarding school in Massachusetts, where he was influenced by Dr. Endicott Peabody, the headmaster. Peabody instilled in his students a sense of Christian duty toward people in need. Dr. Peabody officiated at the wedding of Franklin and Eleanor Roosevelt, and visited the Roosevelts at the White House.[2] As president, FDR wrote to Dr. Peabody, saying, "More than forty years ago, you said. . .something about not losing boyhood ideals in later life. . . . Your words are still with me."[3]

Roosevelt attended Harvard College, and though he didn't excel as a student, he did become editor-in-chief of the *Harvard Crimson*. While Franklin was at Harvard, his fifth cousin, Theodore Roosevelt, was elected president of the United States.

STRICKEN—AND STRENGTHENED

Franklin and Eleanor Roosevelt were married in New York in 1905. Eleanor didn't have to change her last name, because she was already a Roosevelt—Franklin's fifth cousin once removed. Because Eleanor's parents had passed away, her uncle, President Theodore Roosevelt, gave the bride away.

FDR made a bid for the New York State Senate in 1910, running as a Democrat in a Republican district. An aggressive campaigner, he won the seat. He campaigned for Woodrow Wilson in 1912 and was rewarded with an appointment as assistant secretary of the navy.

In 1920, Roosevelt ran for vice president as the running mate of Governor James M. Cox of Ohio, but Cox was beaten by Warren G. Harding. After the defeat, FDR looked forward to spending the summer of 1921 at Campobello Island in New Brunswick. By this time Franklin and Eleanor had five children (a sixth died in infancy).

The Roosevelts owned a fifteen-room waterfront home on the island. The family spent time sailing, swimming, or sunning on the beach. After a few days, Franklin came down with an apparent cold, accompanied by chills and muscle aches. He went to bed and awoke with a fever, dragging his left leg as he walked. A local doctor examined Roosevelt and said he had the flu.

The fever lingered for days, the numbness spread to both legs, and his skin became painfully sensitive. Roosevelt believed he was dying. Eleanor sent for a specialist, Dr. Robert Lovett, an orthopedic surgeon from Boston. Lovett was a leading expert on infantile paralysis—otherwise known as polio. When he examined FDR, he recognized the symptoms. He sent Franklin to New York for treatment.[4]

One of FDR's longtime friends was Frances Perkins (he would later appoint her secretary of labor). In her memoirs, she described how the illness impacted FDR's character:

> Franklin Roosevelt underwent a spiritual transformation during the years of his illness. I noticed when he came back that the years of pain and suffering had purged the slightly arrogant attitude he had displayed on occasion before he was stricken. The man emerged completely warmhearted, with humility of spirit and with a deeper philosophy. Having been to the depths of trouble, he understood the problems of people in trouble. . . .
>
> He was young, he was crippled, he was physically weak, but he had a firmer grip on life and on himself than ever before. He was serious, not playing now.[5]

FDR's grandson Curtis concluded that the paralysis "provided the one thing we all need, deep frustration, that keen sense that you cannot do everything you want to do. The only thing that mattered to FDR [before his illness]. . .was his political ambition, and to have it thrown in his face that it looked impossible must have entered into his soul."[6] In a paradoxical way, FDR's disability had made him stronger as a human being.

Roosevelt refused to accept that his paralysis was permanent. He underwent every known therapy, but nothing helped. He purchased a resort in Warm Springs, Georgia, as a hydrotherapy center for himself and others afflicted with polio-related paralysis.

He told friends and reporters he was improving, though it's doubtful he believed it. He wanted to run for governor of New York, and he thought his paralysis might cost him votes. He was careful not to be photographed in his wheelchair. While there are many photographs of Roosevelt seated at his desk, there are almost no photos that show his disability.

He was elected governor of New York in the 1928 election. By 1932, the country was in the grip of the Great Depression, and President Herbert Hoover was as popular as ants at a picnic. As the popular governor of a populous state, FDR was the logical choice for the Democratic presidential nomination. At the Democratic National Convention, he told the delegates he was committed to "a new deal for the American people."[7]

As unemployment soared and the banking system collapsed, his candidacy was an easy sell. FDR reached out to disaffected minorities and union members, creating a new majority coalition that defines the Democratic Party to this day. He won in a landslide.

When Roosevelt took office, a quarter of the workforce was jobless. Farmers lost everything as the bottom dropped out of food prices. Panic was everywhere. Roosevelt met the challenge with a three-pronged strategy of Relief, Recovery, and Reform—relief programs to alleviate human misery; recovery programs to prop up the economy; and reform programs to provide long-term solutions to the Depression.

Historians and economists still debate whether his recovery and reform programs pulled the country out of the Depression—or prolonged it. One thing is beyond dispute: Roosevelt's social programs provided sustenance for people who had lost everything, including their confidence in the future.

"A Traitor to His Class"

Paul F. Boller Jr., in *Presidential Anecdotes*, tells how Roosevelt's political opponents had to warn each other lest they be taken in by the famed FDR charm. When a New York Republican leader learned that a friend was going to visit then-Governor Roosevelt at the governor's mansion, he almost blew a gasket. "Lookout you don't make the mistake of liking Roosevelt," he warned. "I've seen people taken in by it."

"By what?" the other man asked, puzzled.

"By a perfectly grand political personality, you fool!" snapped the party leader.

FDR's personal magnetism was undeniable, and he used his people skills to serve those who were suffering and needy, just as Dr. Endicott Peabody had taught him.[8] Upon reaching the White House, Roosevelt did all he could to make it the people's house.

Roosevelt believed God had given him the power and position of the presidency so that he could improve the people's lives. One of his first orders as president was that his staff was to be polite and helpful to anyone who phoned the White House for help. Staffers were to listen to the problem then find a way to assist. It was FDR's way of living out the ideals Dr. Peabody had taught him. Eleanor Roosevelt recalled that after FDR's death, she received hundreds of letters from people describing how FDR and his staff had shown them kindness during the worst days of the Great Depression.[9]

Roosevelt did not see himself as promoting a political agenda. He believed he was simply doing what had to be done to lift people out of their misery—hardworking people who had fallen on hard times through no fault of their own.

Once a reporter tried to pin him down about his political ideology. "Mr. President," the reporter asked, "are you a Communist?"

"No."

"Are you a capitalist?"

"No."

"Are you a socialist?"

"No."

"In that case, sir, just what *is* your political philosophy?"

"Philosophy? Philosophy!" Roosevelt snapped. "I am a Christian and a Democrat—that's all."[10]

An indignant socialite once complained that FDR was "a traitor to his class." The remark was picked up in the national press. It was intended as an insult, but Roosevelt wore it as a badge of honor. Though born to wealth and privilege, he understood that America is not about the privileges of position, but fairness and equality. When the word got out that "high society" saw Roosevelt as "a traitor to his class," people loved him all the more.

A BALANCE OF TENDERNESS AND TOUGHNESS

Sometimes Roosevelt's New Deal programs created personality clashes within his administration. He had to apply his people skills to keep his aides and cabinet members focused on serving the people instead of serving their own egos.

Two of the most important relief programs under the New Deal were the Works Progress Administration (WPA) and the Public Works Administration (PWA). The WPA was headed by Harry Hopkins, one of FDR's closest friends (he had served in the New York governor's office). WPA jobs generally went to people who were unemployed. The Public Works Administration, headed by Secretary of the Interior Harold Ickes, also created government jobs, but applicants were not required to be needy.

Because the two projects competed for the same funding, administrators Hopkins and Ickes were locked in a continual feud. President Roosevelt repeatedly brokered peace between the two men, even taking them on a cruise of the Potomac on the presidential yacht. He hoped they would get to know each other and end their feud. No such luck.

In May 1936, a newspaper headline indicated that Ickes's future in the administration was in doubt. Ickes blew up. He cornered President Roosevelt in the Oval Office and complained that Hopkins was plotting against him—and he accused FDR of collusion with Hopkins.

"Harold," the president said ominously, "you're being childish."

Ickes stormed out. After cooling down, he realized he'd been foolish—and he'd probably trashed his White House career. That night Ickes recorded his regrets in his journal, writing, "I responded hotly. I never thought I would talk to a President of the United States the way I talked to President Roosevelt last night."

But Roosevelt had no plans to fire Ickes. He knew Ickes was hot-headed by nature. It would do him good to suffer for a while.

A few days later, during a cabinet meeting, FDR singled Ickes out in front of everyone. Ickes was scheduled to testify before the Senate Appropriations Committee about the PWA. Roosevelt warned Ickes not to disparage Harry Hopkins or the WPA in front of the committee.

Ickes felt humiliated. President Roosevelt had just taken him to the woodshed in front of his peers. It was a public shaming, and Ickes could see out of the corner of his eye that some of his colleagues enjoyed his discomfiture. Yet Ickes could not deny he had it coming.

After the cabinet meeting, Ickes tried to get a few moments in private with the president so he could apologize—but FDR wouldn't see him. Ickes's remorse turned to outrage. He was sure the president planned to fire him. So, in a white-hot fury, he typed up his resignation letter, signed it, and sent it to the president's attention.

The next day, Ickes was in the White House dining room, having lunch and feeling sorry for himself. He looked up and saw the president approaching in his wheelchair. The look in FDR's eyes was part anger, part hurt. The president handed Ickes a handwritten memorandum:

> *Dear Harold—*
> *1. PWA is not "repudiated."*
> *2. PWA is not "ended."*
> *3. I did not "make it impossible for you to go before the committee."*
> *4. I have not indicated lack of confidence.*
> *5. I have full confidence in you.*
> *6. You and I have the same big objectives.*
> *7. You are needed, to carry on a big common task.*

8. Resignation not accepted!
Your affectionate friend,
Franklin D. Roosevelt.

That letter was a masterful demonstration of Franklin Roosevelt's people skills. It was the perfect balance of tenderness and toughness—and FDR achieved his objective. Ickes learned his lesson and later reflected on how his boss had handled the situation:

"What could a man do with a President like that! Of course I stayed."[11]

The Ickes-Hopkins episode is a practical example of one of FDR's own leadership maxims: "Put two or three men in positions of conflicting authority. This will force them to work at loggerheads, allowing you to be the ultimate arbiter."[12]

Frances Perkins admired the people skills of FDR. She wrote, "His capacity to inspire and encourage. . .was beyond dispute. I, and everyone else, came away from an interview with the President feeling better. It was not that he had solved my problem or given me a clear direction which I could follow blindly, but that he had made me more cheerful, stronger, more determined to do [my job]. . . . This is very important in the leadership of a democracy."[13]

FDR's CARS

During his presidency, Franklin D. Roosevelt owned two cars equipped with hand controls so that he could drive them without the use of his legs. Both cars also give us a fascinating window into FDR's people skills.

The first specially equipped car Roosevelt owned was a 1931 Plymouth PA Phaeton, built by the Chrysler Corporation ("phaeton" refers to an automobile body type that is open, windowless, and has no weather protection). A Chrysler designer named W. F. Chamberlain created the hand controls, and Mr. Chamberlain and a mechanic personally delivered the car to the White House. Mr. Chamberlain later told the story of his encounter with FDR to author Dale Carnegie.

"When I called at the White House," Chamberlain said, "the President was extremely pleasant and cheerful. He called me by name, made me feel very comfortable, and particularly impressed me with the fact that he was vitally interested in things I had to show him and tell him. . . . He remarked: 'I think it is marvelous. . . . I'd love to have the time to tear it down and see how it works.'"

A crowd gathered around, including FDR's wife, Eleanor, and Secretary of Labor Frances Perkins. They all wanted to see the president's new car. Chamberlain instructed the president in the operation of the hand controls. Then FDR said, "Well, Mr. Chamberlain, I have been keeping the Federal Reserve Board waiting thirty minutes. I guess I had better get back to work." The mechanic who accompanied Chamberlain was shy and hung back, but FDR sought him out, shook his hand, and thanked him by name.[14]

No wonder FDR was elected to four terms as president! The man was loaded with people skills. He made sure to call Chamberlain and the mechanic by name (every leader should acquire that habit). He praised Chamberlain in front of everyone (public praise is a huge self-esteem builder). He took a vital interest in all of the special features Mr. Chamberlain had added to the car (taking an interest in people's achievements lets them know you value them). If you want a reputation for charm and charisma, study the people skills of FDR.

The second specially equipped car Roosevelt owned was a 1936 Ford Phaeton. FDR used that car to enhance his people skills. The biggest obstacle Roosevelt faced in dealing with world leaders was his physical disability. He felt that confronting a prime minister or a dictator from a wheelchair made him look weak. So Roosevelt came up with an ingenious way of increasing his leadership stature: he drove a car.

By the late 1930s, Roosevelt had replaced the hand-controlled Plymouth with a hand-controlled Ford Phaeton (he liked the phaeton body design because it was lightweight, open, and fast). It was against Secret Service rules for President Roosevelt to drive—but how could the Secret Service order the boss not to drive if he wanted to?

In June 1939, when President Roosevelt hosted England's King George VI and Queen Elizabeth, the Queen Mother, for a weekend at his Hyde Park estate, he treated them to a ride in his Ford. FDR himself did the driving—and he drove *fast*. The Queen Mother later described that ride as more frightening than the London blitz. She told journalist Conrad Black:

> President Roosevelt drove us in his car that was adapted to his use, requiring great dexterity with his hands. Motorcycle police cleared the road ahead of us but the president pointed out sights, waived his cigarette holder about, turned the wheel, and operated the accelerator and the brake all with his hands. He was conversing more than watching the road and drove at great speed. There were several times when I thought we could go right off the road and tumble down the hills. It was frightening, but quite exhilarating. It was a relief to get to the picnic.[15]

(The picnic, by the way, was an all-American repast of hot dogs and baked beans, with strawberry shortcake for dessert.)[16]

Roosevelt merged his people skills with his driving skills—and in the process he replaced the image of a wheelchair-bound paraplegic with the image of a strong, adventurous leader who is going places fast. The King and Queen Mother probably had no idea that FDR was deliberately altering their mental image of him. But if they had come to America expecting to find him in a wheelchair with a shawl around his shoulders, he dispelled that image in a hurry.

Roosevelt had a similar welcome ready for Winston Churchill in June 1942 (this was their second meeting; the first had been in December 1941, not long after the attack on Pearl Harbor). Author Robert Cross describes Churchill's arrival:

> As the small plane carrying Winston Churchill banked over the majestic Hudson River, President Roosevelt waited patiently below in the driver's seat of his blue, hand-controlled Ford. The plane bumped as it landed on the Hackensack airfield near Hyde Park. . . . After greeting his English friend, FDR drove Churchill around his Duchess County estate, talking business and giving the prime minister more than a few scares as the president "poised and backed on the grass verges of the precipices over the Hudson," and drove his car through fields and woods, successfully playing hide-and-seek with his Secret Service guards.[17]

Again, FDR had a serious purpose in scaring the daylights out of visiting dignitaries. After sharing a wild, frightening ride with President Roosevelt, Churchill knew he was dealing with a man of strength, daring, and courage—not a wheelchair-bound invalid. Roosevelt used his specially equipped Ford as a symbol of his leadership—and his formidable people skills.

"He Is the Truest Friend"

One of the toughest challenges for Roosevelt's people skills was Soviet dictator Joseph Stalin. In 1943, Roosevelt flew to Tehran for a summit meeting with Churchill and Stalin. When the two leaders were introduced, Roosevelt found Stalin to be cold and unfriendly. Roosevelt tried working his charm on Stalin, but the Russian leader was made of stone. For the first three days of their summit, Roosevelt could find no way to establish trust between himself and Stalin.

On the fourth day, FDR decided to try a different approach. That morning, before they entered the conference room, he told Churchill, "I hope you won't be sore at me for what I'm about to do." Churchill had no idea what Roosevelt had in mind. Moments later, they joined Stalin in the conference room As Roosevelt later explained:

> I talked privately with Stalin. . . . I said. . ."Winston is cranky this morning, he got up on the wrong side of the bed." A vague smile passed over Stalin's eyes, and I decided I was on the right track. . . . I began to tease Churchill about his Britishness, about

John Bull, about his cigars, about his habits. It began to register with Stalin. Winston got red and scowled, and the more he did so, the more Stalin smiled. Finally Stalin broke out into a deep, hearty guffaw, and for the first time in three days I saw a light. I kept it up until Stalin was laughing with me, and it was then that I called him "Uncle Joe." He would have thought me fresh the day before, but that day he laughed and came over and shook my hand.[18]

The ability to break the ice in order to create trust is an important people skill. Roosevelt had a deep understanding of what makes people tick. He even coaxed a laugh and a handshake out of one of the cruelest thug dictators who ever lived.

In the end, of course, Churchill figured out what his friend, the American president, was up to—and he approved. Churchill not only respected Roosevelt—he treasured their friendship. Perhaps Churchill's experience as a passenger in Roosevelt's Ford helped to strengthen the bond between them.

We catch a glimpse of Churchill's emotional bond with Roosevelt at the Casablanca Conference in French Morocco, January 14–24, 1943. There Roosevelt and Churchill conferred with Free French generals Charles de Gaulle and Henri Giraud and planned their strategy for the next phase of the war against Hitler.

When the conference was over, Roosevelt prepared to return home. Churchill accompanied Roosevelt to the airport and helped him board the plane. Then Churchill turned his back on the plane and said to an aide, "Let's go. I don't like to see them take off. It makes me far too nervous. If anything happened to that man, I couldn't stand it. He is the truest friend; he has the farthest vision; he is the greatest man I have ever known."[19]

The fourth inauguration of Franklin D. Roosevelt was held on January 20, 1945. He left the White House on March 29, traveling to the "Little White House" at Warm Springs, Georgia, for a few weeks' rest. On the afternoon of April 12, he was sitting for a portrait by artist Elizabeth Shoumatoff, when he remarked, "I have a terrific pain in the back of my head." Then he collapsed, having suffered a massive cerebral hemorrhage.

A fitting epitaph was offered by a grieving soldier outside the White House fence. Frances Perkins stopped to chat with him and asked what he thought of the late president. "I felt as if I knew him," the soldier said. "I felt as if he knew me—and I felt as if he liked me."[20]

The test of our progress is not whether we add more to the abundance of those who have much; it is whether we provide enough for those who have too little.
FRANKLIN D. ROOSEVELT

9

POPE JOHN PAUL II

The Force of Forgiveness

---

*What we talked about will have to remain a secret between him and me.
I spoke to him as a brother whom I have pardoned
and who has my complete trust.*
POPE JOHN PAUL II

Ten thousand people thronged St. Peter's Square in Vatican City. Pope John Paul II stood in the back of his white Fiat Campagnola "popemobile" as it slowly passed along the barricade. Cheering people reached up to receive his blessing and hand their babies up to be kissed. It was a little after 5:00 p.m. on May 13, 1981, under a bright blue sky.

Standing among the tourists and pilgrims was a man named Mehmet Ali Ağca. He hid a Browning 9 mm semiautomatic pistol under his jacket. Ağca was a Turkish assassin who had murdered Turkish journalist Abdi İpekçi in 1979. While on trial for that murder, Ağca escaped from a military prison with the help of the terror organization Grey Wolves. Using false passports and multiple identities, he traveled to Rome.

At 5:17, the pope's vehicle passed close to Mehmet Ali Ağca. The assassin raised his gun at close range. He squeezed the trigger. Shots split the air in rapid succession. Pope John Paul II was struck four times, once in the left index finger, once in the right elbow, and twice in his lower intestines. The pope looked surprised but did not cry out. He stood upright for a moment, mouth agape, then fell back into the arms of his aides, a blood stain spreading across the front of his white cassock.

Two women were also hit, neither fatally.

For a moment, the crowd was stunned to silence by the gunshots. A fast-thinking nun knocked the gun from Ağca's hand. A security officer and several spectators swarmed over the gunman and dragged him to the ground. Men in suits surrounded the car, which lurched forward and sped away. People screamed, wept, and prayed.

Pope John Paul II was placed in an ambulance and rushed to Gemelli Hospital. On the way, he prayed—not for himself, but for the crowd that had witnessed the shooting and for the man who shot him. While slipping in and out of consciousness, Pope John Paul II asked God to forgive the gunman.[1]

By the time the pope reached the hospital, he was unconscious, having lost more than half his body's blood supply. He regained consciousness briefly as the doctors prepped him for surgery, and he asked them not to remove the scapular he had worn since boyhood—two symbolic pieces of brown cloth connected by straps over the shoulders, representing the Carmelite order and a deep devotion to Mary. Pope John Paul II spent five hours in surgery.

One factor in favor of the pope's survival was his general good health. The assassination attempt occurred five days short of his sixty-first birthday. He had always been an avid sportsman who enjoyed hiking, skiing, swimming, and soccer. As pope, he had continued his regimen of early-morning jogs in the Vatican gardens.

Following surgery, he was listed in critical but stable condition. His condition quickly improved. Just four days after the shooting, he issued a message of forgiveness for the gunman from his hospital bed. Buoyed by prayers from around the world, he spent three weeks in the hospital, and his doctors pronounced him fully recovered on his release. Even so, he suffered pain and impairment for the rest of his life—a constant reminder of his brush with death.

At trial, Mehmet Ali Ağca was unrepentant. He pled guilty, claimed he acted alone, and was sentenced to life in prison. Two and a half years after the shooting, on December 27, 1983, Pope John Paul II went to Ağca's cell in Rome's Rebibbia Prison. Ağca, unshaven and still unrepentant, said, "So why aren't you dead?"

The pope talked to Ağca for twenty minutes. The prisoner seemed darkly suspicious the entire time. John Paul II told Ağca he was alive because he had been protected by the Lady of Fátima—the Virgin Mary, as she is said to have appeared to three children at Fátima, Portugal, in 1917; the assassination attempt occurred on the Feast of Our Lady of Fátima, May 13. Ağca worried that this "goddess" might come to his prison cell and take revenge against him. The pope assured Ağca that both he and the Lady forgave him, though Ağca never asked forgiveness. Like Jesus on the cross, the pope forgave even though forgiveness was unasked.[2]

Evidence suggests that Mehmet Ali Ağca was paid by the Bulgarian secret services, and that he acted as a proxy for the Soviet KGB. Ağca would eventually tell dozens of versions of his story, making many bizarre and conflicting claims. To this day, his reasons for shooting Pope John Paul II remain a mystery. He was later released and now lives as a free man.

THE PEOPLE SKILL OF FORGIVENESS

In order to lead people, we must be able to understand their weaknesses, empathize with their problems, and be tolerant of their mistakes and failures. Forgiveness is the heartbeat of all the people skills.

An old French proverb states, "To understand is to forgive." People will disappoint us and wound us, and it's easy to resent them for the hurt they cause us. But the more we can understand and empathize with them, the easier it is to forgive.

The value of forgiveness as a people skill has been taught for centuries in our wisdom literature. "A gentle answer turns away wrath, but a harsh word stirs up anger," wrote Solomon (Proverbs 15:1). "Blessed is the one whose transgressions are forgiven, whose sins are covered," wrote the psalmist (Psalm 32:1).

Pope John Paul II exhibited both sides of this crucial people skill. He freely forgave the gunman, and he sought forgiveness from those who suffered injustice at the hands of the institutional church over the centuries. On behalf of the Catholic Church, the pope made public apologies for more than a hundred historic wrongdoings, including the church's persecution of Galileo Galilei for his scientific views; the religious wars following the Protestant Reformation; violations of the rights of women; inaction during the Nazi Holocaust; and the church's inadequate response to sexual abuse by a few in the clergy.

Any organization that is unable to honestly face its own past, with its mistakes and failures, is doomed to repeat those mistakes in the future. Pope John Paul II wanted to cleanse the Church of these stains and prepare the church to demonstrate moral leadership in the future.

HE WHO SAVES A LIFE...

Pope John Paul II was born Karol Józef Wojtyła (pronounced "voy-TIH-wah") in Wadowice, Poland, on May 18, 1920. He was the youngest of three children born to Karol and Emilia Wojtyła. An older sister died before he was born. His mother died of a heart ailment when Karol was eight. Karol idolized his older brother, Edmund, who became a physician. When Edmund was twenty-six, he contracted scarlet fever from a patient and died; Karol, age twelve, was devastated.

Karol and his father lived in a chilly, one-room apartment. His father sewed together a makeshift soccer ball made of rags, and the future pope and his father spent many hours together playing soccer.

Wadowice was a predominantly Catholic town with a substantial Jewish population. Karol's father raised him to be a devout Catholic, kind and openhearted to everyone. Karol enjoyed playing goalkeeper in soccer, and games were often organized pitting Catholics against Jews. Karol often volunteered to play on the Jewish team. A Jewish friend, Jerzy Kluger, recalled that because there were fewer Jews in the town, "somebody had to play on the Jewish team and he was always sort of ready."[3] Kluger would later serve as the pope's unofficial envoy between the Vatican and the government of Israel.

Next to his faith, Karol's great passions in life were poetry and the theater. In 1938, Karol and his father moved to Kraków. There he attended Jagiellonian University, studying literature and philosophy. He founded a small theater company, Rhapsodic Theater, which met in the apartments of its members. He produced, directed, wrote, and acted in its plays. Like Ronald Reagan, the future pope honed his communication skills by performing as an actor.

When Hitler invaded Poland in late 1939, Karol Wojtyła came to know life under an oppressive government. The Nazis shut down the university and forced all young men in Poland to find jobs. Karol had to close down his theater group and take a job in a limestone quarry. His father urged him to study for the priesthood, telling him, "I would like to be certain before I die that you will commit yourself to God's service." In February 1941, his father, age sixty-one, died of a massive heart attack. By age twenty, Karol had lost his entire family.

The Nazis routinely murdered priests and students. Sometimes his friends would vanish without a trace, and he believed it was just a matter of time before the Nazis got him, too. He made up his mind to join the priesthood, though doing so was forbidden by the Nazis. He joined an underground seminary secretly run by the archbishop of Kraków. In February 1944, Karol Wojtyła was on the street when he was struck and severely injured by a speeding German truck. He spent two weeks recovering from head and shoulder injuries, and his survival confirmed to him that God had called him to the priesthood.

On August 1, 1944, the Polish resistance staged an uprising in Warsaw, attempting to liberate the Polish capital from the Nazis. The uprising failed, and on August 6—a day known as Black Sunday—the Gestapo swept through Kraków to prevent a Warsaw-style uprising. More than eight thousand men and boys were rounded up by the Nazis. Karol Wojtyła narrowly escaped being caught in the Gestapo dragnet, as historian Norman Davies reports:

> The Gestapo took no chances. After sweeping the streets. . .they then searched the houses of suspect youngsters. At 10 Tyniets Street, they broke in, but failed to find the twenty-four-year-old Underground actor and aspirant priest, who was praying on his knees, "heart pounding," in a hidden compartment in the cellar. His close colleague had been shot as a hostage only shortly before. . . . [After the Gestapo] left, a young woman guided the fugitive to the archbishop's palace. He was taken in, given the cassock to wear, and was told to present himself as one of the archbishop's "secretaries." In this way, Karol Wojtyla took a major step towards ordination, and in the long term, towards the Throne of St. Peter.[4]

By January 1945, the Soviet Red Army swept across Poland, driving the Nazis back. On the night of January 17, the Germans pulled out of Kraków. The next morning, Karol Wojtyła and his fellow seminary students went to reclaim the old seminary building. They found its tile roof collapsed, windows shattered, heating system broken, and the rooms blackened by smoke from open fires used for makeshift heat. The lavatories were heaped with frozen excrement. Karol Wojtyła volunteered to chop up and haul away the filth.[5]

Karol saved the life of a fourteen-year-old Holocaust survivor, Edith Zierer. Her family was captured during the 1939 German invasion of Poland, and they died in Dachau. Edith went to work in a weapons factory in occupied Poland, laboring twelve hours a day in freezing conditions without shoes. She continued working there until the Germans fled in January 1945.

Once the factory was abandoned, Edith walked outside and made her way to the train station. The people there ignored her. She recalled:

> I was thin, eaten up by lice, tired and exhausted. There wasn't a drop of life in me. I was lying there, apathetic and motionless. . . .
>
> Totally unexpectedly, a young priest made his way through the people and approached me. I looked up and saw a Christian priest in a brown robe standing in front of me, with a great light in his eyes. He turned to me of all the people who were sitting there in the station, and asked, "Why are you sitting here like that?"

That priest was Karol Wojtyła. He brought Edith a sandwich and a cup of tea. When she had eaten, he said, "We're going." Then he picked her up and carried her in his arms. He took her to Kraków and placed her in the care of Lena Kuchler, who rescued many orphans of the Holocaust. Edith Zierer later emigrated to Israel and raised a family.

In 2000, Pope John Paul visited the Yad Vashem Holocaust Museum, and Edith Zierer was there to honor him. She said to him in Polish, "He who saves the life of even one Jew is likened to one who has saved an entire world." She was moved to tears when he placed his hand on her shoulder. "I had closed a circle," she later said.[6]

"WUJEK WILL REMAIN WUJEK"

Karol Wojtyła completed his studies at the seminary in Kraków and was ordained on All Saints Day, November 1, 1946. He continued his studies at the Pontifical International Athenaeum Angelicum in Rome.

In 1947, the young Father Wojtyła went to Foggia in southern Italy. There he attended mass at the friary at San Giovanni Rotondo. He made his confession to the friar there, Padre Pio. During their conversation, Padre Pio told the young Polish priest that he would one day "gain the highest post in the Church." (Karol Wojtyła later believed that Padre Pio's prophecy was fulfilled in 1967 when he became a cardinal. He couldn't imagine holding any higher post than that.)[7]

Karol Wojtyła returned to Poland in 1948 to take up his duties at the Church of the Assumption in Niegowić. On arriving, his first act was to prostrate himself and kiss the ground—a gesture that would become the trademark of his papacy.[8]

He used his people skills to mentor and influence young people, organizing student groups that met for prayer, Bible study, and service to the needy. He also led them on outings that included camping and kayaking.

The end of World War II replaced the tyranny of the Nazis with the tyranny of the Communists. The Communists considered Christianity a "corrupting" influence on the youth, so priests were not permitted to organize youth outings. So, when Father Wojtyła went on these outings, he would remove his collar and ask his young friends to call him "Wujek" (Polish for "Uncle"). The nickname stuck.

In 1958, one of his kayaking trips was interrupted by the news that he had been elevated to bishop. When his young friends asked if this would change their relationship with him, he told them not to worry—"Wujek will remain Wujek."[9]

He then became a cardinal in 1967. And in August 1978, after the death of Pope Paul VI, Cardinal Wojtyła attended his first papal conclave and voted in the election of Pope John Paul I. Thirty-three days into his papacy, John Paul I died at age sixty-six. His death triggered another papal conclave.

On October 16, 1978, the word went out: "*Habemus papam!* We have a pope!" To the astonishment of the world, the new pontiff had an unfamiliar, non-Italian name. He was Karol Wojtyła, the cardinal from Kraków, and he had adopted the Latin name of John Paul II. Cheers went up around the world, especially in the Soviet-oppressed land of Poland.

Pope John Paul II appeared on the balcony and broke tradition by delivering a speech in which he accepted his new role "in the spirit of obedience to Our Lord."[10] Instead of a lavish papal coronation, he chose a simple papal inauguration on October 22, 1978. During the inauguration, at the point where the cardinals were to take their vows on their knees then kiss his ring, Pope John Paul reached out to Stefan Cardinal Wyszyński of Poland and embraced him in a bear hug.

These symbolic breaks with tradition might seem like small matters, but they were powerful examples of the new pope's people skills. Through these gestures, Pope John Paul II was saying loud and clear, "Wujek will remain Wujek."

THE FORCE THAT TOPPLED COMMUNISM

On June 2, 1979, Pope John Paul II flew to Warsaw. On arrival, he went to his knees and kissed the ground. More than a million people lined the motorcade route as he drove to the Old City. There, at Victory Square, he celebrated Mass and delivered a bold homily that indicted the atheist regime of Communist Poland:

> Christ cannot be kept out of the history of man in any part of
> the globe, at any longitude or latitude of geography. The exclusion
> of Christ from the history of man is an act against man. Without
> Christ it is impossible to understand the history of Poland. . . . The

history of the nation is above all the history of people. And the history of each person unfolds in Jesus Christ. In him it becomes the history of salvation.[11]

In response, the people chanted, "We want God! We want God!" It was a cry of spiritual yearning—and a shout of defiance against the atheistic state.

A week later, on June 10, the pope held outdoor mass. Though the government had not allowed any publicity, word of mouth produced a crowd of at least two million people. In his sermon, Pope John Paul II indicted Communism again. Peggy Noonan, President Reagan's speechwriter, later recalled:

> He exhorted the crowd. . ."You must be strong, my brothers and sisters. You must be strong with the strength that faith gives. . . . Never lose your spiritual freedom." . . .
>
> Everyone at that mass went home and put on state-controlled television to see the coverage of the great event. They knew millions had been there. . .[but] state-run TV had nothing. . .[but] a few people in the mud and a picture of the pope.
>
> Everyone looked at the propaganda of the state. . . . And they thought: It's all lies. Everything the government says is a lie. The government itself is a lie.[12]

Pope John Paul II had exposed the rotting underpinnings of Soviet Communism. His sojourn in Poland led directly to the founding of the Solidarity labor movement at the Gdańsk Shipyard in 1980, and the rise of Polish labor leader Lech Wałęsa. By 1989, Eastern Bloc Communism was collapsing like a house of cards. Lech Wałęsa later said of the pope's visit, "We knew the minute he touched the foundations of Communism, it would collapse."[13]

The fall of Communism is the cornerstone of John Paul's legacy. He was part of a concerted effort by several world leaders to consign Soviet Communism to the ash heap of history. Lech Wałęsa was one of those leaders. Czech dissident Václav Havel was another. And Prime Minister Margaret Thatcher of England and President Ronald Reagan of the United States also played key roles.

Pope John Paul II and President Reagan had a strong working partnership. President Reagan hammered away at the Soviet monolith with American "hard power." Pope John Paul II chipped away at the crumbling foundation with spiritual "soft power." Both forms of power were needed to bring down Communism.

In June 1982, President Reagan went on a ten-day tour through Western Europe—a tour that included a lengthy discussion with Pope John Paul in the Vatican. "Hope remains in Poland," Ronald Reagan told the pontiff. "We, working together, can keep it alive."[14]

Ronald Reagan spoke of a special bond between them: both men had barely survived assassination attempts less than six weeks apart. On March 30, 1981, a bullet missed Ronald Reagan's heart by less than an inch; he nearly died from loss of blood. On May 13, 1981, the pope was shot, and he, too, nearly died from loss of blood.

And there are more parallels: both Ronald Reagan and Pope John Paul II publicly forgave the gunmen who shot them. Both men believed God had spared them for a greater purpose. Working together, they both helped bring down Soviet Communism.

Could it be that the people skill of forgiveness was actually the driving force that toppled atheistic Communism?

LEADERSHIP LESSONS AND THE PEOPLE SKILL OF FORGIVENESS

What does the example of Pope John Paul II teach us about the role of forgiveness in leadership? Let me suggest a few principles:

1. *Forgive others to liberate yourself.* Pope John Paul II lived free of bitterness, resentment, and fear. Forgiveness enables us to make peace with our past and move forward with our lives.

2. *Forgiveness is a choice, not a feeling.* Even when you don't feel like forgiving, you can make a choice to forgive. Even when the other person is unrepentant, you can make a choice to forgive. The decision to forgive others doesn't depend on anyone else. It is completely up to you. Very often, when you make a choice to forgive, the feelings of forgiveness soon follow.

3. *As the leader, set an example of forgiveness.* The people in your organization need to know that you don't hold grudges—you forgive. Bitterness and resentment can tear an organization apart. Forgiveness enables teams, organizations, and nations to function smoothly. Like Pope John Paul II, become an inspiring example of forgiveness to the people you lead.

4. *Forgiving does not mean forgetting.* The reason we forgive is precisely because we can't forget. The memory of being hurt will keep hurting us until we make a decision to let it go. You will probably feel wary around a boss, a subordinate, or a coworker who has hurt you. That's normal. Memories and feelings won't immediately change. What *will* change is your determination to let go of all bitterness and resentment.

5. *Forgiving does not necessarily mean maintaining a relationship with someone.* Pope John Paul II forgave the gunman, but he did not become close friends with the gunman. Sometimes the person you forgive is simply toxic to you, and you can't maintain contact. But at least you can let go of the bitterness and get on with your life.

Pope John Paul II led by forgiving, and so should we. Though he forgave, he suffered. His wounds healed, but the pain never completely went away. Later in life, he was afflicted with weakness and tremors due to Parkinson's disease, but his forgiving spirit was strong to the end.

On April 2, 2005, Pope John Paul II died at his apartment in the Vatican. His funeral, held six days later, is believed to be the largest funeral in the history of the world. Almost immediately after his death, people chanted, "*Santo subito!* Sainthood now!" The Church canonized him on April 27, 2014, making him Pope Saint John Paul II.

Of all the saintly qualities that marked his life, I think the greatest was the people skill of forgiveness.

> *A person's rightful due is to be treated as an object of love,*
> *not as an object for use.*
> POPE JOHN PAUL II

The Fourth Side of Leadership

CHARACTER

10

GEORGE WASHINGTON

When the Summons Comes

To the distinguished character of Patriot, it should be our highest glory to add the more distinguished character of Christian.
GEORGE WASHINGTON

You never really know the strength of your character until it has been tested in a crisis. For George Washington, the supreme test of his character occurred during the Revolutionary War, in the winter of 1777–78 in a place called Valley Forge. After an initial victory in the siege of Boston (March 1776), Washington suffered a string of demoralizing defeats—the Battle of Long Island, the retreat across New Jersey, the Battle of Brandywine, and the unsuccessful assault on the British garrison at Germantown. The British captured Philadelphia, prompting many in Congress to call for Washington's removal as commander in chief.

In all of 1777, Washington's forces tasted victory only once, at the Battle of Saratoga, October 7. As winter set in, the war ground to a standstill. Washington led his army of eleven thousand men to Valley Forge, north of Philadelphia, to await the springtime and better fighting weather. Washington's associate, Prussian-born Major General Friedrich Wilhelm von Steuben, conducted drills and tactical training to sharpen the Continental Army's fighting skills. During that winter, Washington's army lost a dozen men per day to disease, hunger, and desertion.

General Washington sent repeated messages to the Continental Congress, requesting food for his troops. Congress, which had moved to York, Pennsylvania, after the British captured Philadelphia, refused to send food. Instead, Congress told General Washington to send his men out to steal from nearby farmers. After all, many farmers were trading beef and corn to the British for gold. By stealing from the farmers, the Continental Army would eat better and cut off provisions to the enemy.

But General Washington refused to steal. First, he considered theft to be a violation of his character and moral principles, which he based on the Bible. Second, while stealing from the farmers might produce a short-term advantage, in the long term it would cause the new American government to be hated by its own citizens.

He told Congress that he not only refused to send men out to steal, but he was warning them that any soldier caught stealing would be hanged. Pulitzer Prize–winning historian James Thomas Flexner wrote, "Congress was more than ever outraged that Washington would not take what the army needed from the inhabitants at bayonet point. The Commander in Chief, had, indeed, more respect for civilian rights than did many legislators."[1]

Though Washington's men often went hungry during the bitter winter months, Dr. Burton W. Folsom of the Mackinac Center for Public Policy observes that his principled stand bore fruit:

> The starving army was impressed by Washington's integrity. His men trained hard that winter, leaving bloody footprints in the snow. The next summer brought a smaller but tougher fighting unit that stood up to the seasoned British army for the first time at the Battle of Monmouth. With that victory, Washington took a giant step in ousting the British and winning independence for his country.
>
> During Washington's presidency, his character would be tested often but it served him and the nation well.[2]

George Washington's character and unyielding principles were rooted in his deep Christian faith. During that bitter winter in Valley Forge, he told his men: "While we are zealously performing the duties of good citizens and soldiers, we certainly ought not to be inattentive to the higher duties of religion. To the distinguished character of Patriot, it should be our highest Glory to laud the more distinguished Character of Christian."[3]

A Life Devoted to Good Character

George Washington was born in Virginia on February 22, 1732, the son of Augustine Washington, a slave-owning tobacco planter, and Mary Ball Washington. Young George grew up on Ferry Farm near Fredericksburg, and he later acquired the plantation on the Potomac River, Mount Vernon, as an inheritance when his older half-brother died.

The most famous anecdote about Washington's childhood is the legend recorded by Parson Mason Locke Weems, in which the boy Washington is said to have chopped down his father's favorite cherry tree. When questioned by his father, young George allegedly said, "I can't tell a lie, Pa; you know I can't tell a lie. I did cut it with my hatchet." George's father supposedly embraced the boy and praised him for telling the truth.

Evidence suggests that Parson Weems made up the story. In fact, one of Parson Weems's own grandchildren claimed that the story was based on an incident in which Weems's own son cut down a favorite rosebush in the garden; the son confessed to the crime—and Parson Weems gave the boy a sound thrashing.[4] The truth about Washington's youthful devotion to character building is far more interesting than any fable about a cherry tree.

By the time Washington was sixteen, he had painstakingly copied, with pen and ink, a document called "110 Rules of Civility & Decent Behavior in Company and Conversation." These 110 rules are based on life rules composed in 1595 by French Jesuits. When you read these rules today, some sound quaint and even strange. For example, "In the Presence of Others Sing not to yourself with a humming Noise, nor Drum with your Fingers or Feet." But many of the rules should never go out of style. Let me give you a sampling with the antique spelling and capitalization intact, followed by my translation in today's vernacular:

"Let your Discourse with Men of Business be Short and Comprehensive." (Be concise.)

"Use no Reproachful Language against any one; neither Curse nor Revile." (Be respectful and keep it clean.)

"Be not hasty to believe flying Reports to the Disparagement of any." (Be skeptical of gossip—don't believe everything you hear.)

"In all Causes of Passion admit Reason to Govern." (In heated situations, keep your cool.)

"Be not Curious to Know the Affairs of Others neither approach those that Speak in Private." (Mind your own business.)

"Undertake not what you cannot Perform but be Careful to keep your Promise." (Don't start what you cannot finish; keep your word.)

"Speak not Evil of the absent for it is unjust." (Don't badmouth people behind their backs.)[5]

Minneapolis *Star Tribune* columnist Katherine Kersten contrasts the way we raise our children today versus the character-focused way Washington was raised:

Washington and his contemporaries knew. . .that human beings who make happiness their goal are very unlikely to find it. For happiness is a byproduct of striving to do what is right. After all his travails, we can be sure that Washington died happy. But this was precisely because he had always aimed at something far greater. . . .

Americans of Washington's generation believed that character training begins in childhood. Our children are likely to spend school hours listing "10 things I like about myself." The youthful Washington, by contrast, laboriously copied 110 "Rules of Civility and Decent Behavior" into his exercise book.[6]

From his earliest years, George Washington trained himself to be a man of character. His sterling character became the foundation of his leadership.

A Growing Reputation for Good Character

In his early years, Washington's character was tested and refined in battle. In 1753, twenty-one-year-old George Washington was given command of a militia unit. Along with a band of Iroquois warriors, Washington's unit attacked the French in the Battle of Jumonville Glen—a decisive victory for Washington and his men.

In 1755, Washington was an aide to General Edward Braddock of England. During an expedition into the Ohio Valley to expel the French, Braddock's party was ambushed by French soldiers and Indian warriors. Braddock was mortally wounded, and his forces were scattered. Without regard to his own safety, Washington rallied his men so that they could retreat safely. Washington's brave exploits in the French and Indian War elevated his reputation for leadership.

Washington was assigned command of the Virginia Regiment, a force of a thousand soldiers. He and his men fought twenty battles over ten months, losing a third of their complement. Though the regiment suffered heavy losses, Washington's reputation as a military leader grew.

In 1758, Washington retired from the regiment and did not return to the military until the Revolutionary War, seventeen years later. His experience taught him valuable lessons in leadership, military discipline, logistics, organization, and battlefield tactics. Those insights would prove invaluable during the war for American independence.

In 1759, Washington married the widow Martha Dandridge Custis, who was twenty-eight years old and a woman of considerable wealth. He became a father to Martha's two children by her late first husband. They lived on Washington's Mount Vernon estate, near Alexandria.

On December 16, 1773, a group called the Sons of Liberty touched off the Boston Tea Party. This action produced a chain of events leading to the battles of Lexington and Concord in Massachusetts, April 19, 1775, which initiated the Revolutionary War. Two months later, Congress created the Continental Army, and John Adams nominated Washington to be commander in chief. In response, Washington humbly replied, "I this day declare with the utmost sincerity, I do not think myself equal to the command I am honored with." Yet he agreed to accept the position because of the unanimous support of the Congress. Refusing any compensation, Washington immediately went to work, forming the various state militias into a cohesive and disciplined Continental Army.[7]

Though Washington won fame for exploits in the French and Indian War, he was even more widely known as a man of *character*. Historian David McCullough explained, "He was chosen because they knew him; they knew the kind of man he was; they knew his character, his integrity. . . . He was a man people would follow. And as events would prove, he was a man whom some—a few—would follow through hell."[8]

George Washington's reputation for character and integrity was so widespread that even British newspapers—which were hostile toward most leaders of the rebellion—actually *praised* the personal character of George Washington. Historian Troy O. Bickham of Missouri State University explains:

> Throughout the American Revolution, the press in Britain portrayed the commander of the rebel army as a model of citizen virtue and an ideal military leader. Most press reports supported the effort to crush the rebellion and considered the Continental Congress a den of self-serving scoundrels but heaped praise on George Washington. . . . The general personified the dilemma that faced many Britons during the conflict: he was a quintessential English-American gentleman, despite being the enemy. He represented much of what the British Atlantic community thought admirable while commanding an army in a cause that many Britons believed would ruin the empire.[9]

While leading the American forces during the Revolutionary War, George Washington lost many battles—in fact, he lost far more battles than he won. Though he sometimes retreated, he never surrendered. When a battle went badly, he always had an escape route so that his men could make a strategic retreat, regroup, then come back and fight another day.

THE IMPRINT OF HIS CHARACTER

He battled the British relentlessly, all the way to the final battle, the Siege of Yorktown, Virginia. There he forced General George Cornwallis to surrender on October 19, 1781. The Revolutionary War was over. America was free. On September 3, 1783, Great Britain signed the Treaty of Paris, officially recognizing the United States of America as a sovereign nation.

On December 4, at Fraunces Tavern in New York, Washington bade his officers farewell. Two days before Christmas, he resigned his commission as commander in chief of the Continental Army; then he returned home, planning to live out his days as a gentleman farmer at Mount Vernon. But his peaceful retirement would not last long.

The electoral college unanimously elected Washington as America's first president in 1789. He took the oath of office on the balcony of Federal Hall in New York.

Washington was careful to avoid any trappings reminiscent of European royalty.

He insisted on a simple, unpretentious title for the position: "Mr. President." When Congress approved a substantial salary for the position, Washington initially declined to accept, but Congress convinced him to take the money to avoid any suggestion that public service was only for the rich.[10] After two terms, Washington declined to run for a third. His example was so influential that all of his successors obeyed the customary two-term limit until Franklin D. Roosevelt broke that tradition in 1940.

In Washington's Farewell Address to the Nation, September 19, 1796, he said that American liberty and prosperity rested on a foundation of strong faith in God and good moral character. "Of all the dispositions and habits which lead to political prosperity," he said, "religion and morality are indispensable supports. In vain would that man claim the tribute of patriotism, who should labor to subvert these great pillars of human happiness, these firmest props of the duties of man and citizens."[11]

Most of the customs we associate with the presidency today bear the imprint of George Washington's character. His towering personal integrity echoes across the years, setting a standard that we the people measure all our leaders against. When we hear that a president has plotted Nixonian crimes or exhibited Clintonian immorality in the Oval Office, we are repulsed, because that behavior defiles the standard of character set by Washington.

As constitutional scholar Thomas Sowell reminds us, "Presidents of the United States lacking character and integrity have inflicted lasting damage on the office they held and on the nation. . . . The nation as a whole is stronger when it can trust its President."[12]

WASHINGTON'S GREAT FLAW

Here we must acknowledge a flaw in our portrait of George Washington. As a Virginia plantation owner, he was also a slave owner. He became a slave owner at the age of eleven, when he inherited ten slaves from the estate of his late father. Though he was born into a world where human slavery was "normal," though he purchased slaves to improve the productivity of his landholdings, his views on slavery began to evolve.

By 1786, three years before he was elected president, it was clear that the idea of slavery had begun to trouble him deeply. On April 12, 1786, he wrote to his friend Robert Morris, the merchant who helped finance the Revolution:

> There is not a man living who wishes more sincerely than I do to see a plan adopted for the abolition of [slavery]; but there is only one proper and effectual mode by which it can be accomplished, and that is by Legislative authority; and this, as far as my suffrage will go, shall never be wanting.[13]

And on September 9, 1786, he wrote to his friend and fellow Virginian John Francis Mercer:

I never mean to possess another slave by purchase; it being among my first wishes to see some plan adopted by which slavery in this country may be abolished by slow, sure, and imperceptible degrees.[14]

You might ask, "Doesn't slave ownership disqualify Washington as a person of character?" Historian Stephen Ambrose points out that, of the nine US presidents who owned slaves, only George Washington set his free. Ambrose goes on to say:

> History abounds with ironies. These men, the Founding Fathers and Brothers, established a system of government that, after much struggle, and the terrible violence of the Civil War, and the civil rights movement led by black Americans, did lead to legal freedom for all Americans and movement toward equality. . . .
>
> Of all the contradictions in America's history, none surpasses its toleration first of slavery and then of segregation. . . .
>
> Slavery and discrimination darken our hearts and cloud our minds in the most extraordinary ways, including a blanket judgment today against Americans who were slave owners in the eighteenth and nineteenth centuries. That the masters should be judged as lacking in the scope of their minds and hearts is fair, indeed must be insisted upon, but that doesn't mean we should judge the whole of them only by this part.[15]

So, even though George Washington is not without his troubling flaws, Stephen E. Ambrose insists that we must assess this man as a whole human being, in terms of his character: "Washington's character was rock solid. He was constant. At the center of events for twenty-four years, he never lied, fudged, or cheated. He shared his army's privations. . . . They respected him, even loved him. Washington came to stand for the new nation and its republican virtues, which was why he became our first President by unanimous choice. . . . He established the thought, 'We can do it,' as an integral part of the American spirit."[16]

It's easy to look back from the vantage point of the twenty-first century, with the hard, bloody battles of the Civil War and the civil rights movement already won, and say, "If I had lived in that era, I never would have owned slaves. I would have fought against slavery and discrimination and hate in all its forms." And perhaps you would have. It's impossible to know how your views would have been shaped by the mood of the times.

But it's heartening to realize that, by 1786, George Washington was afflicted in his conscience over the injustice of slavery. Had he lived longer, perhaps the gnawing in his conscience would have propelled him to take up the cause of abolition. But we'll never know.

A Leader in Winter

When we consider the greatness of George Washington, it's tempting to view him as more of a myth than a man. But those who knew him testify that he was a genuine human being, with real human imperfections, but also with a deep core of character. One man who knew him well, Thomas Jefferson, wrote:

> I think I knew General Washington intimately and thoroughly; and were I called on to delineate his character, it should be in terms like these. . . . His integrity was most pure. . . . He was, indeed, in every sense of the words, a wise, a good, and a great man. . . . On the whole, his character was, in its mass, perfect, in nothing bad, in few points indifferent; and it may truly be said that never did nature and fortune combine more perfectly to make a man great and to place him in the same constellation with whatever worthies have merited from man an everlasting remembrance.[17]

Historian Peter R. Henriques of George Mason University observes that throughout his life, George Washington devoted considerable thought to his own death. "It was not only very important to George Washington to live his life with honor," Henriques writes. "It was also very important to him that he end his life with honor. . . . Washington always confronted the prospect of his own death with remarkable equanimity and composure."[18]

Washington had faced death many times in his life, especially during the French and Indian War and the Revolutionary War. Many times he had heard the whistle of bullets passing near his head, and he had often seen men die in war. Though Washington was not eager for death, he didn't fear it.

In September 1799, Washington learned that his brother Charles had died. In a letter to Charles's son-in-law, Washington contemplated his own eventual death: "When the summons comes I shall endeavour to obey it with a good grace."[19] When he wrote those words, Washington had no way of knowing how soon that summons would come.

On December 12, 1799, Washington rode on horseback around Mount Vernon, inspecting his plantation for several hours in freezing rain. He ate supper that evening without changing to dry clothes. The next morning, he awoke with a sore throat. Medical experts believe he had contracted acute epiglottitis due to a bacterial infection. Henriques writes:

The truly frightening aspect of acute epiglottitis is the obstruction of the larynx that makes both breathing and swallowing extremely difficult. The first thing an infant masters is to breathe and the second is to swallow. To have these two absolutely basic functions dramatically impaired is very frightening to anyone, no matter how brave and courageous he or she might be. Like any mortal, Washington had to face the terror of air hunger, of smothering and gasping for each breath. . . . Essentially, Washington slowly and painfully suffocated to death over many hours.[20]

The medical treatment Washington received, while the best available for that time, only added to his sufferings. He was bled by leeches four times, losing five pints of blood. He suffered from medicines that induced diarrhea, vomiting, and blistering on his skin. His would have been a difficult enough death without these miserable medicines. At one point in his sufferings, Washington said, "I die hard."

Yet, as Peter R. Henriques concludes, the way he went through the process of dying "reveals a great deal about the man and his character." In his final hours, Washington showed compassion to everyone around him. He reassured the nervous doctor who bled him, "Don't be afraid." And when Tobias Lear strained to move Washington to make him comfortable, the dying man apologized for burdening him. Not once did he complain about his suffering. His last words, recorded by Tobias Lear in his journal, were, "'Tis well."[21]

LEADERSHIP LESSONS FROM THE FATHER OF OUR COUNTRY

The example of Washington teaches us that character determines our leadership destiny. Our character determines how we will live, how we will lead, and how we will die. Here are some character principles that emerge from the life of George Washington:

1. *It's not too late—start building character now.* Good character is the accumulated deposit of good moral choices. Every choice you make moves you a step closer to good character—or a step away. Commit yourself to making good choices, day by day and hour by hour, because every choice counts.

2. *Lead by example.* Be conscious of the example you display to others. Leadership is influence. How are you influencing the people you lead? Take pride in your personal excellence, your moral excellence, and in the example you set for others.

3. *Remain humble.* When the Congress chose Washington to lead the Continental Army, he said, "I do not think myself equal to the command I am honored with." Was that false humility on Washington's part? I don't think so. I believe his humility was sincere. An arrogant and overconfident leader is a danger to himself and his followers. Washington never let his authority go to his head. The greater his fame,

the greater his humility.

4. *Take time to reflect.* Washington often pondered his own character and his own mortality. He often wondered how he would face his own death. As painful and difficult as his death proved to be, he faced it with courage and character. When his time came, he was ready.

5. *Obey your conscience in all things.* Washington said that he wished slavery would be abolished by a legislative authority. He said he would never purchase another slave. That's good—but he didn't go far enough.

At the end of the Revolutionary War, Washington had a vast deposit of moral and political capital to spend. People were ready to follow wherever he led. What if, at the height of his popularity, he had said, "I'm going to free all my slaves, and I encourage my countrymen to do the same. Our Declaration of Independence says we believe all men are created equal. Well, do we? We have liberated ourselves from the tyranny of England. Shouldn't we liberate our African-American brothers from the tyranny of slavery?"

I wish Washington had made such a statement. Many slave owners would have rebelled, but many might have joined him. Washington might have been acclaimed not only as the Father of Our Country, but as the Great Emancipator as well.

If your conscience whispers to you, listen carefully—then act. That's your character speaking.

Happiness and moral duty are inseparably connected.
GEORGE WASHINGTON

11

BILLY GRAHAM

Moral Firewalls

---

*The greatest legacy one can pass on to one's children and grandchildren
is not money or other material things accumulated in one's life,
but rather a legacy of character and faith.*
BILLY GRAHAM

When I was an undergrad at Wake Forest University, I hosted an interview show on the campus radio station. In 1962 (my senior year), Billy Graham came to speak. I booked him for an interview, little realizing it would be one of my best-ever sports interviews. I learned that Billy Graham had been a baseball and basketball player in high school and had dreamed of making it to the big leagues as a first baseman.

He told me about the time the great Babe Ruth came to Charlotte, North Carolina, for a personal appearance. It was about 1928, the height of Ruth's career. Billy's dad arranged for the ten-year-old to meet the baseball legend and shake his hand. Billy told Babe Ruth about his goal of playing in the major leagues, and the Bambino replied, "Well, son, you're sure built like a first baseman! Good luck!" For years after that encounter, those words kept Billy fired up to pursue his baseball dreams.

We talked about some of the athletes he knew, especially the ones who were outspoken Christians and had shared their faith at his evangelistic crusades. He was very knowledgeable about a lot of different sports.

During his visit to Wake Forest, Graham also spent time talking to our basketball coach, Bones McKinney. Wake Forest was in the Final Four that week, and in the first game, our team was pitted against Ohio State, headlined by Jerry Lucas and John Havlicek. Graham was on hand as our players boarded the bus for the trip to the airport. Bones turned to him and said, "Billy, I hope you'll be praying for us."

Graham replied, "I will, Bones—but you'd better play good defense on Lucas and Havlicek!"

"JUST AS I AM"

My next personal encounter with Billy Graham came almost a decade later, in June 1971. By then, I was general manager of the Chicago Bulls—and I had been a Christian for about five years. Dr. Graham was bringing his evangelistic crusade to Chicago's McCormick Center, and he invited me to share my faith before an audience of more than forty thousand people.

Billy Graham is an imposing and charismatic man, tall and angular with striking features, piercing blue eyes, and an unmistakable personal magnetism. Whenever he enters a room, conversations go silent and all eyes turn in his direction. At the same time, Billy Graham is the humblest and most self-effacing man I have ever met.

His youngest daughter, Ruth, was once a guest on my local radio show in Orlando. We spent a few moments talking about her illustrious father, and at one point, in her rich North Carolina accent, she gave me a profound insight into her father's character: "My Daddy knows who he is, a flawed human being. In Daddy's mind, he's still just a farm boy from Charlotte, North Carolina."

Billy Graham was raised on a dairy farm, the oldest of four children born to William Franklin Graham Sr. and his wife, Morrow. In 1933, when Prohibition was repealed, Billy's father brought several bottles of beer home and took Billy and his sister Catherine into the kitchen. He opened the bottles and gave one to Billy and one to Catherine. "Drink it," Mr. Graham said. "All of it." Billy was fifteen at the time, and he and Catherine did as they were told—and they hated the taste of the stuff. That's exactly what their dad had in mind.

"From now on," he told them, "whenever any of your friends try to get you to drink alcohol, just tell them you've already tasted it and you don't like it."

Billy later recalled, "His approach was more pragmatic than pious, but it worked."[1]

In 1934, a group of Christian businessmen in Charlotte, including Billy's father, brought evangelist Mordecai Ham to the city for a series of revival meetings in a sprawling five-thousand-seat wooden tabernacle specially constructed for the event. Dr. Ham would be preaching every morning and every night except Mondays for almost three months. Sixteen-year-old Billy wanted nothing to do with those revival meetings, and he told his parents he wasn't going.

One night, Mordecai Ham preached on the subject of teenage immorality. He spoke pointedly about some goings-on around the high school in Charlotte. This angered some students, and they hatched a plan to disrupt the next meeting. Billy and some of his friends decided to show up, sit in the back, and see if there would be a fight.

For some reason, the student protest never materialized. When Dr. Ham preached, young Billy Graham was spellbound. In spite of his inner resistance, the message was getting through to him. Later that night, Billy lay in bed, unable to sleep, unable to turn his mind off.

Billy kept attending the meetings, and, he later recalled, "I became deeply convicted about my sinfulness and rebellion. And confused. How can this evangelist be talking to me, of all people? . . . I had gotten into mischief once in a while, but I could hardly be called wicked. . . . So why would the evangelist always be pointing his bony finger at *me*?"[2] He began to realize he had been depending on his parents' faith and his church membership as proof he was saved. The "miserable realization" dawned on him that he didn't know Jesus Christ for himself.

One night, right around Billy's sixteenth birthday, Dr. Ham invited anyone who wished to come forward and accept Christ as Lord and Savior. In contrast to some of Dr. Ham's fiery sermons, this was a gentle invitation, and he quoted Romans 5:8 (KJV): "But God commendeth his love toward us, in that, while we were yet sinners, Christ died for us." The song leader led the audience in all four verses of "Just as I Am."

Billy Graham got out of his chair and walked down the aisle, feeling strangely weightless. He was one of several hundred people who went forward that night. A man came up beside him, a family friend "with a deep love for souls." The man put his arms around Billy's shoulders and urged him to decide.

And Billy made his decision.[3]

FEELING LIKE A HYPOCRITE

After graduating from high school in 1936, Billy Graham attended Bob Jones College in Cleveland, Tennessee—and was shocked to find an academic environment that was legalistic, intellectually rigid, and autocratically controlled. Graham left Bob Jones College after one semester and continued his studies at Florida Bible Institute.

While Graham was at Florida Bible Institute, the president of the college was accused of immoral behavior. Graham believed the college president (who was a close friend and mentor to him) was innocent. His accusers had an ax to grind, and their stories were inconsistent. Eventually, the scandal passed, the college president remained in office, but a quarter of the student body left. The accusations were never proven but never dispelled, either. The incident left the campus under a pall. "It was a big learning experience for me in many ways," Graham later recalled, "and it taught me to be very careful myself."[4]

Graham was continuing his studies at Wheaton College in Illinois when World War II broke out. He applied to the War Department for acceptance into the Chaplains Corps. The War Department replied that his application would be considered after he completed his studies at Wheaton and took a seminary course. Though he wanted to serve as a chaplain, he never got to the battlefield.

At Wheaton, he met Ruth Bell, the daughter of Presbyterian missionaries to China. At the time, Ruth was inspired to follow the example of Amy Carmichael, an orphanage director and missionary in India who worked for fifty-five years without furlough—and was never married. Billy Graham needed all his powers of persuasion to change Ruth Bell's thinking about marriage. He succeeded in convincing her, and they were married on August 13, 1943, and eventually had five children.

Billy Graham served as a pastor of a Baptist church in Western Springs, Illinois, from 1943 to 1944. In January 1944, he took over the "Songs in the Night" radio program begun by Torrey Johnson. Through that radio ministry, Billy became acquainted with singer and ministry partner George Beverly Shea.

In late 1944, Torrey Johnson told him of his idea for an international youth movement called Youth for Christ International. Through Youth for Christ, Graham became close friends with Charles Templeton. In 1946, Templeton resigned as pastor of a Toronto church and enrolled at Princeton Theological Seminary, believing that he needed to deepen his theological thinking. Templeton had doubts and questions about the authority of the Bible. Graham recalled, "My respect and affection for Chuck [Templeton] were so great that whatever troubled him troubled me also."[5]

Graham had been reading neo-orthodox theologians, such as Karl Barth and Reinhold Niebuhr, and the combination of Templeton's questions and his own reading left him feeling confused. "I never doubted the Gospel itself, or the deity of Christ on which it depended," Graham recalled, "but other major issues were called into question. . . . Could the Bible be trusted completely?"[6]

In 1947, thirty-year-old Graham was hired as interim president of Northwestern Bible College in Minneapolis—making him the youngest president of any American college and university. He would serve in that role until 1952. While Billy Graham was presiding over a Bible school and seminary, and preaching at evangelistic campaigns, he was troubled by doubts about his faith. His struggles left him feeling like a hypocrite.

"A Spiritual Battle in My Soul"

His nagging questions about the Bible reached critical mass in the summer of 1949, as he prepared for the Los Angeles campaign, the largest citywide evangelistic effort of his career so far. He had agreed to a speaking engagement at Forest Home, a Christian retreat center in the San Bernardino Mountains east of Los Angeles. Because of his doubts, he wished he could cancel—yet he felt obligated to keep the speaking engagement.

He went to the conference, which was organized by Miss Henrietta Mears of First Presbyterian Church of Hollywood. Graham's friend, Charles Templeton, was also slated to speak. During the weeklong conference, Billy had many times of prayer and discussion with Miss Mears. She had a deep faith in the authority of the Bible, and he was hungry for any insight she could offer.

Meanwhile, Charles Templeton, with his passion for theological intellectualism, was trying hard to pull Graham in the opposite direction. "Billy," Templeton said, "you're fifty years out of date. People no longer accept the Bible as being inspired the way you do."

During that week, Billy Graham underwent a crisis of faith. He knew he had to settle the question of whether or not he could trust the Bible. If the answer was no, he could not go through with the Los Angeles campaign. In fact, he believed that, as a matter of integrity, he would have to resign as president of the college and give up his ministry as an evangelist.

He got up one evening and took a walk in the moonlight, Bible in hand. He walked through the woods until he came to a tree stump, where he spread out his Bible. It was too dark to read the text, but the open Bible on the tree stump served as his prayer altar. He went to his knees and told God that there was so much in the Bible he didn't understand, there were so many questions he couldn't resolve. Yet he felt God prompting him to say, "Father, I am going to accept this as Thy Word—by *faith*! I'm going to allow faith to go beyond my intellectual questions and doubts, and I will believe this to be Your inspired Word."

When he got up from his knees, Graham sensed God's presence in his inner being. He still had unanswered questions in his mind, but the crisis was firmly resolved. "In my heart and mind," he later said, "I knew a spiritual battle in my soul had been fought and won."[7]

Graham launched the Los Angeles campaign in the fall of 1949. His organization erected a tent auditorium that would seat six thousand people and scheduled the campaign to run for three weeks. For reasons that are unknown to this day, newspaper tycoon William Randolph Hearst—who had never met Billy Graham and was not previously known as a supporter of Christian evangelism—sent a decree to his editors to publicize the Graham crusade. Almost overnight, the Hearst newspapers turned Billy Graham into a household name.[8]

Attendance soared. The Graham organization expanded the tent seating capacity to nine thousand. Graham extended the meeting schedule from three weeks to eight weeks. More than 2,700 people answered Billy Graham's invitation to come forward and make a decision for Christ.[9]

"WE ARE GOING TO STUMBLE INTO HELL"

On July 14, 1950, at President Truman's invitation, Billy Graham and members of his evangelistic team met and prayed with the president in the Oval Office. At one point in their conversation, Billy Graham asked President Truman about his beliefs.

"I try to live by the Sermon on the Mount and the Golden Rule," Truman replied.

Summoning his courage to speak boldly, Graham said, "It takes more than that, Mr. President. It's faith in Christ and his death on the cross that you need."

At that point, President Truman stood and ended the conversation.[10] From then on, Truman was no fan of Billy Graham. He later told Merle Miller, who recorded Truman's oral autobiography, "I hadn't ought to say this. . .but [Billy Graham] was never a friend of mine when I was President. I just don't go for people like that. All he's interested in is getting his name in the paper."[11]

Perhaps it was Graham's blunt question about faith in Christ that soured Truman. Whatever the reason, Truman was the only president who ever openly expressed dislike toward the evangelist. Dr. Graham went on to become a spiritual adviser to several presidents, and he has prayed with every American president from Harry Truman to Barack Obama.

When President Eisenhower was on his deathbed in 1969, he asked Billy Graham how he could know for sure he was going to heaven. He also asked Graham's help in reconciling with his former vice president, Richard Nixon, whose daughter Julie was soon to marry Ike's grandson David. In 1974, President Gerald Ford sought prayer and counsel from Graham before he pardoned Nixon. Immediately after Ronald Reagan was shot in 1981, Nancy Reagan called Graham to the hospital—and he was the first person Mrs. Reagan called when Ronald Reagan died in 2004.[12]

Billy Graham also had a close friendship with Dr. Martin Luther King Jr. He relied on Dr. King for counsel regarding racial tensions in America. Graham and King had several conversations about ending racial segregation in America. Dr. Graham never preached to a racially segregated audience. During his 1953 crusade in Chattanooga, Tennessee, Graham went into the arena hours before the first meeting and personally took down the ropes separating the white and black sections. The head usher of the event resigned in protest, and other segregationists there were enraged. But Billy Graham stuck to his principles.

At the Nashville crusade in 1954, Graham told a mostly white audience, "We have been proud as a race—we have been proud and thought we were better than any other race, any other people. Ladies and gentlemen, we are going to stumble into hell because of our pride." The *Nashville Banner* newspaper transcribed and published every sermon Billy Graham preached during the four-week crusade.[13]

In 1957, Dr. King joined Billy Graham at his New York City crusade. And in 1963, Graham helped Dr. King post bail to get out of the Birmingham jail following King's Good Friday arrest. In 1964, Graham took his crusade to Birmingham's Legion Field, where he preached to an integrated audience of thirty-five thousand people just six months after the bombing of the Sixteenth Street Baptist Church—a terrorist act that killed four girls. Graham later recalled, "The Ku Klux Klan went around and knocked out our signs. The State Police had to send policemen with us wherever we went. . . . They were afraid we would get shot."[14]

Graham conducted a crusade in Durban and Johannesburg, South Africa, in 1973—twenty years after he was initially invited to preach there. He wouldn't agree to preach in South Africa until he was assured that the meetings would be racially integrated. The South Africa campaign showed blacks and whites what their world could become if apartheid were ended.

"Christianity is not a white man's religion," he told the crowd, "and don't let anybody ever tell you that it's white or black. Christ belongs to all people." The blaring front page headline of the *Sunday Tribune*, March 18, 1973, declared, "Billy Graham: Apartheid Doomed."[15]

Over his ministry career, Dr. Billy Graham has traveled to more than 185 countries and territories, preaching the good news of Jesus Christ to live audiences totaling more than 200 million people, plus hundreds of millions more via television, radio, and other media. In a ministry career that has spanned more than six decades, there has never been the slightest hint of moral or financial impropriety. And there's a good reason for that.

THE MODESTO MANIFESTO

In 1948, Dr. Graham and his top advisers—Cliff Barrows, Grady Wilson, and George Beverly Shea—drove to Modesto, California, for a citywide evangelistic campaign. A number of ministers and evangelists had been involved in highly publicized scandals. During a break from the Modesto meetings, Graham assembled his ministry team to talk about the harm these scandals did to the Christian cause. Then he asked them to retire to their rooms for an hour and make a list of all the problems and temptations evangelists faced. They came back together at the end of the hour and found the lists to be nearly identical.

"In a short amount of time," Billy Graham later recalled, "we made a series of resolutions or commitments among ourselves that would guide us in our future evangelistic work."[16] Though this series of commitments didn't have a formal name, it has come to be known as "The Modesto Manifesto."

The commitments focused on several areas. First, they agreed they would never manipulate audiences with emotional appeals to increase donations. Second, they agreed never to exaggerate the size of the crowds to inflate the reputation of the evangelist. Third, they agreed that all the money collected and spent by the ministry belonged to the Lord—and must never be misused. Fourth, they agreed not only to avoid immoral behavior, but also to make sure they were above suspicion at all times. "We pledged among ourselves to avoid any situation that would have even the appearance of compromise," Graham later said. "From that day on, I did not travel, meet, or eat alone with a woman other than my wife."

If you want to make sure you will never be accused of a financial or moral scandal, you have to make some decisions at the outset. You have to build some protective shielding around yourself. You have to lay down some rules for yourself and your organization, and see that those rules are followed at all times without exception. I call these rules "moral firewalls."

A firewall is a barrier designed to prevent the spread of fire and heat. Firewalls prevent structural collapse. Moral firewalls prevent moral collapse. A firewall is a zone of protection you hope you never need, but if the need ever arises, you're glad it's there. It keeps you from ever being scorched by temptation—or burned by false accusation.

Your moral firewall consists of a number of commitments and promises to guard your integrity: "I will never cheat on my taxes," "I will never pad my expense account," "I will never place myself in a compromising position with someone of the opposite sex," and so forth. Here are some suggestions for building your moral firewalls so that you can have a reputation for character like Billy Graham's:

1. *Honestly assess your own situation.* The Modesto Manifesto may be a good starting point for building your own moral firewalls, but you may need to add some additional rules that specifically address your own situation. For example, if you are the driver in a carpool, make a commitment to drop off those of the opposite sex first so that there's never even a hint of scandal.

2. *Be accountable.* Set up a group of "accountability partners" who will ask you tough questions and challenge your actions when necessary. Admit your struggles to them and seek their advice. A wise leader doesn't go it alone. As a leader, you may have hundreds of acquaintances and thousands of admirers, but you still need three or four close, trusted friends who will care enough about you to hold you accountable.

3. *Consider the consequences.* Always weigh the costs and benefits of your actions. Don't simply tell yourself, "I won't get caught." Ask yourself, "If my actions are exposed, what do I stand to lose?" For example, is the momentary gratification of an illicit affair worth losing your marriage, losing the respect of your children, and damaging your reputation for integrity? If you are willing to put your guilty pleasure above all else, you shouldn't call yourself a leader.

4. *Pray.* Maintaining your moral and ethical purity is a spiritual battle. Ask for God's help in rejecting temptation. Don't ever think of yourself as a "victim" of temptation. You are responsible for your moral choices.

I told the story of my Christian conversion to a crowd of nearly fifty thousand people at a 1987 Billy Graham campaign in Syracuse, New York. I was amazed and humbled to again be on the stage with Dr. Graham, Cliff Barrows, and George Beverly Shea. After the event, I returned to my room at the Holiday Inn, still on a spiritual high. I turned on the TV to catch up on the sports scores. As I flipped the dial, a raw pornographic scene flickered on the screen.

People have accused me of being naive, and maybe I am, but I didn't know sexually explicit material was available on a hotel room TV. I didn't have to pay extra for it—it was a free channel. I continued flipping through channels, looking for ESPN—but I remembered what I had seen. I wondered if King David felt this way after his first glimpse of Bathsheba bathing. I hadn't gone looking for temptation, but it had found me. Now I had a choice to make.

I thought, *Why is this happening? I've just experienced the greatest spiritual high of my life!* The battle was on—and I decided to fight it. I fought that battle with weapons of prayer—and prayer won. God's Spirit was victorious over my human weakness.

It was a privilege to meet Dr. Graham, interview him, and share a speaker's platform with him. The Fourth Side of Leadership is character, and there are few greater examples of leadership character than Billy Graham.

I feel sorry for the man who has never known the bracing thrill of taking a stand and sticking to it fearlessly. Moral courage has rewards that timidity can never imagine. Like a shot of adrenaline, it floods the spirit with vitality.
BILLY GRAHAM

12

THEODORE ROOSEVELT

The Man in the Arena

We must have the right kind of character—character that makes a man,
first of all, a good man in the home, a good father, a good husband—
that makes a man a good neighbor.
THEODORE ROOSEVELT

In July 2011, during a speaking trip to Wisconsin, I stayed in Milwaukee's historic Gilpatrick Hotel. In the hotel lobby next to the main entrance, there is a photo display and a bronze plaque on the wall that reads:

ON THIS SPOT,
OCTOBER 14, 1912, AN ATTEMPT
WAS MADE UPON THE LIFE OF
THEODORE ROOSEVELT.

Here's what happened: Theodore Roosevelt, a former Republican who had served two terms as president of the United States, was running for a third term as the standard-bearer of the Progressive Party (nicknamed the Bull Moose party). Roosevelt had just had dinner with his campaign staff and top supporters in the hotel dining room. He and his staff went outside, where a car waited to take him to the Milwaukee Auditorium to speak. He turned to wave to his supporters—

And an unemployed saloon keeper named John Schrank pushed his way through the crowd. Schrank had stalked Roosevelt for weeks, traveling thousands of miles for this chance. He raised a .32-caliber pistol, aimed it at Roosevelt's heart, and squeezed the trigger. He fired from such close range that he could not have missed. Roosevelt stood unflinching.

Roosevelt's stenographer, a six-foot-tall former football player named Elbert Martin, threw himself at Schrank and dragged him to the ground, knocking the gun out of his hand. As Martin and another campaign aide subdued the gunman, Roosevelt pulled the sheaf of speech notes from his vest pocket. The bullet had passed completely through the manuscript pages, which were stained with blood. It was a fifty-page manuscript, folded double, so the bullet had to pass through a hundred layers of paper—not as bulletproof as Kevlar, but very effective.

The bullet had penetrated the muscle directly over the former president's heart. Blood stained his shirt, vest, and the lining of his army coat. It hurt, but he'd felt worse. He turned to his driver and said, "Take me to the auditorium."

Roosevelt's aides urged him to go to the hospital instead—but he wouldn't hear of it. He said, "I am going to deliver my speech." He climbed into the car and it pulled away.

Minutes later, Roosevelt arrived at the Milwaukee Auditorium, stepped up on the stage, and raised the bloodstained manuscript so everyone could see.

"Friends," he said, "I shall ask you to be as quiet as possible. I don't know whether you fully understand that I have just been shot; but it takes more than that to kill a Bull Moose."

A gasp went up from the crowd. Roosevelt waived off the crowd's concern.

"Fortunately," he said, "I had my manuscript, so you see I was going to make a long speech, and there is where the bullet went through. The bullet is in me now, so I cannot make a very long speech, but I will try my best."

The speech he proceeded to give was largely impromptu, departing considerably from his prepared remarks. He spoke for nearly an hour, and was pale and shaky when he finished.

At the hospital. X-rays showed the bullet had buried itself in a rib. Doctors decided to leave it there.

Though he campaigned valiantly, he lost to Woodrow Wilson.[1]

Physical courage, persistence in the face of opposition, and a dogged commitment to a cause—Theodore Roosevelt had these traits in abundance. But he wasn't born with them. Early in his life, he made a decision to build the traits of a leader into his life—or die trying.

"A Sickly and Timid Boy"

Theodore Roosevelt Jr. (nicknamed "T.R.") was born October 27, 1858, in New York City. He was born to wealth and privilege, the son of businessman Theodore "Thee" Roosevelt Sr. and socialite Martha "Mittie" Bulloch Roosevelt. His boyhood was largely shaped by his chronic poor health. Asthma attacks tormented him, especially at night. The sensation of suffocation terrified him.

We don't have to look far to find out what motivated young Theodore's lifelong pursuit of good character traits: he idolized and idealized his father. In a letter to his friend Edward S. Martin, dated November 26, 1900, T.R. wrote:

> *I was fortunate enough in having a father whom I have always been able to regard as an ideal man. . . . [He combined] the strength and courage and will and energy of the strongest man with the tenderness, cleanness, and purity of a woman. I was a sickly and timid boy. He*

*not only took great and untiring care of me—some of my earliest
remembrances are of nights when he would walk up and down with me
for an hour at a time in his arms when I was a wretched mite suffering
acutely with asthma—but he also most wisely refused to coddle me, and
made me feel that I must force myself to hold my own with other boys
and prepare to do the rough work of the world.*[2]

Theodore Sr. encouraged T.R. to take up vigorous exercise to overcome his health
problems. Two family trips abroad—a tour of Europe when he was about twelve and
an extended stay in Egypt when he was about fourteen—deepened his admiration
for his father and helped shape his view of the world.[3] Theodore Sr. gave his son a
role model of character to live up to. As George Grant observes in *The Courage and
Character of Theodore Roosevelt*:

> Roosevelt's father was a man of extraordinary character and ac-
> complishment. A successful businessman, a tireless philanthropist, a
> determined patriot, a committed family man, a refined intellectual,
> a faithful Christian, and an energetic outdoorsman, he was every-
> thing that Roosevelt himself always strove to be.[4]

When Theodore was thirteen, he was traveling alone by stagecoach to meet
friends in Maine for a summer camping trip. During a stop, two bigger boys teased
and taunted him. They circled around him, threatening to beat him up, challenging
him to defend himself. They filled young Theodore with fear. Finally, without regard
for his own safety, he threw himself at them. They held him as he struggled, laughing
as he tried vainly to free his arms and land a punch.

The two bullies didn't hurt T.R., but they humiliated him. His physical weakness
made him deeply ashamed. Later that summer, when he returned home, Theodore
asked his father if he could take boxing lessons. Theodore Sr. didn't ask why his
son wanted boxing lessons, though he probably suspected. Young Theodore took
lessons from a former prizefighter, John Long. He took to the sport with enthusiasm,
and boxing proved to be another experience that solidified his self-esteem and his
character.[5]

A SERIES OF TRAGEDIES

T.R. was educated by tutors at home. In 1876, he passed the challenging entrance
exams for Harvard College, and enrolled in the fall. Before he left for school, his
father gave him a bit of advice about character: "Take care of your morals first, your
health next, and finally your studies." At Harvard, he studied biology and philosophy.
He was active in boxing and rowing, and was an editor of the *Harvard Advocate*. He

graduated from Harvard with a bachelor of arts magna cum laude in 1880.

While Theodore Roosevelt was at Harvard, his father was diagnosed with intestinal cancer. Young Theodore knew his father was ill but had no idea how serious it was. Theodore Sr. didn't want to disrupt his son's studies, so he kept the seriousness of his illness from Theodore Jr. When Theodore Sr. was on his deathbed, the family sent a telegram to T.R., informing him his father was dying, and he should come home right away. The young Roosevelt took the next train home, arriving just a few hours after his father passed away.[6]

Theodore Roosevelt celebrated his twenty-second birthday, October 27, 1880, by wedding Alice Hathaway Lee, the daughter of banker George Cabot Lee. Theodore and Alice had one daughter, Alice Lee Roosevelt, born on February 12, 1884. Two days later, on Valentine's Day, Theodore's mother succumbed to typhoid fever at three in the morning. Later that afternoon, in an upstairs room in the same house, Theodore's wife, Alice, died from kidney failure, which had been masked by the pregnancy.

In a twist of fate too cruel to comprehend, Theodore Roosevelt lost both his mother and his twenty-two-year-old wife on the same day in the same house. That night before he went to bed, a grieving Theodore Roosevelt inscribed a huge black X in his journal then wrote a single tortured sentence: "The light has gone out of my life."[7]

Crushed by grief, Roosevelt placed baby Alice in the care of his older sister, Anna (he would take baby Alice back into his home after she turned three). He dealt with his sorrow by plunging into his work, focusing on state legislative issues and problems of corruption in New York City. Roosevelt's crusade against public corruption won him considerable praise and popularity.

After a while, he found that his workaholism didn't ease his pain. He needed a change—a *big* change. He left New York City and headed west. In the Badlands of the Dakota Territory, he purchased the Chimney Butte Ranch. There he hunted buffalo and lived the life of a working cowboy.

An incident from this part of his career shows how far he had come from that sickly, timid thirteen-year-old who was so easily bullied. Roosevelt was traveling by horseback around the western Dakota Territory and eastern Montana Territory. It was late in the evening when he arrived in Mingusville (now known as Wibaux, Montana). He was tying up his horse in front of Nolan's Hotel when he heard gunfire from the barroom.

"I disliked going in," he later recalled. "But there was nowhere else to go, and it was a cold night." He walked into the bar and found the bartender and several patrons being intimidated by a man Roosevelt described as a "shabby individual in a broad hat with a cocked gun in each hand," pacing the floor and "talking with strident profanity."

Roosevelt sized the man up as a bully. "As soon as he saw me," T.R. recalled, "he hailed me as 'Four Eyes,' in reference to my spectacles, and said, 'Four Eyes is going to treat.' I joined in the laugh and got behind the stove and sat down, thinking to escape notice."

But the bully had selected Roosevelt as his victim. He strode over to where Roosevelt sat, leaned over him with a gun in each hand, and ordered "Four Eyes" to set up a round of drinks.

"Well," Roosevelt replied, rising carefully to his feet, "if I've got to, I've got to."

Then, summoning his boxing training, Roosevelt delivered a quick, hard right jab to the point of the bully's jaw, then a left, then another right. The guns in the bully's fists both fired—though T.R. didn't know if the man was trying to shoot him or if he just clenched his trigger fingers convulsively when struck in the face.

The bully went down like a felled tree, striking the corner of the bar with his head. Roosevelt was ready to drop low if the bully came up shooting—but the man lay still at T.R.'s feet. "I took away his guns," Roosevelt recalled, "and the other people in the room, who were now loud in their denunciation of him, hustled him out and put him in the shed."

The next morning, the bully departed of his own volition on a passing freight train.[8]

Roosevelt was twenty-six at the time and undoubtedly felt a sense of personal redemption in finally having the upper hand over a bully. He had already taken on the bullying of political bosses in New York. Now he had proven he could take on a gun-toting thug of the Badlands. Consciously or unconsciously, he undoubtedly saw his ability to deal a counterblow to oppressors as a sign of character growth.

ROOSEVELT'S ROUGH RIDERS

After several harsh years as a cattle rancher in the Dakotas, Roosevelt returned to New York City. In December 1886, he married his childhood friend Edith Kermit Carow. They had five children; Theodore III, Kermit, Ethel, Archibald, and Quentin. He ran for mayor of New York City and lost, but in the 1890s he became a vigorous foe of crime and corruption as New York City police commissioner.

In 1897, largely on the strength of T.R.'s highly respected book, *The Naval War of 1812*, President William McKinley appointed him assistant secretary of the navy. Roosevelt used his authority to modernize the navy prior to the outbreak of the Spanish-American War.

When the war broke out in 1898, it was clear that the United States Army was still weakened and ill-prepared three decades after the Civil War. Roosevelt resigned his post with the navy and joined with Army Colonel Leonard Wood to create the First US Volunteer Cavalry Regiment. Roosevelt recruited cowboys and college athletes, mostly from the American Southwest. Wood and Roosevelt put the men through intensive training and drilling. The newspapers dubbed them "Roosevelt's Rough Riders."

In May 1898, more than a thousand Rough Riders, along with their horses, mules, and equipment, made their way by rail to Tampa, Florida, where they shipped out for Cuba. The Rough Riders came ashore at Daiquiri, Cuba, on June 23, 1898, with Colonel Wood in command and Lieutenant Colonel Roosevelt as second in command.

In their first encounter with Spanish forces, the Battle of Las Guasimas, the Rough Riders fought an enemy that was well-hidden by trenches, fortifications, and jungle brush. Early in the battle, one of the men reported to Roosevelt that Colonel Wood had been killed in action. Roosevelt gave himself a field promotion to Colonel then rallied his men and led a charge on the fortification at Las Guasimas. After a battle lasting an hour and a half, the Rough Riders won. They counted their casualties—eight dead and thirty-one wounded.

Roosevelt was surprised to find Colonel Wood among the living—the report of his death had been a case of mistaken identity. If Roosevelt had not seized command of the Rough Riders and led the charge, the outcome of the battle might have been different.

The Rough Riders' next encounter with the enemy was the Battle of San Juan Hill. Colonel Roosevelt was given vague orders to seize and hold the San Juan Heights, which were occupied by a thousand Spanish soldiers. He was to hold his position until he received orders to advance up the hill. As time passed and no order came, Roosevelt grew impatient.

Finally, Roosevelt drew his sidearm and told his Rough Riders he was leading them up the hill. Then he went to the captain of the platoons behind them, declared himself the ranking officer, and told the captain to prepare his men to charge up the hill. Then he mounted his horse and rode off, waving his hat and calling his men to follow. The Rough Riders pursued Colonel Roosevelt up the hill.

Behind them, Lieutenant John H. Parker watched the charge unfolding and ordered his three Gatling gun operators to spray the top of the heights with machine-gun fire. Parker's quick thinking prevented the Spanish from launching an effective counterattack. Roosevelt, the only man on horseback, rode back and forth in front of the men so that they would have a visible leader to follow. His visibility made him a target for Spanish gunfire, but on that day he eluded every bullet fired at him. T.R. and his Rough Riders seized and held San Juan Heights.

At the conclusion of the Spanish-American War, Roosevelt returned to New York a conquering war hero. The newspapers and the public called him "Teddy," a nickname he hated. He preferred "Colonel Roosevelt." He was elected governor of New York, serving from January 1, 1899, to December 31, 1900.

In 1900, Roosevelt was elected vice president of the United States as William

McKinley's running mate. Six months into McKinley's second term as president (and Roosevelt's first term as vice president), a misguided anarchist shot President McKinley while he was visiting an exhibit at the Pan-American Exposition in Buffalo, New York. McKinley died eight days after the shooting, and Roosevelt, at age forty-two, became our youngest-ever president (John F. Kennedy, at forty-three, was the youngest ever *elected* president). Roosevelt went on to win a full term in 1904.

Roosevelt's administration focused on guaranteeing a "square deal" for all Americans, including immigrants and the poor. He strengthened America as a global power. His famous slogan "Speak softly and carry a big stick" referred to his philosophy of combining quiet diplomacy with a powerful military that could deter any threats. In spite of Roosevelt's war-hero image, America was at peace throughout his years in office. He brokered an end to the Russo-Japanese War, and this achievement earned him the 1906 Nobel Peace Prize.

One of Theodore Roosevelt's most lasting legacies resulted from a Mississippi bear hunting trip he took as president in 1902. Some well-meaning attendants had used hounds to chase a black bear then had tied the bear to a willow tree for the president to shoot. Appalled, Roosevelt refused to shoot the bear under unsportsmanlike conditions. Political cartoonist Clifford Berryman of the *Washington Post* drew a cartoon depicting President Roosevelt sparing the bear. The cartoon inspired Morris Michtom of the Ideal Novelty and Toy Company to produce cuddly stuffed bear cubs that were initially called "Teddy's Bear" but which soon became known as teddy bears.

T.R. Speaks on Character

The issue of character was close to Theodore Roosevelt's heart from his boyhood to his final breath. He wrote and spoke about character again and again throughout his life. Though few men prized the life of intellect and learning more than Theodore Roosevelt, he placed an even higher premium on strong character. He once said, "Character is far more important than intellect in making a man a good citizen or successful at his calling—meaning by character not only such qualities as honesty and truthfulness, but courage, perseverance, and self-reliance."[9] Here are some of Roosevelt's best insights on building character into your leadership life:

1. *As a leader, exemplify a strong work ethic.* In a speech to the Brotherhood of Locomotive Firemen in Chattanooga, Tennessee, in 1902, he said, "Your work is hard. Do you suppose I mention that because I pity you? No; not a bit. I don't pity any man who does hard work worth doing. I admire him. I pity the creature who doesn't work. . . . If a man does his work well and it is worth doing, then it matters but little in which line that work is done."[10]

During his presidency, Roosevelt spoke to the student body at Groton School, Groton, Massachusetts, May 24, 1904, and said, "The man who wins out must be the man who works. He cannot play all the time. . . . Let him count in the world. When he comes to the end of his life, let him feel he has pulled his weight and a little more. A sound body is good; a sound mind is better; but a strong and clean character is better than either."[11]

For Roosevelt, hard work was a social obligation, the duty we have to our society and our fellow man. When he began his campaign for governor of New York, 1898, he said, "We are face to face with our destiny and we must meet it with a high and resolute courage. For us is the life of action, of strenuous performance of duty; let us live in the harness, striving mightily; let us rather run the risk of wearing out than rusting out."[12]

2. *As a leader, exemplify absolute honesty and integrity.* In his Groton School speech, he said: "To make a good citizen the prime need is to be decent, clean in thought, clean in mind, clean in action. . . . Keep your eyes on the stars, but remember to keep your feet on the ground. Be truthful; a lie implies fear, vanity or malevolence; and be frank; furtiveness and insincerity are faults incompatible with true manliness. Be honest, and remember that honesty counts for nothing unless back of it lie courage and efficiency."[13]

3. *Be a leader of action, not just words.* Roosevelt believed that character traits and moral values had to be translated into action, or they were nothing but empty platitudes. In a letter to western novelist Owen Wister, July 7, 1915, T.R. said, "I have a perfect horror of words that are not backed up by deeds."[14] T.R. also said that to be a person of character and action is to be a person who sometimes makes mistakes: "The only man who makes no mistakes is the man who never does anything."[15]

4. *Ignore your critics and always do what's right.* The most memorable statement of character Theodore Roosevelt ever made was in a speech called "Citizenship in a Republic," delivered at the Sorbonne, Paris, April 23, 1910. This passage of the speech has come to be known as "The Man in the Arena":

> It is not the critic who counts: not the man who points out how the strong man stumbles or where the doer of deeds could have done better. The credit belongs to the man who is actually in the arena, whose face is marred by dust and sweat and blood, who strives valiantly, who errs and comes up short again and again, because there is no effort without error or shortcoming, but who knows the great enthusiasms, the great devotions, who spends himself for a worthy cause; who, at the best, knows, in the end, the triumph of high achievement, and who, at the worst, if he fails, at least he fails while daring greatly, so that his place shall never be with those cold and timid souls who knew neither victory nor defeat.[16]

T.R. lived his life in the arena. He was complete in all Seven Sides of Leadership, and he excelled in the side called character.

FINAL DAYS

In July 1918, Theodore Roosevelt and his wife, Edith, received the news that their twenty-one-year-old son, Quentin, a flyer in France, had been shot down and killed behind German lines. It was a devastating blow to T.R., who had suffered many sorrows over the years. One morning, not long after T.R. received the news, a servant overheard Roosevelt in his grief, murmuring the boyhood nickname of his late son—"Poor Quinikins. Poor Quinikins."

On the night of January 5, 1919, less than six months after his son's death, T.R. experienced breathing trouble. He called his doctor, who came to the Roosevelt home and treated him. The former president felt a little better and went to bed.

"Please put out the light, James," T.R. said to his valet. Those were his last words.

He had evaded bullets during a Montana bar fight and while charging up San Juan Hill. He had survived a would-be assassin's bullet outside a Milwaukee hotel. But at just sixty years of age, he succumbed to a pulmonary embolism, a blood clot in his lung. He died peacefully in his sleep.[17]

Vice President Thomas R. Marshall said, "Death had to take Roosevelt sleeping, for if he had been awake, there would have been a fight."[18] It's true. Death would have had a fight on its hands—because Death is a bully. And battling bullies was in Roosevelt's character.

It is character that counts in a nation as in a man. It is a good thing to have a keen, fine intellectual development in a nation, to produce orators, artists, successful businessmen; but it is an infinitely greater thing to have those solid qualities which we group together under the name of character—sobriety, steadfastness, the sense of obligation toward one's neighbor and one's God, hard common sense, and, combined with it, the lift of generous enthusiasm toward whatever is right.
THEODORE ROOSEVELT

The Fifth Side of Leadership

COMPETENCE

13

THOMAS JEFFERSON

The Competent Polymath

Some men are born for the public. Nature, by fitting them
for the service of the human race on a broad scale,
has stamped them with the evidences of her destination and their duty.
THOMAS JEFFERSON

During his eight years as America's third president, Thomas Jefferson had a retreat home built at Poplar Forest, a plantation he had inherited in 1773. Poplar Forest was located about a hundred miles from his home at Monticello. After his presidency, Monticello became an attraction for sightseers, so Jefferson often sought refuge in his Poplar Forest retreat.

It took Jefferson three days to make the hundred-mile journey by carriage, and he would stay in simple country inns along the way. The innkeepers and the former president greeted each other as old friends, and the people along the way referred to him simply as "Squire."

On one occasion, while traveling alone between Monticello and Poplar Forest, Jefferson stopped at Ford's Tavern for the night. He passed the evening by the fire with a stranger, a clergyman. If they introduced themselves, they apparently only exchanged first names, because the clergyman didn't realize he was speaking with the former president of the United States.

As they chatted, the clergyman mentioned some innovative mechanical operations he'd seen. Jefferson was familiar with the mechanical principles involved, and the clergyman became convinced (as he later told others) that this man was a professional mechanical engineer.

Their conversation turned to agriculture—and the clergyman decided that this stranger must be quite an accomplished farmer. Then the conversation turned to the clergyman's own area of expertise, religion. As they talked, the clergyman decided his companion must have been a clergyman himself, though it wasn't clear what denomination he belonged to.

The clergyman was curious about this stranger who seemed to be an expert in so many fields of knowledge. After Jefferson retired to his room, the clergyman asked the innkeeper the identity of the man.

"What," said the innkeeper, "don't you know the Squire? That was Mr. Jefferson."

"Not *President* Jefferson?"

The innkeeper confirmed that, yes, the clergyman had just spent the evening with the third president of the United States and the drafter of the Declaration of Independence. That clergyman was Reverend Charles Clay, also known as Parson Clay of Bedford, Virginia. The next morning, Reverend Clay introduced himself to the former president, and they became friends and exchanged a number of letters over the years that followed.[1]

This incident illustrates the amazing competence of Thomas Jefferson. He had a depth of knowledge and experience in many spheres of human endeavor. His mastery of so many subjects contributed to his leadership ability. Competence is the fifth of the Seven Sides of Leadership, and the competence of Thomas Jefferson stands out as his most distinctive leadership trait.

QUALIFIED BY COMPETENCE

In December 1962, President John F. Kennedy hosted a gathering of Nobel Prize winners at the White House. In his welcoming remarks, he honored the Nobel laureates as the most distinguished gathering of intellects to have dined at the White House, "with the possible exception of when Mr. Jefferson dined here alone."[2]

In 1948, historian Arthur M. Schlesinger Sr. of Harvard University surveyed fifty-five distinguished historians and asked them to rank the American presidents in order of their greatness. He repeated that survey in 1962, surveying an even larger number of historians.[3] In 1996, his son, Arthur M. Schlesinger Jr. repeated the poll, surveying thirty-two leading historians. In all three surveys, Thomas Jefferson ranked among the top five greatest presidents of all time.[4]

Washington Post columnist George Will offers an even more exalted assessment of Thomas Jefferson:

> Jefferson expressed the American idea: political and social pluralism; government of limited, delegated and enumerated powers; the fecundity of freedom. He expressed it not only in stirring cadences, but also in the way he lived, as statesman, scientist, architect, educator.
>
> Jeffersonianism is what free men believe. Jefferson is what a free person looks like—confident, serene, rational, disciplined, temperate, tolerant, curious. In fine, Jefferson is the Person of the Millennium.[5]

Widely considered one of the most important thinkers of the Enlightenment Age, Jefferson was a polymath—a person with knowledge and expertise that spanned many different subjects. True polymaths are rare and provide a special kind of competency, the ability to draw upon "cross-matrix" or "interdisciplinary" insight. There's a saying that "to a man with a hammer, every problem is a nail." A polymath like Jefferson has a huge intellectual toolbox to draw upon and is better equipped to solve problems that don't respond well to hammering.

Jefferson was keenly interested in the arts, sciences, philosophy, history, literature, religion, and politics. Though never formally trained as an architect, he studied architecture from books. This self-taught expert became one of our nation's most important architects in the classical tradition.

Jefferson was fluent in Latin, Greek, French, Italian, and Spanish *before* he entered college. His language skills served him well as an ambassador and statesman. Though not a good public speaker, his writing skills qualified him to be the "great communicator" of the revolutionary era. His extraordinary mix of talents, knowledge, and skills made him the competent leader he was.

Effective leaders start with an inspiring vision; then they communicate their vision to others, motivate their followers with good people skills, validate their leadership role by their good character, and inspire confidence through their competence as leaders. As Warren Bennis observes, "The leader hasn't simply practiced his vocation or profession. He's mastered it. . . . Mastery, absolute competence, is mandatory for a leader."[6]

A leader of competence is able to function at a very high level and take the organization to increasingly higher levels of success. Competence is not a static condition, but a measure of continual growth and dynamic learning, both as a human being and a leader. People readily grant the authority of leadership to those who demonstrate competence; any sign of incompetence causes that authority to evaporate. An aura of competence is essential to your authority to lead.

"Competence goes beyond words," observes leadership expert John C. Maxwell. "It's the leader's ability to say it, plan it, and do it in such a way that others know that you know how—and know that they want to follow you."[7]

THE EDUCATION OF THE COMPETENT LEADER

Thomas Jefferson was born on April 13, 1743, the third of ten children born to Peter and Jane Jefferson. Peter passed along to Thomas his knowledge of surveying, agriculture, and horsemanship. He died when Thomas was fourteen. Thomas inherited five thousand acres of land (including Monticello), and a number of slaves from his father.

In his autobiography, Thomas Jefferson recalled that, at age nine, he was sent to a small private boarding school where his teacher, a Scottish clergyman named Reverend William Douglas, taught him "the rudiments of the Latin and Greek languages [and] taught me the French." When he was fourteen, he was taught by "the Reverend Mr. Maury, a correct classical scholar, with whom I continued two years."[8]

In the spring of 1760, at the age of sixteen, Jefferson began his studies at William and Mary College, where he was mentored and instructed by a brilliant man named Dr. William Small. It's impossible to overestimate the impact of Dr. Small on Jefferson's life. Through his influence, Jefferson discovered the writings of the British empiricists—Francis Bacon, Isaac Newton, and John Locke.

Dr. Small was personally acquainted with such luminaries as Benjamin Franklin, Erasmus Darwin (the English physician and grandfather of Charles Darwin), Scottish inventor James Watt, theologian John Ash, poet Anna Seward, and British abolitionist Thomas Day. In his autobiography, Jefferson said that Dr. Small's impact was life-changing:

> It was my great good fortune, and what probably fixed the destinies of my life, that Dr. William Small of Scotland, was then professor of mathematics, a man profound in most of the useful branches of science, with a happy talent of communication, correct and gentlemanly manners, and an enlarged and liberal mind. He, most happily for me, became soon attached to me, and made me his daily companion when not engaged in the school; and from his conversation I got my first views of the expansion of science, and of the system of things in which we are placed. . . . He was the first who ever gave, in that college, regular lectures in ethics, rhetoric and belles lettres.[9]

Not only did Dr. Small introduce young Thomas Jefferson to the intellectual rigors of mathematics and science, but he also inspired in Jefferson a love for philosophy, metaphysics, and *belles lettres*—aesthetic literature such as poetry, fiction, and drama. Dr. Small also opened doors for Jefferson, introducing him to George Wythe, a leading expert on law, and Francis Fauquier, the governor of Virginia. Young Jefferson often dined with Dr. Small, Mr. Wythe, and Governor Fauquier, recalling, "I owed much instruction" to those dinner conversations.[10]

George Wythe ignited young Jefferson's interest in the law, and Jefferson recalled, "Mr. Wythe continued to be my faithful and beloved mentor in youth, and my most affectionate friend through life. In 1767, he led me into the practice of the law at the bar of the General Court, at which I continued until the Revolution shut up the courts of justice."[11]

Jefferson completed a four-year course of studies at William and Mary College in only two years, graduating in 1762. He studied law while working as a law clerk for George Wythe and was admitted to the Virginia bar in 1767. Jefferson's college education intensified his lifelong passion for books. In 1770, when Jefferson was twenty-six, his family home in Shadwell, Virginia, burned to the ground, along with the family's two-hundred-book library. Within three years, he replaced the lost library and expanded it by more than a thousand titles.

(Many years later, after the British burned the Library of Congress in 1814, Jefferson cataloged his book collection, numbering more than six thousand titles. He sold the bulk of his collection to the Library of Congress for $23,950 and planned to use the money to pay off his debts. But as he wrote in a letter to John Adams, "I cannot live without books," and he immediately began buying new books and rebuilding his library.)

BUILDING HIS DREAMS

In 1768, Jefferson began construction of his neoclassical home, Monticello ("Little Mountain" in Italian). He studied books on architecture while in college, and his library contained such titles as *I Quattro Libri dell'Architettura* (*The Four Books of Architecture*) by Andrea Palladio, *A Book of Architecture* and *Rules for Drawing the Several Parts of Architecture* by James Gibbs, and *Ten Books on Architecture* by Vitruvius.

Jefferson might have preferred a formal education in architecture, but no American school offered architectural training at the time. Yet his self-education through books left no gaps in his knowledge.

Though it was traditional for plantation owners to build their homes near the river, Jefferson built Monticello atop a mountain. From Monticello, he had a beautiful view in all directions, and he felt closer to the heavens. As a boy, he had often hiked and played on that mountain. Monticello was the fulfillment of a cherished boyhood dream.

Jefferson was an avid student of the violin and is said to have mastered it during his two years at William and Mary. His musicianship was a great asset to his love life.

Around 1770 or 1771, Jefferson began courting Martha Wayles Skelton, a young widow of a Williamsburg attorney. Slender and attractive, still in her early twenties, Martha (whom Thomas called "Patty") had many suitors. It's said that two of her suitors came to call on her, and as they arrived, they heard music—a harpsichord and violin duet. Knowing that Jefferson was the only violinist in the county, they said, "We're wasting our time," and left.

Thomas married Martha on January 1, 1772. During their ten years of marriage, Martha bore six children, only two of whom survived to adulthood. She was physically frail and suffered from diabetes. In 1782, after the birth of their last child, it became clear that Martha was dying. She had lost her own mother when she was young, and she'd had two stepmothers, both of whom she hated. So she begged Thomas not to remarry, because she didn't want him to bring a stepmother into her children's lives. He solemnly promised he wouldn't.

Martha died at age thirty-three. The inscription Thomas had carved on her headstone stated that she was "torn from him by Death, September 6, 1782." Grief nearly destroyed Jefferson. He isolated himself in his room, pacing and weeping, seeing no one for three weeks. For months afterward, he took long carriage rides or would stand on the hilltop at Monticello, staring into the distance, silently grieving. He kept his promise and never remarried.[12]

THE GREAT PARADOX OF JEFFERSON'S LIFE

Thomas Jefferson was a walking contradiction—a slaveholder troubled by the existence of slavery in a nation dedicated to freedom and equality. It was Jefferson himself who inscribed these words into the Declaration of Independence: "We hold these truths to be self-evident, that all men are created equal, that they are endowed by their Creator with certain unalienable Rights, that among these are Life, Liberty and the pursuit of Happiness."

When he wrote those words, he knew they contradicted his lifestyle and the chief source of his income. The Declaration of Independence was the highest expression of Enlightenment ideals. When he wrote that document, his conscience condemned him. For some reason, Jefferson felt he could not, or would not, live up to those high ideals himself.

Thomas Jefferson hated slavery. He feared what slavery was doing to his country. Reflecting on the injustice of slavery in *Notes on the State of Virginia* (1781), he wrote:

> If a slave can have a country in this world, it must be any other in preference to that in which he is born to live and labour for another. . . . And can the liberties of a nation be thought secure when we have removed their only firm basis, a conviction in the minds of the people that these liberties are of the gift of God? That they are not to be violated but with his wrath? Indeed I tremble for my country when I reflect that God is just: that his justice cannot sleep for ever. . . . The spirit of the master is abating, that of the slave rising from the dust.[13]

As a lawyer, Jefferson represented a number of slaves who went to court to win their freedom. One of those cases was his April 1770 defense of Samuel Howell. Opposing counsel was Jefferson's mentor George Wythe. Under the law, Howell was scheduled to be emancipated at age thirty-one on the basis of his mixed race (his grandmother was white). Jefferson argued that Howell should be freed at once, not kept in slavery until the statutory age of emancipation. Arguing from natural law, Jefferson said, "All men are born free [and] everyone comes into the world with a right to his own person and using it at his own will."

The judge cut Jefferson off in midsentence and ruled against his client—a discouraging, but not unexpected, defeat. Jefferson didn't take a fee for defending Samuel Howell. In fact, he gave money to Howell out of his own pocket, which Howell used to escape to freedom a few months later.[14]

How did Jefferson reconcile his Enlightenment ideals with the ownership of more than two hundred slaves? Historian Andrew Burstein grapples with the paradox this way:

> Jefferson saw African-Americans as noble human beings. In the abstract, he could appreciate the African-American's humanity. . . . Thomas Jefferson occupied a particular moral space and within that moral space, he was a liberal who believed that the most humane thing that could be done with the slavery problem was to re-colonize African-Americans back in Africa. . . . Jefferson wanted slaves to have decent lives. He wanted to be the best slaveholder in America. . . . He did not think that America was politically ready [to abolish slavery]. . . . Jefferson. . .was a political pragmatist.[15]

It would be easy to judge Thomas Jefferson by our current moral standards. This is a common logical fallacy called *presentism*—applying present-day values to cultural attitudes of the past. I'm not saying we should practice moral relativism. Slavery has always been evil. I'm only saying that Jefferson's perception was shaped by the times in which he lived.

Thomas Jefferson's father was a slave owner who bequeathed slaves to young Thomas in his will. His father-in-law, John Wayles, was a slave trader. His friend George Washington was a slave owner. Jefferson saw himself as an *enlightened* slave master. The institution of slavery was all he had known. If you had been born into that culture, your perspective might have been similar. We tend to be products of our times.

Something happened to Jefferson that enabled him to transcend his times and write the timeless words of the Declaration of Independence. In 1760, when Jefferson was sixteen, he encountered Dr. William Small. This young scion of a Virginia plantation owner suddenly discovered a much wider world of ideas. Jefferson said that Dr. Small's influence "fixed the destinies of my life." That may have been an understatement.

Dr. Small introduced Jefferson to empirical thinking through the writings of Isaac Newton and other great thinkers. He plunged young Jefferson into the depths of Enlightenment idealism. He introduced Jefferson to philosophers who taught him to empathize with the sufferings of others. As Jefferson absorbed these truths, he came to conclude that equality and liberty were self-evident truths. Someday, he believed, America would live out those ideals, but not in his lifetime. And he would not practice those ideals on his plantation.

That decision left a stain on his legacy for all time.

"I Have Done. . .All That I Could Do"

Elected president in 1800, Jefferson took the oath of office on March 4, 1801. He rode into Washington, DC, on horseback, alone and dressed in the simple clothes of a farmer. He passed along the streets unnoticed. His rejection of the regal trappings of the office contributed to his reputation as "the People's President."

The White House had been completed in 1800, and Jefferson used his architectural skills to expand the building. Jefferson referred to his election as "the Revolution of 1800," and he proceeded to make revolutionary changes. He dramatically cut taxes (his elimination of the whiskey excise tax made him especially popular) and reined in spending by closing unnecessary government offices and cutting defense spending. The only declared war during his two terms in office was the First Barbary War, when Jefferson sent American warships to protect merchant ships from the Barbary pirates of North Africa.

In 1803, at the beginning of the Napoleonic Wars, President Thomas Jefferson struck a bargain with France, authorized the Louisiana Purchase, and doubled the size of the United States with the stroke of a pen. America paid about $15 million for 828,000 square miles of land, which works out to about four cents per acre—the best bargain in American history.

In his post-presidential years, Jefferson devoted much of his time to planning and constructing the University of Virginia in Charlottesville. The institution opened its doors in 1819, and its initial Board of Visitors included three US presidents—Thomas Jefferson, James Madison, and James Monroe. Always mindful of how his education at William and Mary had impacted his competency as a leader, he envisioned the University of Virginia as a leadership academy.

Jefferson suffered a succession of debilitating illnesses in 1826. By May, he was a shut-in, though he continued to manage Monticello from his sickbed. He declined an invitation to go to Washington for the fiftieth anniversary of the Declaration of Independence.

On July 3, Jefferson was stricken with fever. With his daughter and grandson at his side, he gave instructions for a simple private funeral. Then he said, "I have done for my country and for all mankind all that I could do, and I now resign my soul without fear to my God."[16]

Jefferson slept through most of that day, awakening later that evening. He asked, "Is it the Fourth?"—his last words.

His doctor replied, "It soon will be."

Jefferson slept through the night. On July 4, on the fiftieth anniversary of the Declaration of Independence, at ten minutes before one in the afternoon, he died.

He was eighty-three.[17]

Five hours later, in Quincy, Massachusetts, Jefferson's friend John Adams spoke his last words. Unaware that Jefferson had died, Adams said, "Thomas Jefferson survives." Adams died the same day, July 4, 1826.[18]

Jefferson's simple funeral was officiated by his friend, the Reverend Charles Clay. Jefferson's epitaph, which he himself wrote, makes no mention of his presidency:

HERE WAS BURIED THOMAS JEFFERSON,
AUTHOR OF THE DECLARATION OF AMERICAN INDEPENDENCE,
OF THE STATUTE OF VIRGINIA FOR RELIGIOUS FREEDOM,
AND FATHER OF THE UNIVERSITY OF VIRGINIA.

THE LEADERSHIP LESSONS OF JEFFERSON

Let's look at the lessons that emerge from both the brilliance and the defects in Jefferson's leadership legacy:

1. *Seek mentors.* You are never too young or too old to have mentors. Jefferson described his friendship with Dr. William Small as "my great good fortune." Mentors instruct and counsel you, hold you accountable, and open doors of opportunity for you. Jefferson's competence was shaped not only by his formal education, but also by the many informal contacts he made through his mentor. Who is your Dr. Small?

2. *Don't compartmentalize your leadership life from your private life.* Practice your values and ideals at all times. Jefferson allowed his leadership legacy to be called into question because he advocated the abolition of slavery yet refused to relinquish his own slaves. In your leadership life, don't be a walking contradiction. Be consistent in every facet of your life, and leave a legacy that is unstained and beyond reproach.

3. *Become a polymath.* Cultivate a wide-ranging curiosity about many subjects; then become an expert in as many subjects as you can. Be a "cross-matrix" problem solver, drawing insight from a range of subject areas. Become conversant in several languages. Never stop learning and growing in your leadership competence. Never lose your intellectual curiosity.

4. *Read good books.* King Solomon said, "Like the horizons for breadth and the ocean for depth, the understanding of a good leader is broad and deep."[19] Jefferson treasured few possessions more than his library. The wisdom that penned the Declaration of Independence and the competence that made him one of our greatest presidents came largely from books.

Leadership authority Brian Tracy once told me that by reading one hour a day, I could read one book per week. A book per week equals 52 books per year or 520 books per decade. "And Pat," he concluded, "if you read just five books on a specific subject, you can consider yourself a world-class expert on that subject." There's an undiscovered territory of knowledge awaiting you in books. Emulate the wisdom of Jefferson, and read for your life.

Truth advances, and error recedes step by step only; and to do our fellow-men the most good in our power, we must lead where we can, follow where we cannot, and still go with them, watching always the favorable moment for helping them to another step.
THOMAS JEFFERSON

14

BILL GATES

Compute—and Compete

Like my friend Warren Buffett, I feel particularly lucky to do something every day that I love to do. He calls it "tap-dancing to work."
BILL GATES

In 2008, I went to Omaha for a speaking engagement. My driver, Walter, was my guide to all the interesting things to see and do around the city. I asked him about some of the notable people he had squired around town, and he said his most fascinating passengers had been Warren Buffett and Bill Gates.

"Mr. Gates comes to town a lot," Walter said. "He and Mr. Buffett are fanatical about playing bridge. They're great kidders. Once, when I was driving them, Mr. Gates said, 'Please drive carefully, Walter. You don't want to have a wreck with the two of us in this limo. It would adversely affect the global economy.'"

Gates was joking—but it was no joke. At that time, Warren Buffett was number one on the *Forbes* richest billionaires list and Bill Gates was third.[1]

William Henry "Bill" Gates III is the cofounder (with Paul Allen) and former CEO of Microsoft, the largest software company in the world. He began his career as one of the most aggressive entrepreneurs of the personal computer revolution, and since 2006 he's been transitioning out of the software business and into full-time philanthropy through the Bill & Melinda Gates Foundation.

Bill Gates was born in Seattle on October 28, 1955, the son of prominent attorney William H. Gates Sr. and Mary Maxwell Gates. As a boy, he was nicknamed "Trey" after the III in his name. He was curious and competitive from his earliest days. By age eight, he had read the *World Book Encyclopedia* from beginning to end. As an infant, he learned to make his own cradle rock; as a toddler, he loved to rock on a rocking horse; and as an adult, he is famous for sitting in a chair, rocking back and forth to burn off the energy of his constant hyperactivity.[2] Bill Gates has said his boyhood home was "a rich environment in which to learn." It was also a competitive environment, which suited young "Trey" Gates just fine. Biographers James Wallace and Jim Erickson explain:

> His competitive fire was ignited early in life and fanned by childhood games, sports, and the driving ambition of his parents.

Whether racing with his older sister to finish a 300-piece jigsaw puzzle, playing pickleball at the family's annual tournament, or swimming laps with his friends at the country club pool, Gates loved competing—and winning. Just as importantly, he hated losing. . . .

A friend who knew Gates in his early teens said: "Bill loved playing pickleball and was fiercely competitive. He loved playing tennis and was fiercely competitive. He loved waterskiing and was fiercely competitive. Everything he did, he did competitively."[3]

Bill attended Lakeside School, an exclusive prep school in Seattle, when he was thirteen. The Lakeside Mothers Club held a rummage sale to fund a computer terminal and rent computer time on a General Electric mainframe. This was in 1968, long before most schools ever considered providing computer education. Bill took an interest in writing and running programs in the BASIC computer language. Paul Allen, who was two years older than Bill, also spent time in the computer room. They became close friends.[4]

The decision of the Lakeside Mothers Club to support computer education was, at that time, an odd one. In the mid-1960s, few people gave any thought to computers. You might have expected the group to donate books or an overhead projector—but the Lakeside Mothers Club showed amazing foresight. Bill Gates and Paul Allen had their imaginations fired up by what computers could do—and they soon acquired more programming expertise than most university undergrads studying computer science at that time. If not for the Lakeside Mothers Club, Microsoft might not exist today.

"There was just something neat about the machine," Gates recalled in 1996, reflecting on his grade-school fascination with the computer. His skill as a programmer improved to the point where the company that owned the mainframe computer hired him and his friends to write a payroll program.[5]

When Lakeside administrators heard about Bill's aptitude for computer programming, they selected him to write a program for matching students to classes. The administrators did not anticipate the evil genius of young Bill Gates. He exploited his knowledge of computer code to rig his own class schedule. As Gates later recalled, "I had no classes at all on Fridays. And even better, there was a disproportionate number of interesting girls in all my classes."[6] He recalled:

> I can directly trace the founding of Microsoft back to my earliest days [at Lakeside]. . . . Instead of teaching us about computers in the conventional sense, Lakeside just unleashed us.
>
> The experience and insight Paul Allen and I gained. . .gave us the confidence to start a company based on this wild idea that nobody

else agreed with—that computer chips were going to become so powerful that computers and software would become a tool that would be on every desk and in every home.[7]

In 1970, fifteen-year-old Bill Gates formed a partnership with seventeen-year-old Paul Allen. They called their new venture Traf-O-Data. Their homemade computer system tabulated traffic flow data so that city engineers could better program traffic lights. The two boys paid a Boeing engineer to help with the hardware design. They purchased one of Intel's latest microprocessor chips, the 8008, and connected a paper-tape reader to their homemade computer. The system worked brilliantly in practice runs. But when Bill invited a city official over for a demonstration, the computer crashed. As the official turned to leave, Bill turned to his mother and pleaded, "Tell him, Mom, tell him it really works!"

In the end, Gates and Allen landed several clients. Their Traf-O-Data company grossed $20,000 before they folded the venture.[8]

In 1973, Bill Gates scored 1590 out of 1600 on the SAT and enrolled at Harvard. Encouraged by his parents to pursue a law degree, he chose his class schedule accordingly—but he maintained his passion for computers. He devoted most of his time to Harvard's computer lab but maintained passable grades by cramming. Meanwhile, his friend Paul Allen dropped out after two years at Washington State, and, at Bill's urging, moved to Boston and took a programming job at Honeywell.

Paul Allen recalls that Bill Gates engaged in "nightly poker games with the local cardsharps" at Harvard, and in the process he gained "some costly lessons in bluffing; he'd win three hundred dollars one night and lose six hundred the next."[9] Those "costly lessons in bluffing" were about to pay handsome dividends.

In December 1974, Paul Allen hurried to Harvard's Currier House, burst into the dorm room where Bill Gates was cramming for finals, and plunked down the January 1975 issue of *Popular Electronics*. "Check it out!" Allen said. The magazine featured a story on the Altair 8800—the world's first personal computer.

With Allen listening in, Gates phoned the New Mexico–based manufacturer of the computer, MITS, and said they were creating a version of the BASIC computer language to run on the Altair 8800. The software, Gates said, was just about finished and ready to demonstrate. MITS officials were eager to see a demonstration, but they were still debugging the memory cards for the Altair. They'd be ready for a demo in a month. Gates said their software would be ready around the same time.

Of course, Bill Gates's pitch to MITS had been pure bluff. All those poker nights hadn't been wasted after all. They hadn't written a single line of code. But as soon as Gates got his finals out of the way, they headed for the Harvard computer lab. Working day and night, they figured out how to emulate the Altair 8800 and they produced a version of BASIC that did everything they claimed it would.[10]

At the appointed time, Gates and Allen flew to Albuquerque and demonstrated the program to the MITS honchos at their Albuquerque strip mall headquarters. MITS offered to set Gates and Allen up in their own office. Soon after that, Bill Gates dropped out of Harvard, and together with Paul Allen, they founded their new software company, headquartered next door to a vacuum cleaner showroom in Albuquerque.[11]

They founded Microsoft on April 4, 1975—though they didn't immediately incorporate. At first, the company was "Paul Allen and Bill Gates doing business as Micro-Soft." The Microsoft (or Micro-Soft) name was Allen's idea, a combination of "microprocessor" and "software." In 1995, Gates and Allen recalled those early days in a *Fortune* magazine interview:

> GATES: "We put a credit line in the source code of our first product that said, 'Micro-Soft BASIC: Bill Gates wrote a lot of stuff; Paul Allen wrote some other stuff.'" . . .
>
> ALLEN: "We had talked about a lot of different names back in Boston, and at some point I said, 'Well, the totally obvious name would be Microsoft.'"
>
> GATES: "We also had mentioned names like Outcorporated Inc. and Unlimited Ltd., but we were, you know, joking around. We talked a lot about whether we should call it Allen & Gates, but decided that was not a good idea. . . . It seemed like a law firm or like a consulting company to call it Allen & Gates. So we picked Microsoft even before we had a company to name."[12]

Gates and Allen worked as independent contractors, writing software exclusively for MITS. By late 1976, they had hired employees and were developing software for other computer systems. On January 1, 1979, Microsoft moved from Albuquerque to Bellevue, Washington. As Microsoft grew, Gates continued to manage the business end of the company while overseeing quality control for Microsoft products. "In the first five years," Gates recalled, "I didn't let any line of code get out of the company that I hadn't reviewed."[13]

THE POWER OF COMPETENT COMPLEMENTARY PARTNERSHIPS

Do you know what "pancake sorting" is? I have to confess, I haven't a clue. In *Fun with Algorithms*, mathematicians Paolo Boldi and Luisa Gargano define pancake sorting as "sorting algorithms that use prefix-reversals, with focus on upper-bounds on the number of reversals used in sorting an arbitrary permutation."[14] Well, I'll take their word for it.

In his sophomore year at Harvard, Bill Gates came up with an algorithm for solving mathematical problems using pancake sorting. He later coauthored a paper with computer scientist Christos Papadimitriou (who was then at Harvard; now at UC Berkeley). Papadimitriou once described Bill Gates as "the smartest person I've ever met." He explains:

> Gates was fascinated with a math problem called pancake sorting: How can you sort a list of numbers, say 3-4-2-1-5, by flipping prefixes of the list? . . . For a list of n numbers, nobody knew how to do it with fewer than $2n$ flips. Bill came to me with an idea for doing it with only $1.67n$ flips. We proved his algorithm correct, and we proved a lower bound—it cannot be done faster than $1.06n$ flips. We held the record in pancake sorting for decades. . . .
>
> Two years later, I called to tell him our paper had been accepted to a fine math journal. He sounded eminently disinterested. He had moved to Albuquerque, New Mexico, to run a small company writing code for microprocessors, of all things. I remember thinking: "Such a brilliant kid. What a waste."[15]

There is no denying Bill Gates's technical brilliance, but Paul Allen's contribution to the early success of Microsoft has been grievously underreported. Their friendship was complex, and their personalities were sometimes complementary and other times at odds.

Bill Gates was the extrovert, the driven monomaniac, the hardheaded, uber-competitive son of a successful lawyer. Paul Allen was introverted and laid-back, the technical innovator, the studious son of a librarian. Though both Gates and Allen wanted to make money and both were tech geeks from the get-go, Gates had the business instincts of a shark while Allen was closer to, say, a starfish.

Yet Paul Allen pulled off some huge business coups of his own. When Steve Jobs's Apple II appeared in 1977, it was powered by a MOS Technology 6502 microprocessor—and Microsoft had no software that could run on that processor. Paul Allen devised a plug-in card for the Apple II that enabled Microsoft products to run on Apple computers.

Paul Allen pulled off an even bigger coup in 1981, when IBM sought an operating system for its personal computers. Paul Allen had connections with a tiny Seattle-based software developer that produced a primitive operating system called QDOS (for "Quick and dirty Disk Operating System"). Allen bought the rights to QDOS and used it to build a more powerful operating system called MS-DOS (Microsoft DOS). IBM adopted MS-DOS as its operating system, making it the industry standard. As John Naughton observed in the *Guardian*, Paul Allen's coup gave Microsoft "a license to print money—which it has been doing ever since."[16]

Bill Gates never fully acknowledged Paul Allen's contribution. Early on, Gates proposed that the ownership split between the two Microsoft founders should be 60 percent for Gates, 40 percent for Allen. Gates later chopped his partner's share even further, to 64/36.[17]

Highly successful business partnerships frequently follow the yin and yang pattern of Bill Gates and Paul Allen. One partner tends to be the extroverted, entrepreneurial salesman of the team, while the other tends to be the introverted, stable, innovative technician. We see this complementary relationship between the extroverted, visionary entrepreneur Walt Disney and his quiet, pragmatic financier brother, Roy Disney. In the Ben & Jerry's ice cream empire, Ben Cohen was the extrovert, the deal maker, the outside salesman, while Jerry Greenfield was the introvert who was content to stay behind the scenes, testing recipes and manufacturing the product. At Hewlett-Packard, David Packard was the driven extrovert while William Hewlett was the easygoing, behind-the-scenes technical innovator.

When forming your business partnership, think yin and yang. Find a partner who complements you, merge your respective competencies and personality strengths—then go out and achieve great things together.

WINDOWS INTO BILL GATE'S SOUL

Microsoft launched its Windows operating system in November 1985. With its point-and-click graphical user interface (or GUI), Windows was designed to compete with the GUI-based operating system of Apple's Macintosh computers. The Apple operating system was based on GUI-based capabilities of a programming language Steve Jobs had seen in operation at the Xerox PARC facility in Palo Alto. When Jobs learned that Microsoft's Windows would compete head-to-head with Apple's Macintosh, Jobs hit the roof. Malcolm Gladwell explains:

> Windows. . .used the same graphical user interface—icons and mouse—as the Macintosh. Jobs was outraged and summoned Gates from Seattle to Apple's Silicon Valley headquarters. "They met in Jobs's conference room, where Gates found himself surrounded by ten Apple employees who were eager to watch their boss assail him," [Walter] Isaacson writes. "Jobs didn't disappoint his troops. 'You're ripping us off!' he shouted. 'I trusted you, and now you're stealing from us!'"
>
> Gates looked back at Jobs calmly. Everyone knew where the windows and the icons came from. "Well, Steve," Gates responded. "I think there's more than one way of looking at it. I think it's more like we both had this rich neighbor named Xerox and I broke into his house to steal the TV set and found out that you had already stolen it."[18]

This is a telling portrait of Bill Gates, the ultimate competitor. Facing an infuriated Steve Jobs, Gates is calm and imperturbable—like a chess master who moves his piece, smiles, and softly says, "Checkmate." Gates doesn't raise his voice; he doesn't have to. He simply tells Jobs a little parable, and he has made his point. And he has won.

If there is one central pillar of Bill Gates's personality, it is *competition*. Competitiveness is the key to Bill Gates's competence as a leader. Embedded in the word *competence* is that equally important word *compete*. When you, as a leader, demonstrate this all-important fifth side of leadership, you assure your followers that you can make them competitive—and you can lead them to victory.

In the early 1980s, Fred Thorlin was director of APX, the software marketing division of Atari. Back in Bill Gates's Albuquerque days, Thorlin introduced the young software CEO to a two-player computer game. Thorlin and Gates played each other again and again. The result: Thorlin won thirty-five out of thirty-seven games. Thorlin came back through Albuquerque about a month later, and they played again. This time Gates won or tied every game. Thorlin concluded, "He had studied the game until he solved it. That is a competitor."[19]

On June 15, 2006, Gates announced his plan to transition out of day-to-day involvement with Microsoft, while transitioning into the role of a full-time philanthropist. Gates and his wife established the Bill & Melinda Gates Foundation with a $36 billion endowment. There are many causes that interest him, from global poverty to climate change to the threat of terrorism. But closest to his heart are problems of malnutrition, infectious diseases, and inadequate health care in poor countries. Gates told *Rolling Stone*:

> I want to focus on things where I think my experience working with innovation gives me an opportunity to do something unique. The majority of the foundation's money goes to a finite number of things that focus on health inequity—why a person from a poor country is so much worse off than somebody from a country that's well off. It's mostly infectious diseases. There's about fifteen of those we're focusing on—polio is the single thing I work on the most. And then, because of the importance of nutrition and because most poor people are farmers, we're in agriculture as well.[20]

Much of Gates's concern about health inequity can be traced to a visit he made in the 1990s to the South African township of Soweto. There he visited a hospital ward filled with patients dying from tuberculosis. "This was hell with a waiting list," he later recalled. "But seeing this hell didn't reduce my optimism, it channeled it."[21] He also channels his optimism toward the elimination of AIDS, malaria, and polio.

When asked why he devotes so many resources to these diseases instead of seeking a cure for cancer, Gates replies, "The world is putting massive amounts into cancer, so my wealth would have had a meaningless impact on that." He believes that the foundation gives him leverage to negotiate lower prices on medicines and vaccines, so that the benefits of these medicines can be spread to more people in poor countries, especially children. "We are super-smart about what we pay. We get price reductions. We can track how many kids get the vaccines."[22]

Bill Gates has also challenged the treatment of women as second-class citizens in some countries. Invited to speak in Saudi Arabia, he was shocked to face an audience segregated by gender. On the left, about four-fifths of the audience consisted of men. On the right, about one-fifth of the audience consisted of women, all cloaked and veiled in black. A partition separated them.

After his talk, Gates took questions from the audience. One man said Saudi Arabia hoped to become one of the top ten technology countries in the world. Gates replied, "If you're not fully utilizing half the talent in the country, you're not going to get too close to the top ten."[23]

The women's side of the room erupted in cheers. The men's side remained silent. It takes time to change the world. But Bill Gates is very competitive that way.

LESSONS FROM A COMPETITIVE, COMPETENT LEADER

Here are some lessons about the Fifth Side of Leadership that emerge from the life of Bill Gates:

1. *Competent people are competitors.* Competence is more than knowledge, more than skill, more than experience. Competence entails competitive drive. Some people seem to be born with a naturally competitive personality—but competitiveness can also be learned. Competition is a natural urge and a positive force if it is not carried to a cutthroat extreme. As complete seven-sided leaders, we don't want to win at any cost, but we absolutely want to win.

Teams and organizations mold themselves to the character of the leader. So leaders need to be competitors if they want their organizations to compete. By being a role model of a competitive mind-set, we enable our followers to achieve a higher level of excellence. Raising the bar of excellence benefits everyone—those who win the competition, certainly, but even the also-rans benefit. And the public benefits from better quality products and services. As Bill Gates once said of Steve Jobs, "We spurred each other on, even as competitors."[24] That's a competitive, competent attitude.

2. *Encourage the next generation to acquire the skills for tomorrow, not yesterday.* Our world has been impacted by the foresight and generosity of the Lakeside Mothers Club back in 1968. If they had not introduced two teenagers named Bill Gates and Paul Allen to the world of computers, the world might be very different today.

What's the next big wave in science, medicine, technology, economics, philosophy, or the arts? You may be in a position to influence the next Bill Gates of medicine (cure for cancer!), the next Bill Gates of statesmanship (peace in the Middle East!), or the next Bill Gates of science (colonies on Mars!). Few people have ever heard of the Lakeside Mothers Club, yet they helped change the world. What can *you* do to encourage the next generation of world changers?

3. *Leverage the power of competent, complementary partnerships.* Neither Bill Gates nor Paul Allen could have founded Microsoft alone. They needed each other. They completed each other; each supplied what the other lacked. Separately, Bill Gates and Paul Allen were brilliant individuals. As a team, they conquered the world. Every Bill Gates needs a Paul Allen, at least in those early entrepreneurial days. Do you have a leadership partner who supplies what you lack?

4. *Always seek wider, nobler worlds to conquer.* After Bill Gates conquered the software universe, he decided to devote himself to a bigger challenge: alleviating human suffering and tragedy in poor nations. His Silicon Valley nemesis, Steve Jobs, in a weird inversion of logic, disparaged Bill Gates for transitioning out of the software world and into the world of philanthropy. "Bill is basically unimaginative," Jobs told his biographer Walter Isaacson, "and has never invented anything, which I think is why he's more comfortable now in philanthropy than technology. . . . He'd be a broader guy if he had dropped acid once or gone off to an ashram when he was younger."[25]

Malcolm Gladwell points out that the fact that Bill Gates is now more interested in eradicating poverty and disease than in "overseeing the next iteration of Word" is not evidence of being "unimaginative." It's evidence of a scope of vision and imagination that goes beyond the product-focused, tech-obsessed vision of the late Steve Jobs, as brilliant as he was. Jobs, said Gladwell, endlessly refined "the same territory he had claimed as a young man."[26] Bill Gates sought new worlds to conquer. And so should we.

> *Some people, through luck and skill, end up with a lot of assets.*
> *If you're good at kicking a ball, writing software,*
> *investing in stocks, it pays extremely well.*
> BILL GATES

15

DWIGHT D. EISENHOWER

Competent to Decide

---

*The one quality that can be developed by studious reflection
and practice is the leadership of men.*
DWIGHT D. EISENHOWER

Young Dwight Eisenhower and his older brother Edgar got into a fight in the kitchen while their mother, Ida, was baking. Soon Edgar had Dwight down on the kitchen floor, pounding and punching the younger boy. Their mother continued working at the stove.

"Give up?" shouted Edgar, sitting astride Dwight.

"No!" Dwight wheezed.

Edgar pummeled him again then grabbed Dwight's hair and slammed his head against the floor. Dwight flailed uselessly, yelling for help. Ida went on about her business at the stove.

Finally, Dwight's younger brother Earl rushed into the room and tried to pull Edgar off of Dwight. "Earl," Ida said sharply, "let them alone." And Dwight was left to fend for himself.

David and Ida Eisenhower encouraged their six sons to solve their own problems, to stand up for themselves, to be self-reliant and competitive. If an older son was pounding the stuffing out of a younger son, the younger son would just have to learn to fight his own battles.

The Eisenhower family was a deeply religious family, steeped in the Mennonite tradition of pacifism. The Eisenhower boys were taught never to fight with other children in the neighborhood (why pacifism was not enforced *inside* the Eisenhower home is not clear).

One time, Dwight (who was nicknamed "Little Ike") was being chased down the street by a neighborhood boy just as Dwight's father, David, was arriving home from his job at the creamery. David called Dwight to him and demanded, "Why do you let that boy run you around like that?"

"Because," Dwight said, breathless from the chase, "if I fight him, you'll give me a whipping whether I win or lose!"

David pointed to the neighborhood boy, who stood gloating by the street, and he said sternly, "Ike, you chase that boy out of here!" And he did so.[1]

In the Eisenhower home, Mennonite pacifism clearly had its limits. Dwight's parents didn't want the boys to be bullies or start fights with the neighborhood kids— but neither did they want the boys to run away or get beaten. Historian Stephen Ambrose explains:

> In a family of six boys, competition was the natural order of things. Who could do the best job at this or that task? Who could run the fastest? Jump the highest? Lift the heaviest weight? Read the Bible aloud most accurately? Daily, in countless ways, the boys tested themselves against one another. David and Ida encouraged this competition, encouraged them to be ambitious to do the best. Most of all, each of the boys wanted to be the toughest, and they fought among themselves to find out who was the best scrapper.[2]

The school subjects that most appealed to young Ike Eisenhower were spelling and arithmetic. He especially enjoyed spelling contests, because they were competitive, and he loved to excel. The appeal of mathematics lay in its simple logic and certainty: an answer could be right or wrong, but there were no gray areas.

The subject that he most avidly pursued on his own time was history—especially military history. In spite of his pacifist upbringing, young Ike consistently preferred wars over chores. The family library contained a number of books on history, and Ike read and reread the sections dealing with great military leaders. The heroes he admired most were Hannibal, the great Carthaginian military commander, and George Washington, who prevailed over the British even though his cause often seemed hopeless.

Young Dwight Eisenhower was naturally curious, intensely competitive, self-reliant, and confident. Growing up with five brothers and learning to stand on his own provided a solid foundation for a competent, confident military leader. But he still had much to learn and experience on his way to becoming a great military leader on a global stage.

"THE BEST OFFICER IN THE ARMY"

Eisenhower graduated from Abilene High School, class of 1909. Ike and his brother Edgar both wanted to attend college, but their family couldn't afford it. So Ike and Edgar worked out a plan to alternately put each other through college. As Edgar went off to college, Ike went to work as a night supervisor in the creamery.

In September 1910, Ike learned that an examination was being offered for applicants to the two service academies, West Point and Annapolis. Of the eight Abilene candidates taking the exam, he scored second and won an appointment to West Point. Though his Mennonite mother was anguished over his decision to become a soldier, both she and Ike's father saw him off as he boarded the train.

For Dwight Eisenhower, going to West Point was the fulfillment of a boyhood dream. On arriving at the academy, he was awestruck by the history of the place. During the Revolutionary War, it had been the site of Fort Clinton, guarding the Hudson against the British Navy. General George Armstrong Custer and General Winfield Scott were buried in the West Point Cemetery, and he could go to the barracks and visit the rooms where Grant, Lee, Sherman, and other legends of American history had studied the lessons of leadership.

Eisenhower was part of the fabled West Point graduating class of 1915, known as "the class the stars fell on." Of the 164 graduates of the class of '15, 59 achieved a rank of brigadier general or higher. One of Ike's best friends at West Point was Omar Bradley, who would distinguish himself as field commander in North Africa and Europe during World War II, and would, like Eisenhower himself, become a five-star general. Ike did not stand out as a West Point grad, ranking 61st academically and 125th in discipline, but he made a name for himself on the varsity football team, starting at running back and linebacker.[3]

Ike married Mamie Geneva Doud of Boone, Iowa, in 1916, while he was stationed in Texas. They had two sons, Doud, who was born in 1917 and died at age three, and John, who joined the army and retired as a brigadier general. Ike rarely discussed the sorrow of losing their first son.

Once Ike assumed his duties as a commissioned officer, his superiors began to recognize him as a competent administrator. In 1917, in view of his exceptional organizational abilities, he received an appointment as commander of the tank training center at Camp Meade, Maryland. Though he regretted not seeing combat during World War I, he made a significant contribution to future war efforts. An innovative thinker, he devised a new strategy of speed-oriented tank warfare. His radical ideas were initially resisted by his superiors then adopted, and have been proven in combat from World War II through Desert Storm.

In 1926, having achieved the rank of major, he graduated from Command School at Fort Leavenworth, Kansas, first in a class of 275. Two years later, he graduated first in his class at Army War College.

In 1933, Eisenhower was assigned as an aide to army chief of staff General Douglas MacArthur. He would ultimately spend seven years under MacArthur, much of it in the Philippines. MacArthur was a bombastic, egotistical officer with a flair for the dramatic. Eisenhower served faithfully and efficiently under MacArthur. In a fitness report MacArthur wrote in the early 1930s, he said of Eisenhower, "This is the best officer in the Army. When the next war comes, he should go right to the top."[4]

MacArthur inexplicably put the brakes on Eisenhower's military career—possibly because he saw Eisenhower as an eventual rival. MacArthur valued Eisenhower's leadership skills, keeping Ike at his side for years while denying him promotions. Years later, after Eisenhower became a five-star general, MacArthur dismissed him as "the best secretary I ever had." For his part, Eisenhower observed that he once studied "dramatics" under MacArthur.[5]

Historian Matthew F. Holland observed that Eisenhower's experience dealing with MacArthur's outsized ego and prickly personality prepared him well for his unique role in World War II "when he had to work with such egotistical characters as Franklin D. Roosevelt, Winston Churchill, Charles de Gaulle, George S. Patton, and Bernard Montgomery."[6] And those skills would serve him well in the White House as well.

SEALING THE DECISION

By late 1939, Eisenhower was rising in prominence. In 1941, Ike was promoted to full colonel and appointed commander of the Third Army. By September of that year, he was a brigadier general. As the United States entered World War II in the wake of the attack on Pearl Harbor, December 7, 1941, army chief of staff George Marshall appointed Eisenhower to the War Plans Division in Washington. Ike's responsibilities under Marshall included preparing a strategy for Allied invasions of Europe and Japan. Historian Stanley Weintraub observed:

> Serving fourteen of his thirty-seven years in the Army under both men, Eisenhower was an assistant to MacArthur—invisible, and painfully aware of going nowhere—and then deputy to Marshall, who rocketed him to responsibility and to prominence. In seven years with MacArthur, laboring in the arid peacetime vineyards, Eisenhower earned a promotion of one grade, from major to Lieutenant Colonel, changing the oak leaves on his collar from gold to silver. In seven months under Marshall. . .he earned a constellation of stars and a major command.[7]

In March 1942, Ike was promoted to major general and named head of the Operations Division of the War Department. In May, General Marshall sent Eisenhower to England to assess the readiness of the European theater command. Ike returned with a pessimistic report. In June, Marshall sent him back to London—this time as commanding general, European Theater of Operations. In giving Eisenhower that appointment, he passed over 366 more senior officers—an impressive testimony to Marshall's opinion of Eisenhower's competence to lead.

In November 1942, Eisenhower took command of the campaign in North Africa. The early phases of the North Africa campaign were an organizational nightmare, in which Eisenhower commanded a mismatched collection of forces from several Allied nations—yet Eisenhower was able to impose a unified command that successfully coordinated invasions of Tunisia, Sicily, and Italy. Through his organizational and strategic skills, he racked up such an impressive record of success that in December 1943, he was appointed supreme allied commander of the Allied Expeditionary Force.

In December 1943, President Roosevelt chose Eisenhower to be supreme allied commander in Europe. When Roosevelt's son James asked why he chose Eisenhower, FDR replied, "Eisenhower is the best politician among the military men. He is a natural leader who can convince other men to follow him, and this is what we need in his position more than any other quality."[8]

Eisenhower's responsibility was nothing less than to oversee the invasion and liberation of Western Europe. The campaigns in North Africa, Sicily, and Tunisia served as a valuable training ground for Eisenhower as he faced one of the most challenging military campaigns in human history.

The invasion plan was code-named Operation Overlord. The Allied invasion force would consist of 4,400 ships, 11,000 planes, and nearly 155,000 assault troops. The biggest X factor was the weather. Eisenhower had originally selected June 5, 1944, as the date for the assault, but high winds and heavy seas forced a postponement until June 6. A predicted break in the storm over the English Channel would enable the Allies to catch the enemy by surprise. But if the operation went forward and the storm didn't break, the D-Day assault might end in catastrophe.

Early on the morning of June 5, General Eisenhower, Field Marshal Montgomery, and other senior members of the Allied high command gathered in the map room of Southwick House, near Portsmouth. They studied intelligence reports and weather reports, and Eisenhower invited all opinions—but the decision whether to proceed with the invasion or abort was Ike's alone to make. At that moment, ships were steaming toward France. Before long, it would be too late to recall them. The fate of nations hung on Eisenhower's decision.

Finally, Ike said, "Okay, let's go." And the decision was sealed.

Eisenhower knew his decision might end in disaster. He prepared a note that read, in essence, "Our landings have failed and I have withdrawn our troops. If any blame or fault attaches to the attempt, it is mine alone."

Advance troops parachuted into France just after midnight on June 6. The landing craft and amphibious tanks of the main invasion force reached the beaches just after sunrise. Allied troops came ashore in the face of heavy fire from German artillery and machine guns. They scaled cliffs and cut through coils of barbed wire. By the time the invasion had secured some eighty square miles of French coastline, more than ten thousand soldiers were dead, missing, or wounded.

Eisenhower's note proved unnecessary. Operation Overlord was costly but successful, and it paved the way for an ultimate Allied victory.

"That Awful Thing"

The liberation of Europe was a slow, grinding, bloody process. On April 30, 1945, as the Soviet Red Army rolled through Berlin, Adolf Hitler committed suicide. On May 7, 1945, German general Alfred Jodl arrived at Eisenhower's headquarters in Reims, France, to sign an unconditional surrender. Contemptuous of the Nazi high command, Eisenhower refused to be present for the signing. He delegated that task to his chief of staff, Walter Bedell Smith.[9]

It was the end of the war in Europe.

When Allied forces opened up the Nazi concentration camps and discovered the horrors within, Eisenhower ordered camera crews to document the evidence of war crimes for the Nuremberg trials. Eisenhower himself toured the concentration camps. He wanted to be able to testify of his own personal knowledge of the full extent of the Holocaust. He hoped that by so doing, he could prevent future acts of atrocity and genocide. He also ordered every American soldier in the vicinity to tour the camps and bear witness to what they had seen. He didn't want anyone to be able to deny the reports of the Holocaust.

In July 1945, Secretary of War Henry L. Stimson was at Ike's headquarters in Germany. A number of high-ranking army and War Department officials were present. During the after-dinner conversation, Secretary Stimson received a telegram. He read it to the group, all of whom had top security clearances. It said that the army had successfully tested the first atomic bomb. The bomb was ready to be dropped on Japan. Eisenhower later recalled:

> I listened, and I didn't volunteer anything because, after all, my war was over in Europe and it wasn't up to me. But I was getting more and more depressed just thinking about it. Then he [Stimson] asked for my opinion, so I told him I was against it on two counts. First, the Japanese were ready to surrender and it wasn't necessary to hit them with that awful thing. Second, I hated to see our country be the first to use such a weapon. Well. . .the old gentleman got furious. And I can see how he would. After all, it had been his responsibility to push for all the huge expenditure to develop the bomb, which of course he had a right to do, and *was* right to do. Still, it was an awful problem.[10]

America dropped the first atomic bomb on Hiroshima on August 6, 1945, then dropped a second on August 9, 1945. The surrender of the Empire of Japan on September 2, 1945, brought World War II to a close.

LEADERSHIP LESSONS FROM A CONFIDENT, COMPETENT LEADER

In 1948, Eisenhower accepted a position as president of Columbia University. In December 1950, he accepted an appointment as supreme commander of the North Atlantic Treaty Organization (NATO). He retired from active service as a general in the army on May 31, 1952 so he could run for president. He was inaugurated president of the United States on January 20, 1953, and served two terms, from 1953 until 1961. I could write volumes about Ike's presidential years, and I haven't even touched on them. But the example he set in his military career is rich in leadership lessons:

1. *To learn competence, practice being decisive.* The fate of great nations and countless lives depended on Ike's lonely D-Day decision. Where did he find the strength to make that decision? The answer may sound paradoxical, but it's true: He learned decision making by making decisions.

With every decision you make, the decision-making process gets easier. Every time you make a good decision, your confidence ratchets up. And every time you make a bad decision, you learn how to fix it with another decision and go on. As your responsibilities increase, the magnitude of your decisions grows—and so does your confidence.

Eisenhower observed, "Without confidence, enthusiasm, and optimism in the command, victory would scarcely be obtainable."[11] To obtain victory in all your leadership arenas, build your decision-making competence by increasing your confidence. And confidence comes from doing.

2. *Pay your dues.* Douglas MacArthur knew that Dwight Eisenhower had the makings of a great leader. He said so in an early fitness report. Yet MacArthur held back Eisenhower's career and prevented him from being promoted. Ike did his job without complaint. Even while his career was stalled, he was building his competence. One of his most important leadership lessons was learning how to deal with a prima donna like MacArthur. If he could endure seven years under Douglas MacArthur, dealing with de Gaulle or Churchill would be a cinch. Ike paid his dues and earned his leadership authority the hard way.

3. *Take on tough challenges.* In early 1942, General George Marshall appointed Brigadier General Dwight Eisenhower to the War Plans Division, where he was placed in charge of preparing invasion strategies. Brigadier General Dwight Eisenhower probably would not have felt competent to make the D-Day decision. He needed to spend time mapping strategies. Then he had to get out in the field and take on the decision-making responsibility for the invasions of Tunisia, Sicily, and Italy. Each job tested him in new ways; each job was a little harder than the one before. Every new challenge built his competence and boosted his confidence.

When the time came to launch Operation Overlord, he was already in the habit of making momentous, life-and-death decisions. D-Day was his biggest challenge by far—but by the time he reached that stage in his career, he was up to it.

4. *Build trust in your leadership through personal caring.* In the lead-up to D-Day, Eisenhower visited his troops on a regular basis. He wanted to make sure that when those brave soldiers hit the beaches of Normandy, they had confidence in themselves, confidence in their mission, and confidence in the leaders who sent them there. If the soldiers had any doubt in themselves or their leaders, the mission could be lost.

Eisenhower was a "soldier's general" who loved spending time with his troops. "I belonged with troops," he said. "With them I was always happy."[12] And in a wartime speech at the British Royal Military Academy, he said: "You must know every single one of your men. . . . You must be their leader, their father, their mentor."[13] The more you genuinely care for the people you lead, the more they will trust you—and the farther they will follow you.

5. *Remind your people of the cause they fight for.* Instead of saying, "Do what I say," give them a compelling reason to follow you. Stephen Ambrose gives us this glimpse into Eisenhower's thinking:

> Discipline and training "lie at the foundation of every success in war," he explained to a friend, but morale was just as important. In the prewar Army it was axiomatic that morale came from *esprit de corps*. Eisenhower still believed this, but he now realized that something more was needed. The battlefields of Tunisia and Sicily and Italy had made a deep impression upon him. So had talking with the men at the front and seeing the conditions under which they lived and fought. Eisenhower had decided that for an army to have morale "there must be a deep-seated conviction in every individual's mind that he is fighting for a cause worthy of any sacrifice he may make."[14]

To those who think that leadership requires us to scream and belittle our followers, Ike says, "You do not lead by hitting people over the head—that's assault, not leadership."[15] Eisenhower didn't assault or insult; he inspired.

As the troops boarded their transports for the Normandy invasion, each soldier was handed a sheet of paper, the Order of the Day signed by General Eisenhower. It read, in part:

> You are about to embark upon the Great Crusade, toward which we have striven these many months. The eyes of the world are upon you. The hopes and prayers of liberty-loving people everywhere march with you. . . .
> I have full confidence in your courage, devotion to duty, and

skill in battle. We will accept nothing less than full Victory!

Good luck! And let us beseech the blessing of Almighty God upon this great and noble undertaking.

Stephen Ambrose interviewed many soldiers who received a copy of Eisenhower's Order of the Day for the D-Day invasion. He recalled, "I cannot count the number of times I've gone into the den of a veteran of D-Day to do an interview and seen it framed and hanging in a prominent place."[16] That piece of paper told those men what they were fighting for, and Ike's order sustained them through the battle.

6. *Decide firmly, and don't look back.* People want to follow confident, competent leadership. If they sense in you the slightest doubt about the decision you've made, they'll have second thoughts about following you. Ike once said, "History does not long entrust the care of freedom to the weak or the timid."[17] Competent leaders make confident decisions; then they look straight ahead to the successful outcome of that decision.

Ike's wife, Mamie, once asked him how he summoned the nerve to make the D-Day decision. He told her, "I had to. If I let anybody, any of my commanders, think that maybe things weren't going to work out, that I was afraid, they'd be afraid too. I didn't dare. I had to have the confidence. I had to make them believe that everything was going to work."[18]

The next time you face a big decision, first gather your facts, then listen to your intuition, and finally take a moment to remember Eisenhower's lonely D-Day decision. Then decide—and don't look back.

Leadership is the art of getting someone else to do
something you want done because he wants to do it.
DWIGHT D. EISENHOWER

The Sixth Side of Leadership

BOLDNESS

16

Rosa Parks

Tired of Giving In

I have learned over the years that when one's mind is made up,
this diminishes fear; knowing what must be done does away with fear.
Rosa Parks

A lot of people have Rosa Parks all wrong.
Take, for example, the *New York Times*. After Mrs. Parks died in October 2005, the *Times* published a story about the mourners at the Capitol rotunda, where her body lay in state. The story referred to Rosa Parks as "the accidental matriarch of the civil rights movement."[1]

Accidental? There was nothing accidental about Rosa Parks and her leadership role in the civil rights movement. Long before that December day in 1955 when she refused to surrender her seat on the Cleveland Avenue bus, Rosa Parks was fighting for civil rights. Throughout her life, Rosa Parks was a role model of bold leadership.

That's why I placed Rosa Parks first in the section on the Sixth Side of Leadership: boldness. Rosa Parks epitomized bold leadership. Boldness means committing yourself to action, confronting danger, enduring hardship, and withstanding opposition in the pursuit of a worthwhile goal. There was nothing accidental about the way Rosa Parks lived her life.

She once told an interviewer, "I did not get on the bus to get arrested. I got on the bus to go home."[2] That's true—but long before the incident on the bus, she had been fighting for the right to vote. She had raised money to defend the Scottsboro Boys (nine black Alabama teens who were railroaded on rape charges in 1931). A dozen years before the bus incident, she had been serving as the secretary of the Montgomery chapter of the NAACP. And she had taken part in organizing activism following the murders of teenager Emmett Till and activists George W. Lee and Lamar Smith.

"The *accidental* matriarch of the civil rights movement"? Rosa Parks was a bold, determined civil rights leader. Her actions were no accident. She *led*.

Standing Up to Pharaoh

Rosa Louise McCauley was born on February 4, 1913, in Tuskegee, Alabama, where Booker T. Washington founded the Tuskegee Institute. For as long as she could remember, Rosa McCauley was drawn to the church and to her deep Christian faith. "The church," she once said, "with its musical rhythms and echoes of Africa, thrilled me when I was young. . . . God is everything to me."[3] Raised in the African Methodist Episcopal (AME) Church, Rosa loved to sing hymns and memorize Bible verses. In her book *Quiet Strength*, she recalled:

> My belief in Christ was developed early in life. I was baptized when I was a baby in the African Methodist Episcopal church. . . . I was never pressed, against my will, to go to church—I always wanted to go. I enjoyed dressing up and meeting people. During the service, I paid close attention to the minister's words, the prayer, and the other speakers. . . .
>
> Daily devotions played an important part in my childhood. Every day before supper, and before we went to services on Sundays, my grandmother would read the Bible to me, and my grandfather would pray. We even had devotions before going to pick cotton in the fields.[4]

The same scriptures that brought young Rosa McCauley such peace and joy also gave her a sense of worth and dignity, and taught her to take a bold stance against injustice. "From my upbringing and the Bible," she said, "I learned people should stand up for rights, just as the children of Israel stood up to the Pharaoh."[5]

Rosa's father, James McCauley, was an itinerant carpenter, builder, and bricklayer. Her mother, Leona Edwards McCauley, was a schoolteacher who blessed Rosa with a love of learning. Leona was an admirer of Booker T. Washington, and she kept two books in a place of prominence in the house: the Bible and Booker T. Washington's *Up from Slavery*. Leona preached Washington's values of hard work, thrift, and moral living to young Rosa. She also taught Rosa that the segregationist state motto of Alabama—*Audemus jura nostra defendere*: We dare defend our rights—can also stand as a statement of African-American pride.

James McCauley's work took him away from the family for weeks at a time—and around the time Rosa turned two, he stopped coming home. "My mother and father never got back together," she recalled. "They just couldn't coordinate their lives together, because he wanted to travel and she wanted to be situated in a permanent home."[6] So Leona took Rosa to her tiny hometown of Pine Level, Alabama, where she spent her early years.

Little Rosa McCauley enjoyed nursery rhymes, playing hide-and-seek with her little brother, and exploring the creeks and woods that surrounded her little flyspeck-size town. Rosa liked growing up in Pine Level. But when she was ten, she learned about the hidden dangers in that town.

Rosa was walking along the road when she encountered a white boy named Franklin. For no reason, he insulted her and threatened to hit her. Rosa reached down and picked up a brick.

"Go ahead," she said. "Hit me. I dare ya."

Franklin thought it over—then hurried away.

Rosa didn't give the incident much thought. The next morning, she mentioned it to her grandmother. "Franklin said he'd hit me," she said, "so I picked up a brick."

Her grandmother was horrified. She scolded Rosa and warned her that you don't act that way around white folks.

"But if he threatens me," Rosa said, "I'm in my rights to defend myself!"

Her grandmother replied that Rosa was risking getting lynched.

Rosa was hurt. She felt her grandmother was taking Franklin's side. Only much later did she understand that her grandmother scolded her out of fear—and love:

> My grandmother. . .knew it was dangerous for me to act as if I was just the same as Franklin or anybody else who was white. In the South in those days, black people could get beaten or killed for having that attitude.
>
> I didn't have too many other run-ins with white children. Mostly, white children kept to themselves and black children kept to themselves. We went to different schools and different churches and came into contact with each other only once in a while.[7]

There were many unwritten rules that African-Americans were expected to observe in those Jim Crow days. Black men, for example, were expected to address whites as "Mister" or "Miss." Rosa's grandfather enjoyed flouting the rules of segregationist etiquette, and he would joke about whites behind their backs. It was her grandfather's way of practicing civil disobedience, and Rosa learned by observing how he related to whites.

But Rosa's grandfather knew better than to push his luck too far. The Ku Klux Klan was resurgent, lynchings were on the rise, and the Klan would sometimes parade up and down the street in front of Rosa's house. Rosa's grandfather was determined to protect his family. "By the time I was six," Rosa remembered, "I was old enough to realize that we were not actually free. The Ku Klux Klan was riding through the black community, burning churches, beating up people, killing people."[8]

When the threat from the Klan was high and some of their neighbors were facing attacks, Rosa's grandfather would stay up through the night with a double-barreled shotgun close by, loaded and ready. "I don't know how long I would last if they came breaking in here," he told her, "but I'm getting the first one who comes through the door." Rosa and other family members went to bed fully clothed, ready to flee if trouble came—though Rosa confessed that if anything happened, she wanted to see it. "I wanted to see him shoot that gun," she said.[9]

Rosa recalled that her grandfather never seemed to be afraid—and he taught her not to live in fear. "He never looked for trouble," she said, "but he believed in defending his home."[10] Like her grandfather, Rosa Parks never went looking for trouble—but she believed in defending her rights. Her grandfather's boldness and courage clearly influenced Rosa's own leadership style.

The Bible was another source of courage and comfort for Rosa during those threatening times. Her favorite passages were Psalms 23 and 27—psalms of boldness and courage. Psalm 23 promises, "Even though I walk through the darkest valley, I will fear no evil, for you are with me; your rod and your staff, they comfort me" (verse 4 NIV). And Psalm 27 says, "The LORD is my light and my salvation—whom shall I fear? The LORD is the stronghold of my life—of whom shall I be afraid? When the wicked advance against me to devour me, it is my enemies and my foes who will stumble and fall" (verses 1–2 NIV).

Rosa McCauley Parks didn't give in to hate. She refused to condemn the entire white race, even though the rules of segregated society made race hatred seem pervasive. Some whites didn't seem to be a part of Jim Crow society. Rosa recalled the kindness of one white woman in town who would take her fishing and give her crawfish tails to bait her hook so she could catch bass. The woman treated Rosa and her family as if race simply wasn't an issue. Rosa also remembered a white soldier who came through town after World War I. He patted Rosa on the head and said, "What a cute little girl you are." That evening, her family marveled that the soldier had not treated Rosa like a little *black* girl, but simply like a little girl.[11]

Rosa didn't even hate the white people who sometimes called her names and hurled rocks at her as she was walking to school. She felt God's comfort in the presence of her enemies. She actually felt sorry for them. Her childhood was preparing her for the leadership challenge ahead.

"GET OFF MY BUS!"

Rosa attended a one-room segregated school from first through sixth grade. Public education wasn't offered to black schoolchildren beyond the sixth grade, but Rosa's mother sacrificed to send eleven-year-old Rosa to Miss White's Montgomery Industrial School for Girls. It was a school for African-American girls taught by white teachers. After one semester, Rosa was awarded a scholarship in exchange for chores such as sweeping and cleaning classrooms. In addition to academic courses and Christian education, Miss White's school taught Rosa skills in sewing, cooking, office work, and caring for the sick. Rosa would later credit the school with instilling in her a sense of pride and self-respect.[12]

In 1932, nineteen-year-old Rosa McCauley married Raymond Parks, who was active in the NAACP. In 1941, she got a job at Maxwell Field, an Army Air Corps base, and experienced what it was like to live in a fully integrated environment. President Franklin D. Roosevelt had banned segregation on military bases, and Rosa enjoyed riding around the base on a fully integrated trolley. But when she left the base, she rode home on a segregated bus. She wanted to do something to fight segregation, though she wasn't sure what she could do.[13]

In 1943, she joined the Montgomery chapter of the NAACP, becoming a youth leader and serving as secretary to the chapter president for fourteen years. That same year she had a troubling experience on a Montgomery municipal bus.

On a rainy day in November 1943, Rosa Parks boarded a crowded bus. The driver was—remember this name—James F. Blake. After she paid her fare, Blake ordered her to exit the bus and reboard by the rear door ("colored" people were not allowed to walk down the center aisle). She replied that she was already aboard, and she didn't need to get off and get on again.

Blake warned that if she didn't do as he said, he would put her off the bus. For emphasis, he grabbed her coat sleeve and tugged her toward the exit. She warned Blake not to strike her—she would go of her own accord. Blake repeated, "Get off my bus!"

Mrs. Parks got off the bus and walked toward the rear door—but the bus pulled away, leaving her at the curb to walk home in the rain.[14]

For a dozen years, Mrs. Parks carefully avoided riding any bus driven by James F. Blake.

"She Won't Stand Up"

On December 1, 1955, Rosa Parks finished her work at the Montgomery Fair department store and boarded the Cleveland Avenue bus. Only after boarding did she realize that the bus driver was James F. Blake, the driver who had put her off the bus twelve years earlier.

Mrs. Parks took her seat with three other African-Americans in the fifth row— the first row of the "coloreds" section of the bus. After a few stops, the first four rows—the "whites" section—filled up with white passengers. One white man was still left without a seat.

According to the segregation laws, blacks and whites could not sit in the same row. In order to accommodate *one* white passenger, *all four* blacks in the fifth row had to get up and move to the back of the bus. Three black passengers got up. Mrs. Parks did not.

Blake approached her and said, "Are you going to stand up?"

"No, I am not," she replied.

"I'm going to have to call the police."

"Go ahead."

A few minutes later, two police officers boarded the bus. Blake pointed to Mrs. Parks and said, "She won't stand up."

As the police officers approached, Mrs. Parks said, "Why do you push us around?"

"I don't know," one officer said, "but the law is the law, and you are under arrest."[15]

A myth has grown up around Rosa Parks, suggesting that she remained seated simply because she was physically too tired to stand after working all day. She responds, "People always say that I didn't give up my seat because I was tired, but that isn't true. I was not tired physically, or no more tired than I usually was at the end of a working day. . . . No, the only tired I was, was tired of giving in."[16]

News of Rosa Parks's arrest spread quickly among her friends in the civil rights movement. One of her friends, union organizer Edgar Nixon, bailed her out of jail.

The following night, Montgomery's black community leaders met in the basement of the white-trimmed, redbrick Dexter Avenue Baptist Church. The pastor of that church was twenty-six-year-old Martin Luther King Jr. The community leaders quickly devised an action plan to use Mrs. Parks's arrest as leverage to desegregate Montgomery's city buses. The meeting was held on a Friday night, and Rosa Parks was scheduled to appear in court on Monday—so they needed to act quickly. With amazing speed and efficiency, they mobilized the entire African-American community of Montgomery to action.

Jo Ann Robinson, a leader in Montgomery's Women's Political Council, mimeographed more than fifty thousand leaflets calling for a one-day boycott of city buses on Monday, December 5, the day of Mrs. Parks's court appearance. Teams of volunteers fanned out into Montgomery's black community, distributing the leaflets. Montgomery's broadcast media and weekend newspapers carried stories about the planned boycott, further publicizing the event. Dr. King and other black ministers spread the word to their congregations on Sunday.

The results were astonishing. On the day of the boycott, African-American ridership on the buses fell by 90 percent. Mostly empty buses rolled around the streets, costing the city money. Dr. Martin Luther King Jr. saw the hand of God in the effectiveness of the boycott. "A miracle had taken place," he said later. "The once dormant and quiescent Negro community was now fully awake."[17]

At her trial that day, Mrs. Parks answered charges of disorderly conduct and violating the city's segregation law. The trial lasted half an hour, and she was found guilty. The fine was ten dollars plus four dollars in court costs.

Dr. King and other leaders realized they had reached a critical moment. Should they continue the boycott? Clearly there was momentum for change. If they didn't seize that moment, an opportunity like this might never come again. The leaders formed a group called the Montgomery Improvement Association (MIA) and elected Dr. King as their leader. They called a community-wide meeting at Montgomery's historic Holt Street Baptist Church.

Five thousand people crowded into the sanctuary to hear Dr. King speak. "There comes a time," he said, "when people get tired of being trampled over by the iron feet of oppression." They took a vote of everyone present at the Holt Street meeting. The decision was unanimous: continue the boycott.

Nearly all of Montgomery's black bus riders participated. Many began walking miles to work. Activists organized a carpool of more than two hundred cars to get people to and from work. Community activists held fundraisers to cover fuel and car repairs for the carpool vehicles. White employers threatened many African-Americans with firing—but like Rosa Parks herself, they refused to be intimidated.

The boycott lasted 381 days, ending on December 20, 1956, when the Supreme Court ordered the Montgomery buses desegregated. After the ruling, Dr. King and the MIA knew that many whites in Montgomery would resent the new rules of desegregation, so they issued suggested guidelines for the African-American community to follow:

> In all things observe ordinary rules of courtesy and good behavior.
>
> Remember that this is not a victory for Negroes alone, but for all Montgomery and the South. Do not boast! Do not brag!
>
> Be quiet but friendly; proud, but not arrogant; joyous, but not boisterous.
>
> Be loving enough to absorb evil and understanding enough to turn an enemy into a friend.[18]

Rosa Parks demonstrated bold, courageous leadership the day she refused to give up her seat on the bus. There was nothing "accidental" about her decision. Leadership is never accidental. Her bold, deliberate action led to the Montgomery bus boycott, which launched the civil rights movement and elevated Dr. Martin Luther King Jr. to prominence.

Mrs. Parks didn't know that her refusal to stand would spark such a chain of events. She only knew that she was tired of giving in, and she had to do something. So she boldly defied an unjust law, and she boldly dared them to arrest her.

By acting boldly, deliberately, and decisively, Rosa Parks altered the flow of history.

LESSONS IN BOLDNESS FROM ROSA PARKS

The Sixth Side of Leadership is essential to every leader. Leadership must be bold and courageous. "Timid leadership" is a contradiction in terms.

Courage, of course, is not the absence of fear, but the mastery of fear. As Ralph

Waldo Emerson once said, "Do the thing you fear, and the death of fear is certain." To lead others, you must face your fears, conquer them, and lead confidently and boldly. By doing so, you will embolden the hearts of your followers.

Here are some leadership lessons from the example of Rosa Parks:

1. *Draw inspiration and confidence from your faith.* From her earliest years, Rosa Parks was devoted to her Christian faith. The Psalms gave her comfort and a sense of God's protection in the presence of her enemies. The Old Testament story of the children of Israel and their struggle for liberation from Egypt gave her a biblical prototype for civil disobedience.

Throughout her childhood, Rosa Parks faced threats and insults no child should ever have to deal with. Her faith gave her a sense of dignity and self-worth that racist threats could never take away. Prayer and the comfort of scripture gave her the strength to boldly confront the system of segregation.

2. *Draw inspiration from role models of boldness.* As a child, Rosa Parks was influenced by the example of her grandfather. She never forgot how he sat in his living room, shotgun in hand, ready for trouble. She learned from his example that a bold leader doesn't go looking for trouble but remains vigilant and prepared in case trouble comes.

Mrs. Parks was prepared that day in December 1955, and her refusal to stand was a bold act of righteous defiance and nonviolent resistance to injustice. She always remembered that her grandfather was never afraid—and she refused to be afraid as well.

3. *Don't give in to hate.* Rosa Parks refused to judge the entire white race by the actions of some. She treated people as individuals, not as members of a homogenized group. In this way, she managed to defeat her segregationist enemies without becoming like them.

4. *Rely on friends and supporters to embolden you in a crisis.* On the day Mrs. Parks refused to stand, she knew she was not alone. For years she had been involved with the civil rights movement. She had many friends in the movement, and as soon as she was arrested, word spread quickly throughout the Montgomery civil rights community. Knowing she was not alone made it easier for her to hold firm in the face of arrest.

5. *Use the past as a springboard for future action.* Rosa Parks's combative spirit was emboldened when she saw that the driver of the bus was James F. Blake. He had treated her abusively before, and she had spent twelve years avoiding him. But this time she wasn't going anywhere. Blake represented everything that was evil about the system of segregation, and this time she confronted him head-on.

Let past wrongs inspire present action. Don't be ruled by anger or resentment, but channel your righteous indignation into effective action.

6. *Accept the consequences of bold leadership.* Don't expect your bold decisions

always to bring victory. Before Rosa Parks experienced victory, she had to go through the humiliation of an arrest, jail, an unjust conviction, and sentencing. The boycott took more than a year to bring results. Mrs. Parks and the African-American community had to endure the wrath of an unjust system in order to overturn it.

Don't waste time complaining about the unfairness of the system. Confront the system and take the risks that come with leadership. In the process, you may just change the world.

How far will your boldness take you?

> *Each person must live their life as a model for others.*
> ROSA PARKS

17

Harry S. Truman

The Buck Stops Here

Men make history and not the other way around. In periods where there
is no leadership, society stands still. Progress occurs when courageous,
skillful leaders seize the opportunity to change things for the better.
Harry S. Truman

In the early 1990s, when I broadcast my radio show live from a restaurant in
Orlando, I had Colonel Paul W. Tibbets Jr. as my guest. During World War II, he
flew the mission that dropped the atomic bomb on Hiroshima. It was sobering to
hear him describe the fateful mission that ended the war.

I asked if he could feel any effects from the bomb as he flew away from Hiroshima.
He said that when the bomb exploded, he felt a tingling in the fillings of his teeth.
As he banked the B-29 Superfortress, the *Enola Gay*, and turned toward home, he
looked out the side window and saw the towering mushroom cloud and realized
that an entire city had disappeared. Still, he was relieved that the bomb would end
the war, and millions of Americans and Japanese would live out their lives instead of
dying in an invasion of the Japanese mainland.

Then I asked if he had ever met Harry Truman. "Once," he said. "After the war,
President Truman invited me to the White House for a short visit. He thanked me
for completing my mission; then he said, 'Don't lose any sleep over it. You did what
you had to do. The decision to send you was mine.'"

That decision could not have been easy for President Truman. It was a bold
decision, a decision that is still controversial today. But Harry Truman understood
that wartime leaders must make bold, courageous decisions. They must accept the
consequences of those decisions, including criticism and condemnation.

President Harry Truman demonstrated an abundance of the Sixth Side of
Leadership. But if you look at his life story, you see that his early years hardly suggest
the makings of one of the most bold, decisive leaders of the twentieth century. Harry
Truman's life followed a meandering path that somehow led him into the most
momentous pages of the history books.

His story is encouraging to us all. If a nearsighted, piano-playing haberdasher
from Missouri can become one of the greatest presidents of all time, there's hope for
you and me.

Boldness under Fire

Harry S. Truman was born in Lamar, Missouri, on May 8, 1884. His middle initial *S* doesn't stand for anything—Harry S. Truman is his full legal name. His parents were John Anderson Truman, a farmer and livestock dealer, and Martha Ellen Young Truman.

As a boy, young Harry was very close to his mother, who encouraged his interests in reading (especially history) and music. Harry took twice-weekly piano lessons, getting up at five every morning to practice for two hours. He was partial to classical composers—Mozart, Beethoven, Chopin, Debussy—but he also enjoyed the jazz-inspired compositions of Gershwin. During his presidency, while playing the piano for a women's group, he winked at the ladies and said, "When I played this, Stalin signed the Potsdam Agreement."[1]

When Truman was six, his parents moved to Independence, Missouri. He graduated from Independence High School in 1901, hoping to obtain an appointment to the United States Military Academy at West Point. He was barred from West Point, however, by poor eyesight. So he swallowed his disappointment and went to work as a timekeeper on the Santa Fe Railroad. Living on his own, he often slept in hobo camps near the rail yards.

In 1905, Truman joined the Missouri Army National Guard. Though his uncorrected vision was 20/50 in his right eye and 20/400 in his left (considered legally blind), he passed his vision examination by memorizing the eye chart. He served in the Guard until 1911.

David Gergen, who served as an adviser to Presidents Nixon, Ford, Reagan, and Clinton, noted that President Harry S. Truman "never thought of himself as a leader, nor did anyone else. . . . [Due to his poor eyesight,] Truman couldn't try out for school sports and mostly stayed at home, working the farm, reading, or playing the piano. . . . [He was] the only president of the twentieth century who never went to college."[2]

When the United States became involved in World War I, Truman rejoined the Guard, where he was commissioned a captain and placed in charge of an artillery battery. Before deploying to France, the army sent Truman to Fort Sill, Oklahoma, for training. There he became acquainted with Lieutenant James M. Pendergast, nephew of notorious Missouri political boss Tom Pendergast.

Captain Truman shipped out to France as the commander of an artillery battery that was infamous for disciplinary problems—D Battery, 129th Field Artillery, 60th Brigade, 35th Infantry Division. "When I first took command of the battery," he later remembered, "I called all the sergeants and corporals together. I told them I knew they had been making trouble for the previous commanders. I said, 'I didn't come over here to get along with you. You've got to get along with me. And if there are any of you who can't, speak up right now and I'll bust you right back now!' . . . We got along."

Truman drilled his men and whipped them into shape. Soon, D Battery was the fastest-loading, best-disciplined unit in the 129th Field Artillery. But the biggest test of Harry Truman's leadership ability came in the heat of battle in France.

On the evening of August 29, 1918, Truman's unit took up a position on the slopes of the Vosges Mountains in eastern France, near the border with Germany. Just after dark, the soldiers pulled the horses back from the artillery, and D Battery unleashed a barrage of poison gas shells—about five hundred rounds.

The plan was for the men to bring the horses back as soon as the final round was fired. The horses would be hitched to the artillery pieces and the guns moved out of range of the German artillery. Truman and his artillerymen waited half an hour, but the soldiers didn't return with the horses. An infuriated Truman ordered his artillerymen to lug the artillery pieces out.

Truman climbed up onto his horse, intending to ride to the rear and bring back the horses—but his horse stumbled in a shell hole and went down. Captain Truman was trapped under his horse when he heard German artillery shells exploding along the mountainside. The Germans were firing high explosives and poison gas.

COURAGE IS CONTAGIOUS

With impending death for added motivation, Truman clawed his way out from under his horse. He heard his sergeant call out, "Run, boys! They've got a bracket on us!"

Truman leaped to his feet and yelled at his men. "I got up and called them everything I knew," he said later. "Pretty soon they came sneaking back."

The men pulled the artillery out of harm's way, camouflaging the guns with branches. Truman would later cite his men (with the exception of the sergeant) for "cool courage" under fire—though the truth is that they feared Truman more than they feared German poison gas.[3]

Where did Harry Truman learn the art of bold decision making? How did he acquire the Sixth Side of Leadership? David Gergen believes Truman's trial by fire in the Vosges Mountains refined him as a bold leader. "For the first time in his life he was forced to lead men through moments of mortal danger," Gergen observed.

Truman ultimately got his men through the war unscathed. Throughout his command of D Battery, not a single man was lost. For the rest of their lives, said Gergen, those men "were loyal to Harry Truman, their leader who refused to back down. . . . Truman discovered two vitally important things about himself that night. First, that he had plain physical courage; and second, that he was good at leading people."

Gergen also quotes historian David McCullough, who wrote that Truman learned through that experience that "courage is contagious. If the leader shows courage, others get the idea."[4] Truman's experience under fire in World War I undoubtedly prepared him for leadership as president in World War II. He had gone into the war having never tested the limits of his courage and leadership skills. He emerged from the war a proven leader.

Harry S. Truman won the respect of his superiors and subordinates—and his war record served him well when he ran for public office.

A WINDING ROAD TO THE WHITE HOUSE

After the war, Truman returned home to Independence, Missouri, where he went into business with a longtime friend, Edward Jacobson. Truman and Jacobson opened a men's clothing store in downtown Kansas. On June 28, 1919, Truman married Bess Wallace. Harry and Bess had one daughter, Mary Margaret, born in 1924.

Truman's retail venture with Edward Jacobson flourished for two years but went bankrupt during the recession of 1921. Truman would spend more than a decade paying off his debts from his business failure. The friendship between Truman and Jacobson survived the bankruptcy, and Jacobson became a trusted adviser to Truman. During and after World War II, Jacobson advised Truman on matters relating to the Holocaust, Zionism, and the establishment of the nation of Israel.

In 1922, thanks to Truman's wartime friendship with James Pendergast, Truman became acquainted with James's uncle, political boss Tom Pendergast. With the aid of the Kansas City Democratic Party political machine, Truman won election as a County Court judge. He won a presiding County Court judgeship in 1926, was reelected in 1930, and was appointed Missouri's director for the Federal Re-Employment Program (one of FDR's New Deal programs) in 1933. In that position, Truman became acquainted with FDR's longtime friend Harry Hopkins.

In 1934, Truman was elected United States senator from Missouri. Widely known as a machine politician beholden to Tom Pendergast, he was often referred to as "the senator from Pendergast." This derisive title chafed at Truman. Even worse, he once attended a political dinner in which the evening's entertainment was provided by a ventriloquist. The dummy joked that his relationship to the ventriloquist was like Senator Truman's relationship to Tom Pendergast. The audience roared. Truman wasn't amused.[5]

In 1939, Pendergast was indicted for failing to pay taxes on bribes. Though Truman was not involved in the scandal, his association with Pendergast left him vulnerable to a primary challenge. Truman faced two opponents in the 1940 primary. Had he only faced one challenger, he would have lost, but the two challengers split the anti-Pendergast vote. Truman went on to win reelection.

In late 1940, Truman chaired a Senate committee investigating war profiteering. His leadership of the Truman Committee elevated him to national prominence. His efforts reportedly saved the government up to $15 billion—and landed him on the cover of *Time*. These accomplishments eradicated the stain of the Pendergast scandal.

In 1944, Franklin D. Roosevelt and the Democratic Party needed a replacement for Vice President Henry Wallace. The liberal and labor-friendly Wallace had been the perfect FDR running mate during the Great Depression. But the leftist views of Wallace were seen as a bad match for the war years. Truman's war record and political accomplishments made him the perfect running mate for the times.

The FDR-Truman ticket won by a landslide. Truman was inaugurated as vice president on January 20, 1945. Throughout the campaign and in the opening months of his vice presidency, Truman had very little contact with President Roosevelt. As a result, he didn't realize that Roosevelt's health was failing.

"The Buck Stops Here"

On April 12, 1945, about three months after the inauguration, the nation was stunned by the news that President Roosevelt had died of a massive stroke. After fewer than a hundred days' as vice president, Harry S. Truman found himself the chief executive of a nation at war. During his brief time on the job, he had received no briefings on matters related to the war. He had not even been told about the existence of America's secret weapon, the atomic bomb.

The day after taking office as president, Truman told reporters, "Boys, if you ever pray, pray for me now. I don't know if you fellas ever had a load of hay fall on you, but when they told me what happened yesterday, I felt like the moon, the stars, and all the planets had fallen on me."[6]

President Truman felt the weight of the challenges he faced as FDR's successor. Yet he knew that the times called for bold leadership. Historian David McCullough records that Truman told his cabinet that he "welcomed their advice. He did not doubt that they would differ with him if they felt it necessary, but final decisions would be his, and he expected their support once decisions were made."[7]

Truman presided over the Allied victory in Europe; then he made the decision to drop atomic bombs on Hiroshima and Nagasaki, ending the war in the Pacific. In the postwar period, he dealt with record-high inflation, a crippling national railway strike, the creation of the United Nations, the beginning of the Cold War, implementing the Marshall Plan to rebuild Europe, the Berlin Airlift, recognition of the state of Israel, the Korean War, and more.

In 1960, eight years after leaving office, Truman said, "I have been asked whether I have any regrets about any of the major decisions I had to make as President. I have none."[8] When asked if he agonized over the atomic bomb decision, Truman always replied that the decision was not complicated. The atomic bomb, he said, "was merely another powerful weapon in the arsenal of righteousness. The dropping of the bombs stopped the war [and] saved millions of lives. It was a purely military decision."[9] Much more difficult, he said, was the decision to enter the Korean War.

Though Truman appeared to make decisions quickly and firmly, historian Alan Axelrod notes that Truman was never hasty:

There was never anything "automatic" about the decisions he made. But he was so incisive and absolute a decision maker that it often appeared as if he breezed through the process. He was not a man who agonized, at least not visibly. The president's job, Truman believed, was to make decisions, and he was very good at his job. Instead of a nameplate on his desk, he had his famous sign proclaiming, "The Buck Stops Here." He explained in 1952: "The papers may circulate around the government for a while but they finally reach this desk. And then, there's no place else for them to go. The president—whoever he is—has to decide. He can't pass the buck to anybody." . . .

The idea, of course, was always to make the *right* decision. But this was less important than making *some* decision. . . . Truman wrote, "Presidents have to make decisions if they're going to get anywhere, and those presidents who couldn't make decisions are the ones who caused all the trouble." Of course, the *right* decision was the best decision, but the worst possible outcome did not result from a *wrong* decision. It resulted from the failure to decide.[10]

Many historians have studied the presidency of Harry S. Truman, seeking the secret of his bold, decisive approach to leadership. But Truman has explained his philosophy quite simply in his book *Mr. Citizen*:

Whenever I felt a mistake had been made, I always tried to remedy the mistake by making another decision. Everybody makes mistakes and the important thing is to correct them, once they are discovered. Sometimes you have a choice of evils, in which case you try to take the course that is likely to bring the least harm.

I am not one who believes it does any good to cry over past mistakes. You have got to keep looking ahead and going straight ahead all the time, making decisions and correcting the situation as you go along. This calls for a fundamental policy, a basic outlook, for the making of major foreign and domestic decisions. Otherwise the operations of the government would be reduced to improvisation—and inevitable trouble. . . .

The man who keeps his ear to the ground to find out what is popular will be in trouble. I usually say that a man whose heart is in the right place and who is informed is not likely to go very far wrong when he has to act.[11]

Our political leaders, corporate leaders, and religious leaders face crises on every hand. The world cries out for bold leadership. As our civilization is increasingly rocked by threats of war and terrorism, economic upheaval and social collapse, moral corruption and spiritual malaise, we see one leader after another failing the boldness test. Our government is paralyzed by political division and indecision. The people around us are like sheep without a shepherd. They look for leaders—and find none.

We need leaders who are complete in all Seven Sides of Leadership. But we especially need leaders who are strong in the Sixth Side of Leadership, leaders who are bold, courageous, and decisive. We need leaders with the boldness of Harry S. Truman.

Who will step up? Why not you?

The Leadership Lessons of Harry S. Truman

Truman was not a born leader. He had to acquire leadership skills the same way you and I do: experience, testing under fire, making tough decisions, learning from mistakes, and seeking bigger, tougher challenges all the time. Here are some of the lessons in bold leadership we can learn from the example of Harry S. Truman.

1. *Don't let your "limitations" limit you.* Truman never went out for sports, was hampered by poor eyesight, and never went to college. As a businessman, he went bankrupt. He refused to let his "limitations" limit his future. I don't recommend cheating on your eye exam, but Truman showed he was willing to do anything to achieve a military career. Once in the military, he excelled as a leader. He discovered depths of character and leadership ability he never knew he had. What are the "limitations" that hold you back as a leader? And what can you do to overcome them?

2. *You don't have to be liked—but must be respected.* When Truman took command of D Battery, he knew he was dealing with a poorly disciplined unit. He intended to change that, so he called together his sergeants and corporals and laid down the law. It was essentially the old "my way or the highway" speech—and after Truman delivered his ultimatum, he got the cooperation he demanded.

Many leaders fail because they have a neurotic need to be liked. I'm not recommending that you become a tyrant. But a bold leader must make tough decisions—decisions that will make you about as popular as a skunk at a garden party. Leadership is not a popularity contest. Sometimes your harshest critics will be the very people you are trying to help.

Harry S. Truman was not always popular as president. In fact, he very nearly lost the 1948 election. Today, however, he is widely regarded as one of our greatest presidents. If you believe you're on the right path, stay on it. If you lead boldly and decide firmly, you may not always be popular, but odds are, you will ultimately be respected.

3. *To increase your boldness as a leader, continually accept bigger and more difficult*

leadership challenges. For Truman, leadership was a series of stepping-stones up a mountainside, leading to the pinnacle. He had to follow that path, step-by-step, stone by stone. He had to go to France and learn leadership under fire. He had to try his hand in business—and even failure taught him something about himself. He got into politics, and with each new position, he increased his ability to lead boldly. When thrust into the White House by the death of FDR, he may not have felt prepared to lead. But Truman had the ability to make bold decisions and to stick by them. That's why Harry S. Truman was the indispensable leader for his times.

Are you growing in your leadership skills and strengths? Are you accepting the leadership challenges that come your way? Are you following the stepping-stones that will lead you to your leadership destiny?

4. *Don't dither—decide.* Truman understood that a failure to decide was far worse than any wrong decision he might make. A wrong decision can be corrected; there's no way to correct indecision.

Truman also understood that good decision making is guided by principles—what Truman called, "a fundamental policy, a basic outlook." When you have a framework of values and principles to guide your thinking, decision making becomes much easier. Your options become clearer. You make high-quality decisions based on sound and proven principles.

The leader who tries to make decisions without a clear set of principles must make it up as he goes along, basing his decisions on all the wrong considerations: Which decision will make me popular? Which option will benefit me the most in the short term? Which decision requires the least effort to implement? Which is the least risky option?

When your decisions align with your guiding principles, you can be confident you're making the right decision. Every decision you make will be firm, final, and confident. At the end of each day, when your head hits the pillow, you'll sleep well, knowing you did your best and you have no regrets.

There has been a lot of talk lately about the burdens of the Presidency.
Decisions that the President has to make often affect the lives of tens of millions
of people around the world, but that does not mean that they should take longer
to make. Some men can make decisions and some cannot. Some men fret and delay
under criticism. I used to have a saying that applies here, and I note that
some people have picked it up, "If you can't stand the heat, get out of the kitchen."
Harry S. Truman

18

Margaret Thatcher

The Lady's Not for Turning

Being prime minister is a lonely job. . . . You cannot lead from the crowd.
Margaret Thatcher

It was nearly three in the morning on October 12, 1984.

Mrs. Margaret Thatcher, the prime minister of the United Kingdom, was working late in her room at the Grand Hotel in Brighton. As she was putting the finishing touches on the speech she was to deliver the next day—

Thud! The room shook violently. Windows shattered. Plaster rained from the ceiling.

Mrs. Thatcher knew that a terrorist bomb had exploded—though she mistakenly thought it was a car bomb in the street. The bomb had exploded in the room above hers. She would have died if the terrorists hadn't put the bomb in the wrong place.

Within seconds, members of her staff came into the room to make sure that she and her husband, Denis, were unhurt. Detectives from her security detail arrived and told Mrs. Thatcher they should stay put for the moment. There was always the possibility of a second bomb, timed to kill people fleeing the first explosion.

About fifteen minutes after the blast, firemen led Mrs. Thatcher's group down the main staircase and out through the foyer—other exits were blocked by rubble. Arriving in the foyer, Mrs. Thatcher realized the seriousness of the explosion. Debris had fallen from the upper floors and was piled near the entrance. The air was gray with cement dust that settled on her clothes and her tongue.

Once outside the hotel, Mrs. Thatcher, her husband, and several aides were placed in a police car and rushed to Brighton Police Station. Other members of her entourage soon followed, and the police provided them with tea and kept them informed as news became available.

Mrs. Thatcher knew who had planted the bomb. For a quarter century, Great Britain had endured a campaign of terror bombings carried out by the Irish Republican Army. Over the years, the IRA had wounded more than two thousand civilians and killed more than a hundred.

A little later, Mrs. Thatcher and her staff were taken to Lewes Police College, where she changed into a dark blue suit and turned on the television, hoping for news. She invited "Crawfie" (her longtime personal assistant Cynthia Crawford) to kneel and pray with her.

Finally, she took a fitful nap then awoke at six-thirty and checked the news. It was bad. Several were confirmed dead—all friends—and there were many injuries.

Mrs. Thatcher informed her staff and security that she intended to go forward and give her speech to the conference. She needed transportation immediately.

Later, at her scheduled speech, she said she would not dwell on the attack, but she did want to say, on behalf of the British people, that the bombing was "an attempt to cripple Her Majesty's democratically elected Government. . . . The fact that we are gathered here now, shocked but composed and determined, is a sign not only that this attack has failed, but that all attempts to destroy democracy by terrorism will fail."[1]

Mrs. Thatcher's speech received an emotional, thunderous ovation.

In all, five people were killed, including Member of Parliament Sir Anthony Berry and three wives of government officials. Thirty-four were injured, including Mrs. Thatcher's friend Margaret Tebbit, who was paralyzed from the neck down.

After this attempt on her life, Prime Minister Thatcher's bold leadership demonstrated not only her own unyielding will, but the unbreakable spirit of the British people.

THE IRON LADY

Margaret Thatcher served as prime minister of the United Kingdom from 1979 to 1990, the longest-serving prime minister of the twentieth century. She led the Conservative Party from 1975 to 1990 and retired from the House of Commons in 1992. Queen Elizabeth II granted her a life peerage as Baroness Thatcher of Kesteven in the county of Lincolnshire.

Mrs. Thatcher was born Margaret Hilda Roberts in Grantham, Lincolnshire, on October 13, 1925. Her parents, Alfred and Beatrice Roberts, owned two grocery shops. Margaret and her older sister, Muriel, were raised in the flat above the larger of the two shops. She was raised in the Wesleyan Methodist faith and remained a devout Christian throughout her life.

When she was nine, Margaret received a prize for excellent schoolwork. When a grown-up suggested she was "lucky" to have received the prize, she responded, "I wasn't lucky. I *deserved* it."[2]

Margaret won a scholarship to Kesteven and Grantham Girls' School, where she attended from 1936 through 1943. She was awarded a scholarship to study chemistry at Somerville College, Oxford, arriving in 1943. She was elected president of the Oxford University Conservative Association in 1946. While at Oxford, she was influenced by free market writers, and especially by Friedrich von Hayek's *The Road to Serfdom* (1944),[3] a book that also influenced Ronald Reagan. She graduated in 1947.

Margaret Roberts specialized in the study of X-ray crystallography, using X-rays to study the atomic and molecular structure of crystals in salts, metals, and minerals. Though she would later gain fame as the first woman prime minister, she said she was actually prouder of being the first prime minister with a science degree.[4]

In 1948, she applied for a job at Imperial Chemical Industries (ICI), the largest chemical manufacturer in Britain. ICI rejected her application, and the personnel department placed these comments in her application file: "This woman is headstrong, obstinate and dangerously self-opinionated."[5] In other words, she had the makings of a bold leader.

After a brief career as a research chemist, Mrs. Thatcher studied law. She was elected a member of Parliament representing Finchley (an area of North London) in 1959. She served as secretary of state for education and science under Prime Minister Edward Heath. In 1975, she defeated Heath for the Conservative Party leadership.

On January 19, 1976, Mrs. Thatcher delivered a speech at Kensington Town Hall titled "Britain Awake." It was a blistering denunciation of Soviet expansionism. She said:

> The Russians are bent on world dominance, and they are rapidly acquiring the means to become the most powerful imperial nation the world has seen.
>
> The men in the Soviet politburo don't have to worry about the ebb and flow of public opinion. They put guns before butter, while we put just about everything before guns. They know that they are a super power in only one sense—the military sense. They are a failure in human and economic terms.
>
> But let us make no mistake. The Russians calculate that their military strength will more than make up for their economic and social weakness. They are determined to use it in order to get what they want from us.[6]

She made these remarks during the era of détente, when it was considered impolite for Western politicians to denounce the Soviets. She delivered the speech *seven years* before Ronald Reagan's controversial "Evil Empire" speech in 1983.

In response to Mrs. Thatcher's speech, the Soviet Defense Ministry newspaper *Krasnaya Zvezda* (*Red Star*) labeled her "the Iron Lady." The Soviets intended it as an insult. Mrs. Thatcher accepted it as a compliment. In fact, the Soviet reaction elevated her prominence and increased her stock with the British people. Her biographer Charles Moore explained:

> The Soviets, her implacable foes, gave Mrs. Thatcher the big

break her image needed. . . . The Red Army newspaper *Red Star* reported on a tough speech she had made about the weakness of NATO's defenses and described her as the Iron Lady. With a bit of "little woman" playfulness, she seized the moment: "I stand before you tonight in my Red Star chiffon evening gown, my face softly made up and my fair hair gently waved, the Iron Lady of the Western world." . . . The idea of the Iron Lady caught fire and, as the years passed, spread across the whole world.[7]

From then on, Margaret Thatcher was known among friends and foes alike as the Iron Lady. The nickname suited her well, especially in regard to her iron-hard yet ladylike leadership style—a bold approach to leadership if ever there was one. Margaret Thatcher went on to win election as prime minister in 1979.

"The Lady's Not for Turning"

Mrs. Thatcher was elected during the "Winter of Discontent" in early 1979, a time of economic hardship in Great Britain. The world was in the grip of an OPEC-engineered energy crisis, and widespread strikes by public-sector labor unions threatened to cut off the coal supply during a record cold winter. Prime Minister James Callaghan and his Labour government had no answer for these economic woes.

Mrs. Thatcher and the Conservatives mocked the Labour government's disastrous record with the slogan "Labour Isn't Working." When the Callaghan government lost a no-confidence motion, Britons elected the Conservatives to a forty-four-seat majority in the House of Commons—and made Margaret Thatcher their prime minister.

Arriving at No. 10 Downing Street, Mrs. Thatcher told reporters, "I would just like to remember some words of St. Francis of Assisi which I think are particularly apt at the moment. 'Where there is discord may we bring harmony; where there is error, may we bring truth; where there is doubt, may we bring faith; and where there is despair, may we bring hope.'"[8]

Government documents from 1979, made public in 2011, revealed that Mrs. Thatcher and her husband Denis lived an amazingly frugal lifestyle at No. 10. In June 1979, a Labour member of Parliament demanded an accounting of government spending, including the Thatchers' accommodations. Typically, a new prime minister will order changes and refurbishments costing tens of thousands of pounds. By contrast, Mrs. Thatcher submitted a bill of £464 for linen and pillows, and £209 for new crockery. A line item of £19 for an ironing board was crossed out and Mrs. Thatcher had written, "I will pay for the ironing board." Another note in Mrs. Thatcher's handwriting explained the modest expenses: "We use only one bedroom."[9]

Mrs. Thatcher introduced a program of free market economic initiatives (anticipating "Reaganomics" by two years) intended to cure Britain's recession woes. Her policies emphasized lower taxes, spending restraint, deregulation, and loosening the grip of Britain's trade unions on the economy. During her first two years in office, as economic indicators were slow to budge, her popularity dipped. Yet Mrs. Thatcher, confident her policies would bring prosperity, maintained her course.

By the fall of 1980, as the economy remained in the doldrums, many in the media and the Labour Party demanded Mrs. Thatcher perform a "U-turn" and reverse her economic policies. In a bold speech to the Conservative Party Conference on October 10, 1980—widely considered the defining moment of Margaret Thatcher's political career—she said, "To those waiting with bated breath for that favorite media catchphrase, the U-turn, I have only one thing to say: You turn if you want to. The lady's not for turning."

She delivered that line like a hammer blow, and the hall erupted in cheers. At the end of her speech, she basked in a five-minute standing ovation. Liz Kulze of the *Atlantic* wrote that Margaret Thatcher "pulverized her opponents through the strength of her own preponderant will. . . . Yet, iron-fisted as she was, she managed to maintain that special brand of feminine sass all the way through."[10]

By early 1982, the economy was improving—but in April, the ruling junta in Argentina launched an invasion of the Falkland Islands. The Iron Lady sent a Royal Navy task force to kick Argentina out. Her bold response to the Falklands invasion sent her approval rating soaring.

She was deeply aware of the cost of war and keenly felt the loss of British lives. After the sinking of the HMS *Sheffield*, in which twenty British sailors lost their lives, she sat on her bed at No. 10 weeping. Her husband Denis, a WWII veteran, sat beside her and said, "That is what war is like, love. It is bloody. I know. I've been in one."[11]

Because of her bold leadership at home and at war, Margaret Thatcher was easily reelected in 1983. A vastly improved economy won her a third term in 1987. The Sixth Side of Leadership prevailed.

What Was She Like?

The best way to illustrate Margaret Thatcher's leadership style is through stories told by those who knew her.

Her biographer Charles Moore describes her as a feminine woman who enjoyed the company of strong, powerful men. She especially enjoyed going head-to-head in debates and clashes with strong, powerful men. "She did not have many close women friends," Moore wrote. "It was always men that excited her attention, affection, and competitiveness." She admired great men like Ronald Reagan, Mikhail Gorbachev, and France's François Mitterrand. It was Mitterrand who described her as having "the eyes of Caligula and the lips of Marilyn Monroe." Moore adds, "She was always on the lookout for 'great men' and was wont to say that 'when a big man has a big idea I never like to stand in his way.'"[12]

Margaret Thatcher and Ronald Reagan met a couple of times in the 1970s before either of them had become a head of state. Reagan called on her at the House of Commons in April 1975 and again in November 1978.[13] During their conversation over tea in 1978, Reagan told Mrs. Thatcher that he "intended to try and become President." In reply, Mrs. Thatcher boldly predicted, "I *am* going to become Prime Minister."[14]

James Baker, Reagan's chief of staff, recalled, "President Reagan recognized Margaret Thatcher as a philosophical soul mate. . . . When Prime Minister Thatcher took office, the clock had run down on Britain's post-war experiment in socialism. . . . But Prime Minister Thatcher and President Reagan shared an optimistic dream of what she later called 'boundless opportunity built on enterprise, individual effort, and personal generosity.'"[15]

Sir Malcolm Rifkind, a Conservative politician who was secretary of state for Scotland under Thatcher during the late 1980s, observed that Mrs. Thatcher had an excellent relationship with Ronald Reagan even though she loudly disagreed with him on a number of issues—proof that leaders can express bold positions and still remain friends. Rifkind noted that Thatcher disagreed with Reagan over the Reykjavik summit (she thought he made too many concessions to the Soviets). She was livid when the United States invaded Grenada without advance notice to Great Britain. She called Reagan in the Oval Office to give him the rough side of her tongue.

Reagan was meeting with his staff when the call came in, and they could hear the bawling out their boss was getting from the prime minister. At one point, Reagan put his hand over the mouthpiece and said to his aides, "Gee, isn't she marvelous?"[16] Even on the receiving end of her high dudgeon, Reagan admired her.

In 1992, debate raged over the Maastricht Treaty, which created the European Union. Mrs. Thatcher was no longer prime minister, but she was involved in the debate in the House of Commons—and she opposed the treaty. Prime Minister John Major sent Conservative politician Michael Forsyth to talk her into supporting the treaty. When Forsyth arrived, Mrs. Thatcher had a marked-up copy of the treaty in her hands.

"Michael," she said, "which section of the treaty would you like to discuss?"

Forsyth replied that he hadn't come to discuss the content of the treaty. Instead, he was concerned that she was hurting herself politically by her opposition to it. He later recalled, "It was a stupid mistake and I should have known better. There followed an almost thermonuclear explosion during which I was asked in forceful terms if I thought she had ever cared about herself rather than her country. . . . I crawled under the door, thoroughly ashamed of myself."[17]

Here is one of the keys to Margaret Thatcher's bold leadership: She didn't care about her own political interests. She didn't care if she was praised in the press. She didn't care if she was popular. She cared only about what was best for her country. Her lack of self-interest made her bold where others would have been timid.

Bernard Ingham, Mrs. Thatcher's longtime press secretary (1979 through 1990), said, "She did not crave to be loved. God save me from politicians who want to be loved. It is sufficient to be respected. Margaret Thatcher was respected."[18]

Even some of Mrs. Thatcher's most bitter opponents respected her. After her death, Paddy Ashdown, leader of the Liberal Democrats from 1988 through 1999, told the *Guardian*, "I didn't like her politics. . . . I fought, sometimes mistakenly, against elements of her agenda. . .but there's no question that she was one of the great prime ministers of our century."[19]

Mrs. Thatcher's boldness served to embolden others in the Conservative Party. Kenneth Clarke, health secretary under Thatcher, said, "We were all believers in free-market economics; we all thought the trade unions were a dreadful, over-powerful vested interest. . . . [But] if it hadn't been for Margaret, I'm not sure many of us would have had the courage of our convictions. She gave us all the courage to do what we all believed ought to be done."[20]

Underneath Margaret Thatcher's boldness was a captivating (and underrated) feminine charm. Geoffrey Howe, foreign secretary during the Thatcher years, recalled a European summit in Copenhagen in December 1987. The delegates could not come to an agreement. Tempers were frayed. French president François Mitterrand rose and delivered a dour monologue, saying the summit was over and no solutions were in sight.

Then Mrs. Thatcher stood and cheerily replied, "No, it hasn't been like that at all, President Mitterrand. It's been a very good meeting. We haven't quite solved it, but we will."

Mitterrand responded, "I sometimes think Mrs. Thatcher is even more beguiling when she is saying yes than when she is saying no."

Howe was also present at the first meeting between Margaret Thatcher and Mikhail Gorbachev in 1984. Thatcher was the first Western leader to recognize Gorbachev as a different kind of Soviet leader. At the end of their time together, she said, "Here is a man with whom I can do business." Soon after that meeting, Mrs. Thatcher met with Ronald Reagan. Howe was present, and he reflected, "Margaret's most important contribution to the world was her ability to convince Reagan. . .that Gorbachev was a guy with whom he could do business, too."[21]

Mikhail Gorbachev remembers Margaret Thatcher as a bold and daring leader who contended forcefully for her views. Gorbachev especially appreciated Mrs. Thatcher's statement about him, and the fact that he and Mrs. Thatcher could disagree intensely while growing closer as friends. "For me," he concluded, "she was 'a person one can deal with.'"[22]

"This Is No Time to Go Wobbly"

On August 2, 1990, Prime Minister Thatcher was preparing to give the closing remarks at the Aspen Institute Symposium in Colorado. Her top foreign policy adviser, Charles Powell, called her and told her that Saddam Hussein's forces had just crossed the border into Kuwait. She told Powell to determine the location of British ships and aircraft in the region, and find out what resources could be diverted to the area. During a crisis, she once said, a leader must "take some action quickly, and you want first to know the facts."

Her next step was to take a walk to clear her thoughts. Then she went to see President George H. W. Bush, who was staying in the Aspen home of the American ambassador to Britain. President Bush welcomed her and said, "Margaret, what do you think?"

"Aggressors must be stopped," she replied, "and not only stopped, but they must be thrown out. An aggressor cannot gain from his aggression." Her experience in the Falklands had confirmed this principle. The experience of World War II also confirmed it, for the Nazis had been emboldened by a failure to "deal firmly enough with Hitler in the early stages."

President Bush was receiving conflicting advice. Arab leaders told Mr. Bush to allow time for an "Arab solution" to work. Colin Powell urged sanctions. Mrs. Thatcher knew that an "Arab solution" meant endless stalling, while sanctions could take years to work.

"You often receive conflicting advice," Mrs. Thatcher reflected. "That's why it is so vital to get your own ideas sorted out and the reasons for them. You don't have to accept advice which you think is unsound, but it is vital that you work out what you think has to be done and the reasons for it."

Mrs. Thatcher could see that President Bush lacked clarity. So she said, "Look, George, this is no time to go wobbly." She knew that the United States and Great Britain had to stand firm. Saddam Hussein had to be evicted from Kuwait.[23]

Because of the bold leadership of the Iron Lady, President Bush committed American forces to the region. Mrs. Thatcher left office on November 28, 1990, less than a hundred days before coalition forces launched the ground assault that began the liberation of Kuwait.

Mrs. Thatcher died on April 8, 2013. When she passed into history, the world mourned the loss—and remembered the legacy—of a bold, courageous leader.

Lessons in Leadership from the Iron Lady

The life of Margaret Thatcher is rich in lessons on the Sixth Side of Leadership: Boldness. Here are some important insights:

1. *Physical courage is a leadership asset.* It is one thing for a leader to put a career, a reputation, or finances on the line. It is quite another thing for a leader to demonstrate

courage in the face of suffering, tragedy, or mortal peril. A leader who demonstrates the kind of physical courage Margaret Thatcher did—going on with the conference after the Brighton bombing—sets an inspiring example for everyone to follow.

I'm not suggesting you should engage in reckless behavior or exploit a personal tragedy. But when events put you to the test, you have an opportunity to become a role model of bold courage. Your trials and tragedies can be opportunities for influencing others.

2. *Dare to speak the truth that others refuse to face.* Margaret Thatcher delivered her bold "Britain Awake" speech in 1976, when most politicians muted their criticism of the Soviet Union. Mrs. Thatcher defied convention and told the truth as she saw it. Though some were aghast, others applauded her boldness. The Soviets responded by dubbing her the "Iron Lady"—and she wore the sobriquet as her trademark. Let your boldness be your leadership trademark.

3. *Set bold goals and pursue them with confidence.* When Ronald Reagan told Margaret Thatcher he was going to "try" to become president, she replied, "I *am* going to become Prime Minister." She dreamed an extreme dream—then she pursued a step-by-step plan for turning her leadership dream into a reality.

Lech Wałęsa, leader of the Solidarity movement in Poland, was grateful for Margaret Thatcher's support. He recalled, "Observing her at work was a great opportunity to learn how to achieve goals. Once she gave me advice: 'Write down the ten steps from where you are now to where you want to be.' It was a good lesson."[24]

4. *Eliminate habits that undermine your boldness.* In 1975, critic Clive James criticized Margaret Thatcher's voice, saying she sounded "like a cat sliding down a blackboard."[25] Mrs. Thatcher responded by hiring a consultant, former television producer Gordon Reece. Mr. Reece, while on a train from Brighton to London, encountered actor Laurence Olivier. The actor gave Reece the name of a renowned speech coach at the National Theatre. After working with the speech coach, Mrs. Thatcher eliminated the shrillness of her voice and developed a dramatic, almost Shakespearean style of speaking. By the time she became a national leader, her voice was no longer a liability—it was one of her strongest leadership assets.[26]

On two occasions, I was in the audience when Mrs. Thatcher spoke in Orlando. Though she was not a dynamic, high-energy speaker, she was compelling. Everyone in the audience was captivated by her passion, her wit, and her stories about great people and great events. She walked us around the world and talked about nations and issues that would confront the West in years to come. I came away saying, "That was the best political science class I've ever attended!" It's encouraging to realize that her speaking ability was not a natural gift, but a skill she acquired, practiced, and improved on with the help of professional coaching.

5. *In times of crisis, don't go wobbly.* Don't abandon your principles in the crucible of testing. Margaret Thatcher believed that free market principles would turn the

economy around if given enough time to work. By the fall of 1980, her policies had been in place a little more than a year—yet her critics demanded that she make a "U-turn." Her bold reply: "The lady's not for turning." If you know in your heart that your principles are worth fighting for, don't go wobbly. Silence your critics by proving them wrong.

When Saddam Hussein invaded Kuwait, Margaret Thatcher's first response was to take a walk, clear her thoughts, and recall her core principles. By clarifying her principles, her decision became clear. People who lack core principles have very little basis for decision making. They are uncertain and indecisive—they make it up as they go along. Crises catch them by surprise, and they often delay decisions until it is too late. A well-defined set of principles will clarify your options and serve you well in a crisis.

A leader must not go wobbly. A leader is not for turning. Leaders must be bold.

If you set out to be liked, you would be prepared to compromise
on anything at any time, and you would achieve nothing.
Margaret Thatcher

The Seventh Side of Leadership

A SERVING HEART

19

GANDHI

The Great Soul

My life is dedicated to service of India through the religion of nonviolence.
GANDHI

The train was moving as Mohandas Gandhi jumped aboard. He climbed the steps, tripped—and one of his shoes slipped off and fell beside the track. Without hesitating, he yanked off the other shoe and heaved it away in the direction of the lost shoe.

A fellow passenger asked, "Why did you throw away your other shoe?"

Gandhi said, "The poor man who finds the one shoe will now have a pair he can wear."

The Seventh Side of Leadership is a serving heart. Many leaders find this the hardest dimension of leadership to grasp. There are a lot of five- and six-sided leaders in the world. They are visionary leaders, and they're skilled at communicating their vision. They have excellent people skills, and they work hard at building good character traits. They are competent and bold.

But tell them they have to become *servants* to the people they lead, and they look at you with blank incomprehension. We don't lead to be served. We lead to serve others. Our job as leaders is to put on a servant's apron every day. If we don't understand serving, we don't understand leadership.

More than ever before, in our corporate offices, in our churches, on our campuses, on our military bases, and in our marble-columned halls of power, we need leaders with serving hearts. We're up to *here* with bosses. We are desperate for authentic seven-sided leaders.

So the leadership example of Gandhi has never been more relevant than it is today.

THE FAILED BARRISTER

Mohandas Karamchand Gandhi led an amazingly successful movement to liberate India from British colonial rule—and he did so entirely through nonviolent civil disobedience. Gandhi's example inspired such leaders as Dr. Martin Luther King Jr. and Nelson Mandela. He is often referred to as Mahatma Gandhi (Mahatma is a Sanskrit title of blessing meaning "great soul" or "venerable"). The Indian people also referred to him as Bapu ("Papa").

Gandhi was born October 2, 1869, in Porbandar, a coastal town in western India. His father, Karamchand Gandhi, was a local government official and a Hindu, and his mother, Putlibai, was from an offshoot sect of Hinduism, Pranami Vaishnava.

As a boy, Gandhi viewed plays and read stories based on the epic tales of Shravana and King Harishchandra. In his autobiography, Gandhi recalled:

> My eyes fell on a book purchased by my father. It was *Shravana Pitribhakti Nataka* (a play about Shravana's devotion to his parents). I read it with intense interest. There came to our place about the same time itinerant showmen. One of the pictures I was shown was of Shravana carrying, by means of slings fitted for his shoulders, his blind parents on a pilgrimage. . . . "Here is an example for you to copy," I said to myself.[1]

King Harishchandra was a legendary ruler who, it is said, never told a lie and never broke a promise. In the tales of Harishchandra, his virtue is tested again and again by various painful ordeals, yet he always maintains his integrity. Gandhi recalled:

> This play—*Harishchandra*—captured my heart. I could never be tired of seeing it. . . . It haunted me and I must have acted Harishchandra to myself times without number. "Why should not all be truthful like Harishchandra?" was the question I ask myself day and night. To follow truth and to go through all the ordeals Harishchandra went through was the one ideal it inspired in me. I literally believed in the story of Harishchandra. The thought of it all often made me weep.[2]

In May 1883, Mohandas was married at the age of thirteen to a bride of fourteen. The marriage was arranged by their parents. He recalled, "I am inclined to pity myself. . . . I can see no moral argument in support of such a preposterously early marriage."[3]

Mohandas was an unexceptional student. It took him several tries to pass the examination to attend Samaldas College in Bhavnagar, Gujarat. His parents urged him to become a barrister (lawyer), so he went to London to study law at the Inner Temple, one of the four Inns of Court for English barristers. At the time, Gandhi was a rather worldly young man, eager to adopt English ways. In "Reflections on Gandhi," novelist George Orwell observed, "Gandhi started out with the normal ambitions of a young Indian student. . . . There was a time, it is interesting to learn, when he wore a top-hat, took dancing lessons, studied French and Latin, went up the

Eiffel Tower, and even tried to learn the violin—all this with the idea of assimilating European civilization as thoroughly as possible."[4]

Gandhi completed his law studies and was called to the bar in June 1891. He returned to India and established a law practice in Bombay. In his first appearance in court, he was unable to cross-examine witnesses due to stage fright. "I stood up," he recalled, "but my heart sank into my boots. My head was reeling. . . . I could think of no question to ask. . . . I sat down and told the [defendant]. . .that I could not conduct the case."[5]

In time, this tongue-tied young lawyer would become one of the greatest leaders on the world stage—and his words would shake the foundations of the British Empire.

SOUTH AFRICA AND THE BIRTH OF SATYAGRAHA

In 1893, at age twenty-four, Gandhi accepted an employment contract as a legal representative for an Indian company in Pretoria, South Africa. Though he planned to spend only one year in South Africa, he would ultimately stay twenty-one years. Those years would shape his moral, ethical, and leadership views.

The Indian population in South Africa was divided between Muslims, who were mostly wealthy, and Hindus, who were generally poor and oppressed. In Gandhi's mind, an Indian was an Indian, regardless of religion or caste.

In South Africa, Gandhi encountered racism and segregation. Once, while traveling by train to Pretoria, he was sitting in a first-class rail compartment. The train stopped to take on passengers. A European passenger entered the compartment, saw that Gandhi was a "colored" man, and left the compartment to find a railway official. He returned with a couple of railway employees, and one of them said, "Come along, you must go to the van compartment"—the luggage compartment at the end of the train.

Gandhi protested, "But I have a first-class ticket."

The officials insisted he had to go to the van compartment. When Gandhi refused, the railway officials called the constable, who bodily removed Gandhi and his luggage from the train. So Gandhi watched the train chug away, leaving him stranded with a first-class ticket in his hand.[6]

That was one of many incidents that enabled Gandhi to empathize with poor, oppressed, and marginalized people. On another occasion, while traveling by stagecoach from Charlestown to Johannesburg, he ran afoul of an ill-tempered, racist stagecoach driver. The driver didn't want Gandhi to sit with the white passengers, so he made Gandhi sit outside on the coach box. To avoid confrontation, Gandhi swallowed his pride and did as the man said.

At one stop, the coachman continued to insult Gandhi and order him around, calling him "Sami" (a term of racial derision). When Gandhi refused to accept any more of the man's bullying, the driver gave Gandhi a beating. The man only stopped pummeling Gandhi when the white passengers begged him to stop.

As they continued on their way, the driver told Gandhi that when they reached their next stop, "I shall show you what I do." Gandhi sat speechless and prayed for God to help him.[7]

Events like these shaped Gandhi's social and ethical awareness, and caused him to question his place in the British Empire.

In 1894, he helped to establish the Natal Indian Congress, to give the Indian community in South Africa a sense of identity and political power. His efforts to empower the Indian community in South Africa made him unpopular with white settlers. In January 1897, he arrived in Durban—and a crowd gathered around him, shouting "Gandhi, Gandhi!" The crowd swelled—and soon they began pelting him with rocks, sticks, and rotten eggs. It became a full-scale riot, and one of the rioters ripped the turban from his head while others punched and kicked him.

The crowd might have lynched him if a woman named Mrs. Alexander hadn't happened by. She was the wife of the police superintendent, and she knew Gandhi. When she heard the rioters yelling his name, she placed herself between Gandhi and the mob, opened her parasol as a shield, and ordered the mob to disperse. The rioters ordered Mrs. Alexander out of the way.

Meanwhile, an Indian teenager ran to the police station and returned with the police superintendent, Mr. Alexander, and a number of officers. They formed a cordon around Gandhi and led him to the police station, saving his life.

Mr. Alexander offered to let Gandhi take refuge at the station, but Gandhi declined. In his autobiography, Gandhi recalled saying, "They are sure to quiet down when they realize their mistake. I have trust in their sense of fairness."[8] That's a remarkable statement from a man who is covered in blood and bruises, smelling of rotten eggs.

In 1906, the Transvaal government enacted the Transvaal Asiatic Registration Act, requiring Indian and Chinese residents to register or be deported. Gandhi believed this requirement humiliated and threatened the safety of the Indian community. By this time, Gandhi had been formulating his ideas of nonviolent resistance. He called this methodology *satyagraha*, which means "devotion to the Truth." He taught the Indian community the principles of satyagraha, and urged his fellow Indians to defy the Registration Act—and to *accept the consequences* of that defiance.

Many nonresisting Indians were beaten, flogged, jailed, or killed. Yet the Indian community believed in Gandhi's teachings. In the face of violent persecution, many steadfastly refused to register. Others publicly burned their registration cards as a solemn act of defiance.

In time, the government's abusive treatment of Indian protesters stung the conscience of South African whites. It was hard for South African citizens to see peaceful, unresisting Indians being beaten and arrested. After seven years of peaceful Indian protests, South African leader Jan Christiaan Smuts negotiated a compromise agreement with Gandhi—the Smuts-Gandhi Settlement of 1914. It was the first vindication of Gandhi's principles of satyagraha.

Tolstoy Farm

Gandhi's concept of satyagraha was heavily influenced by the philosophical and religious writings of Russian novelist Leo Tolstoy (1828–1910). Tolstoy had made an intense study of the life and teachings of Jesus of Nazareth, particularly his Sermon on the Mount. While Gandhi waged his nonviolent fight against oppression in South Africa, a "Tolstoyan movement" took hold in Russia, America, and Europe.

In 1910, Gandhi founded Tolstoy Farm, a cooperative agrarian colony outside of Johannesburg. Gandhi's partner in founding Tolstoy Farm was a wealthy German-born Jewish architect, Hermann Kallenbach, who provided the land and funding for the project. Kallenbach was a devoted follower of Gandhi's principles of satyagraha. He saw Tolstoy Farm as a pilot project that could lead to greater understanding and equality among all people. Kallenbach designed the main farmhouse and called it Satyagraha House.

People in the Tolstoyan movement put the teachings of Jesus into practice—and they tried to do so as literally as possible. Tolstoyans lived simple lives, practicing vegetarianism, pacifism, and the avoidance of alcohol, tobacco, and sexual sin. They rejected the state (which, in Tolstoy's view, was built on coercive force). Tolstoy's definition of following Jesus, based on the Sermon on the Mount, could be summed up in five principles:

1. Love your enemies (Matthew 5:44).
2. Do not be angry (Matthew 5:22).
3. Do not resist an evil person (turn the other cheek; Matthew 5:39).
4. Do not lust (Matthew 5:28).
5. Do not swear an oath (Matthew 5:34–37).

This radical brand of Christian thought merged seamlessly with Gandhi's brand of Hinduism, which had largely been shaped by the idealism of his childhood heroes, Shravana and King Harishchandra. As a boy he had asked himself, "Why should not all be truthful like Harishchandra?" He later reflected that the notion of following truth and enduring all the trials of Harishchandra was the one ideal that inspired him as a child. The radical Christian message of the Tolstoyans gave Gandhi a way to translate his childhood ideals into a mature plan of action.

Swadeshi and the Salt Satyagraha

Gandhi returned to India in 1915 and began organizing peasants and laborers to protest injustice. His work in South Africa had gained for him an international reputation as a protest organizer. He took over as head of the Indian National Congress in 1921, and his goal was nothing less than swaraj—Indian independence and self-rule. Under Gandhi's leadership, the Indian National Congress pushed for reforms to ease poverty, build religious and ethnic tolerance, and end the designation of some people as *Dalits* (untouchables).

In 1921, Gandhi adopted the loincloth that became his trademark. Made from homespun khadi cloth, it not only symbolized Gandhi's identification with the poorest of his people, but it served as a "sign of mourning"—a symbol of Gandhi's ongoing grief over British colonial oppression. Gandhi didn't expect his followers to wear the loincloth—he intended it only for his personal expression. The loincloth had the paradoxical effect of elevating him as a saint, a holy man, a Mahatma.[9]

Gandhi's loincloth was a shock to the sensibilities of Britons, because his seeming return to "nakedness" made Gandhi seem primitive and uncivilized. He insisted on wearing the loincloth during his audience with King George V at Buckingham Palace. A reporter asked him, "Mr. Gandhi, do you think you are properly dressed to meet the King?" Gandhi replied, "Do not worry about my clothes. The King has enough clothes on for both of us."

The loincloth became a trademark for Gandhi's new nonviolent "weapon"— *swadeshi*. This term comes from a conjunction of two Sanskrit words, which together mean "of one's own country." The swadeshi policy was composed of two parts: (1) The Indian people were to boycott foreign-made goods, especially cloth goods from Great Britain. (2) The Indian people were to wear homespun khadi instead of imported textiles. Swadeshi quickly became a symbol of pride, and all Indians, both rich and poor, began to spin khadi.

During one of Gandhi's frequent stays in the guest accommodations of the colonial prison, he invented a portable spinning wheel. The December 1931 issue of *Popular Science* featured a photo of Gandhi with his invention.[10]

The taxation of salt by Great Britain had been a sore point for decades. On March 12, 1930, as a symbolic protest against taxes on salt, Gandhi began his march from Ahmedabad to the seacoast village of Dandi. Many Indians joined the march along the way. It was a violation of British law for anyone to go to the seashore and make their own salt without paying the tax. After traveling on foot for twenty-four days, Gandhi reached the sea on April 5, 1930, and began making salt.

He planned another act of civil disobedience at the Dharasana saltworks, south of Dandi, but the British arrested him on May 4. Gandhi's followers continued the Salt Satyagraha for a year. During that time, the colonial government imprisoned more than sixty thousand Indians. These arrests did not surprise Gandhi. He expected Britain to overplay its hand. By arresting so many peaceful demonstrators for simply making salt, the British government looked thuggish and ridiculous. These heavy-handed actions won sympathy and support for the people of India.

Finally, the British colonial government, represented by Lord Edward Irwin, the viceroy of India, negotiated with Gandhi. The result was an agreement, the Gandhi-Irwin Pact, signed in March 1931. Under terms of the agreement, the British government would free all political prisoners—and Gandhi would suspend his civil disobedience movement. The British government invited Gandhi to attend the Round Table Conference in London, leading him to believe that Indian independence would be on the agenda—but the subject never came up.

One month after the Gandhi-Irwin Pact was signed, Lord Irwin was replaced by Lord Willingdon, a hardliner who steadfastly opposed Indian independence. Soon after Gandhi returned to India from England, he was arrested once more.

THE ROAD TO SWARAJ

Gandhi's vision for India was an independent India in which Hindus and Muslims would live together in peace. He was committed to a unified India based on religious pluralism and religious unity. During the war years, however, a new Muslim identity began to assert itself, demanding a separate Islamic homeland.

World War II came to an end in the summer of 1945. Two years later, on August 15, 1947, Great Britain granted independence to India—but not as Mahatma Gandhi envisioned it. India was partitioned into two separate countries, a Hindu nation called India, and a Muslim nation called Pakistan. This created a crisis for people in the border regions. Many Hindus, Sikhs, and Muslims suddenly found themselves on the wrong side of the border line. The result was religious violence, hordes of refugees flowing in both directions, and as many as a half million killed in riots.

This was not Gandhi's dream. This was Gandhi's nightmare. Historian Stanley Wolpert, in his book *Gandhi's Passion*, gives us a glimpse of Indian independence as it must have appeared through Gandhi's eyes:

> "Who listens to me today?" a despondent Gandhi muttered. . . . To disillusioned devotees, the Mahatma ("Great Soul") freely confessed his "bankruptcy," admitting that he lived in "a fool's paradise." Nonetheless, the seventy-seven-year-old little Father (Bapu) of his nation did not surrender to sorrow. Great Soul that he was, Gandhi carried on, passionately ignoring daily threats to his life, refusing to silence his criticism of the government, and rejecting appeals to remain in New Delhi to celebrate the dawn of India's freedom at midnight on the Fifteenth of August, 1947. "What is there to celebrate?" This "vivisection of the Mother," as he called partition, was fit only for prayer and "deep heart-searching," not for fireworks, proud speeches, and songs.[11]

In many ways, Gandhi had achieved a remarkable success. Together, he and the Indian people had thrown off British colonial rule without a bloody revolution. His principles of satyagraha had been amazingly effective. Gandhi had succeeded magnificently—but he went to his grave believing he had failed.

On the evening of January 30, 1948, Gandhi walked through the garden of the Birla House in New Delhi, accompanied by a number of followers and family members. Gandhi had lived at Birla House for nearly half a year, ever since India had won its independence from Great Britain. He was on his way to deliver an invocation at a prayer meeting.

At 5:17 p.m., a man named Nathuram Godse, a Hindu nationalist, stepped forward. He pointed a Beretta 9 mm pistol at Gandhi's chest and fired three times at point-blank range. Gandhi cried out as he fell, "*Hē Ram*," which means, "O God!"—not an oath, but a prayer. Gandhi died at age seventy-eight.

The gunman killed Gandhi in the mistaken belief that the Indian leader favored Muslims over Hindus. It was an irrational view, but then, so much of the violence in this world is perpetrated by people with irrational views.

LESSONS FROM A LIFE OF SERVING

As George Orwell points out, Gandhi was a man who could have done anything with his life. "Inside the saint, or near-saint," he wrote, "there was a very shrewd, able person who could, if he had chosen, have been a brilliant success" in business or politics.[12] Instead, Gandhi chose to be a servant. By leading, he served. By serving, he led. Some of his simplest and humblest acts, such as stooping to make his own salt, were among his greatest acts of leadership. Putting on a homespun loincloth was his version of the Declaration of Independence.

Leadership takes many forms and is expressed many ways. Let's look at some of the surprising leadership lessons that are woven into his life:

1. *Make serving others your first inclination.* Practice serving others until servanthood is your default switch, your instinctive reaction. When Gandhi lost his shoe while boarding the train, he didn't take time to think about what he should do. His reaction was instinctive. He removed his shoe and threw it away, preserving the pair for someone else's use.

If you're in a meeting and there aren't enough chairs, should you send someone for chairs—or get them yourself? Imagine the example you'll set for your people if you go and get chairs and set them up yourself. The leader sets the tone for the organization. If you build an organization where everybody pitches in and nobody says, "This job is beneath me," you build a winning organization. Set an example of serving, and you'll build an organization that serves.

2. *Spread epic stories of servanthood.* As a boy, Gandhi was influenced by the epic tales of Shravana and King Harishchandra. Stories inspire us and teach us. We

measure ourselves against the heroes of our stories. If you want to inspire servanthood in your organization, tell stories that highlight serving acts. Tell about people in your organization who do great acts of service. Tell stories of servanthood you read in *Fortune* or *Fast Company*. Share these stories in your newsletter or public speaking. Use stories to create a culture of serving.

3. *Practice the spirit of satyagraha.* Some people mistakenly define satyagraha as "passive resistance." There's nothing passive about it. Satyagraha is warfare. It's nonviolent, but it's warfare. The person practicing satyagraha will engage in acts of disobedience, acts that may entail consequences and suffering, acts of absorbing violence without hitting back. Your goal is to win without harming your opponent. Your goal is to defeat your enemy by serving.

Practicing satyagraha means you refuse to participate in unjust systems. Satyagraha requires you to align yourself with the truth. If you are a leader in the government, then satyagraha demands that you take a stand against corruption, deception, and the waste of taxpayer money. If you are a leader in business, satyagraha demands that you treat your employees, customers, suppliers, and even the government according to the truth—no cheating, no cutting ethical corners, no lies, no excuses. Satyagraha is "truth force," it is absolute truth implemented as policy in every aspect of your leadership life.

4. *Trademark yourself as a serving leader.* Gandhi's loincloth was his trademark. I suggest you find a *different* trademark, but find some visual way of letting your people know you are ready to serve them. Let them know your door is always open by taking the door off its hinges. Wear a T-shirt or ball cap with an "At Your Service" logo. Find an unforgettable image or a catchphrase that sticks in the mind and make that your personal theme. Let your people know you are a leader with a serving heart.

Another Gandhi trademark was the spinning wheel. The next time you see the flag of India, take note. In the middle of the flag's white center stripe is a navy blue twenty-four-spoke wheel. By law, the flag must be manufactured out of hand-spun cloth.

The wheel represents the spinning wheel, Gandhi's invention that he designed to set his people free of foreign domination. The very cloth the flag is made of is the hand-spun cloth Gandhi urged his people to make and wear. The Indian flag is a symbol of independence from foreign domination. Symbols are powerful. In your leadership life, find meaningful symbols that will convey your serving heart to the people you lead.

5. *Don't trust your emotions.* After the partition of India, Gandhi was despondent. He felt he had failed. His utopian dream of the Indian nation at peace with itself had become a nightmare of riots and fleeing refugees. Gandhi ended his life in disillusionment.

Though India still has far to go, it would be wonderful if Gandhi could see how far India has come. Much of the credit for India's progress can be traced to the self-sacrificing leadership of the Mahatma, the Great Soul.

There will be times in your leadership life when you have served and sacrificed, and you'll feel it was all for nothing. You'll feel depressed and disillusioned. Don't trust your feelings. Give yourself time to gain a clear perspective on your leadership life.

Keep serving. Keep leading. Keep living out the truth force in your life as a leader.

Nonviolence in its dynamic condition means conscious suffering. It does not mean meek submission to the will of the evil-doer, but it means the putting of one's whole soul against the will of the tyrant. Working under this law of being, it is possible for a single individual to defy the whole might of an unjust empire to save his honor, his religion, his soul and lay the foundation for the empire's fall or its regeneration.

GANDHI

20

MOTHER TERESA

In Service to God's Holy Poor

Do not wait for leaders; do it alone, person to person.
MOTHER TERESA

Shortly before Christmas 1985, Mother Teresa visited Sing Sing Correctional Facility in Ossining, New York. There she met three prisoners with AIDS. They were young men ages twenty-seven to thirty-six, all serving sentences for robbery. These young AIDS sufferers reminded her of the lepers of Calcutta.

She went to the office of Mayor Ed Koch and asked his help in creating a hospice for AIDS patients at St. Veronica's Church in the West Village. She would start with the three prisoners. Mayor Koch enlisted the help of Governor Mario Cuomo, who told her, "We have forty-three AIDS cases in the state prison system—I'd like to release them all to you."

Mother Teresa replied that, for now, she'd better start with three. Then she described the eventual size of the hospice facility she envisioned. "Would you like to pay for it?"

"Okay," Governor Cuomo found himself saying.

Then Mother Teresa turned to Mayor Koch and said, "Today is Monday. I'd like to open the hospice on Wednesday. We'll need some permits cleared. Can you arrange that?"

Amazed at her chutzpah, he said, "As long as you don't make me wash the floors."[1]

She probably weighed all of ninety-eight pounds, yet to these two men, she was a steamroller. They couldn't say no. This little Albanian-born servant was quite a leader.

INSPIRATION DAY

Mother Teresa was born Anjezë (Agnes) Gonxhe Bojaxhiu on August 26, 1910, in Skopje, Republic of Macedonia (then part of the Ottoman Empire). From her earliest years, she was fascinated by stories of the lives of missionaries. By age twelve, she had decided to devote her life to the service of God and others. At age eighteen, she joined the Sisters of Loreto, answering the call to become a missionary.

She arrived in India in 1929 and underwent her novitiate training in Darjeeling, taking her vows as a nun in 1931. She took the name "Sister Teresa" after Saint Thérèse de Lisieux (1873–97), the patron saint of missionaries. For nearly two decades, she taught at Saint Mary's, the Loreto convent school in Calcutta (Kolkata), becoming headmistress in 1944.

On September 10, 1946, Sister Teresa was traveling by train from Calcutta to the Loreto convent in Darjeeling for her annual spiritual retreat. During the journey, she experienced a series of inward conversations. She believes she heard the voice of Jesus speaking directly to her soul. Jesus revealed his heart to her—his compassion for those who suffer the most. She sensed that Jesus was calling her to carry his love to the poorest of the poor in the slums of Calcutta. "Come," he told her, "be my light."

In early October, she returned to Calcutta and talked to her spiritual adviser at the convent, Jesuit Father Céleste Van Exem, and told him about her experience on the train. She had made a solemn vow to the Loreto order. Now it appeared that God was calling her to a new ministry—but she would not go back on her vow unless Father Van Exem gave his blessing. Only with his blessing could she be certain God's hand was in this undertaking.

Father Van Exem told Sister Teresa to renounce this new idea, and put it out of her mind—but he was actually putting her new calling to a test, to see if it was a delusion or a genuine call from God. By January 1947, Father Van Exem was convinced that her calling had truly come from God—and he released her from her vows.[2]

For the rest of her life, Mother Teresa would look back on September 10, 1946, as "Inspiration Day." Biographer Joseph Langford observed, "Though no one knew it at the time, Sister Teresa had just become *Mother* Teresa."[3]

THE MAKINGS OF A SHREWD BUSINESSWOMAN

Mother Teresa was an admirer of Mahatma Gandhi, and she had studied his life and leadership style. She understood how important symbols were to Gandhi's leadership—the spinning wheel, the homespun cloth, the loincloth. So from the outset, Mother Teresa chose visual symbols that would help her new religious congregation, the Missionaries of Charity, to make a distinct impression.

She went to a local bazaar and purchased three Indian saris made of white cloth and edged with three blue stripes. Now, instead of a traditional black or white nun's habit, the Missionaries of Charity would wear habits that symbolically represented the culture of India.[4] It was a brilliant act of "branding" that would make Mother Teresa one of the most recognizable figures on the world scene.

In 1948, one year after India achieved independence from British colonial rule, Mother Teresa became a naturalized citizen of India. She took some basic medical instruction then began her work among the poor. Soon she was joined by other nuns who shared her burden for the poorest of the poor.

The early years were a time of financial struggle. Mother Teresa had to devise creative approaches to fund her work. On one occasion, she went to a Calcutta grocery store that catered to upscale clientele. Though she had no money, she proceeded to load shopping carts with food—about $800 worth. When she reached the cashier, she loudly declared that she was buying food for starving people—and she was not moving out of line until the people behind her came up with donations to pay for the food. She left the store with her groceries paid for.[5]

Mother Teresa found value in scrounging for money and supplies daily. She found that her struggles helped her identify with the poor. While looking for a house to serve as a shelter for the poor, she wrote about her struggle in her diary: "The poverty of the poor must be so hard for them. While looking for a home I walked and walked till my arms and legs ached. I thought how much they must ache in body and soul, looking for a home, food and health."[6]

While finding creative ways to make ends meet, Mother Teresa discovered that she had the makings of a shrewd businesswoman. She learned that the city government of Calcutta was looking for a solution to one of its biggest public relations problems—the destitute and dying people in the city streets. So much unsightly human misery was bad for tourism. So Mother Teresa went to the city officials and offered them a deal: If the city would give her a house, free and clear, she would help take the destitute and dying people off the streets.[7]

One of Mother Teresa's most important priorities was hospice care for the terminally ill. In 1952, the city of Calcutta provided an abandoned Hindu temple, which she converted into a free hospice called Nirmal Hriday, the Place of the Immaculate Heart. Mother Teresa's biographer, Kathryn Spink, explains:

> The sick and the destitute, the beggar picked up from the streets, the leper rejected by his family, the dying man refused admittance to a hospital—all were taken in, fed, washed and given a place to rest. In the beginning, conditions in the home for the dying were rudimentary in the extreme. There were times when Mother Teresa transported people in dire need in a workman's wheelbarrow. Of those brought in, those who could be treated were given whatever medical attention was possible; those who were beyond treatment were given the opportunity to die with dignity, having received the rituals of their faith: for Hindus, water from the Ganges on their lips; for Muslims, readings from the Koran; for the rare Christian, the last rites. . . . "A beautiful death," [Mother Teresa] maintained, "is for people who lived like animals to die like angels—loved and wanted."[8]

The Missionaries of Charity established a number of clinics throughout Calcutta for people suffering from Hansen's disease (leprosy). In 1955, she opened the first of many orphanages, the Children's Home of the Immaculate Heart. By the 1960s, the ministry of the Missionaries of Charity had spread across India in the form of hospices, leprosy clinics, and orphanages. From the 1960s on, the Missionaries of Charity have expanded their work into 133 countries around the world.

Mother Teresa ministered in relative obscurity until 1969, when British journalist Malcolm Muggeridge (a longtime agnostic who had recently converted to Christianity) profiled her in a documentary titled *Something Beautiful for God*. As a result of this publicity, Mother Teresa soon became a household name.

She was awarded the Nobel Peace Prize in 1979 for her service to the poor and terminally ill. Poverty and human misery, the Nobel committee said, constitute a threat to peace. She accepted the medal but declined the traditional ceremonial banquet, and she directed that the $192,000 prize be given to the poor.

Mother Teresa was always looking for people she could enlist in the struggle against poverty and disease. This typical incident, recalled by Father Dwight Longenecker, speaks volumes about the kind of servant she was:

> Father Dwight and his friend Father James had both grown up in India, so in 1985, they made plans for a three-week journey through India. Before leaving, they took up a collection in England that they intended to present to Mother Teresa in person.
>
> When they arrived in Calcutta, their driver took them to the mission house where Mother Teresa lived. They went inside and presented the check to the nun at the reception desk. She offered to introduce them to Mother Teresa. Minutes later, Mother Teresa emerged and greeted Father Dwight and Father James warmly.
>
> "Have you come to give your life in service to God's holy poor?" she asked.
>
> The question caught them off guard. They stammered, "We're Anglican priests from England."
>
> "We have many people working with us from England," she said. "Perhaps you will stay and work for just a few years?"
>
> "We have parishes in England we need to return to," they replied.
>
> "I understand," Mother Teresa said. "Go in peace, and thank you for coming."
>
> At the time, the idea of setting aside all their plans to serve alongside Mother Teresa seemed unthinkable. But years later, Father Dwight had to ask himself, "What if . . . ?" [9]

Those who lead by serving are always trying to raise up a new generation of serving leaders to come after them, to replace them, to carry on their work. Recruitment was a big part of Mother Teresa's ministry.

MISSION TO BEIRUT

In 1982, Jeanette Petrie and Ann Petrie began shooting a documentary titled simply *Mother Teresa*, released in 1986 and narrated by Richard Attenborough. They were on hand to record one of the most harrowing incidents of Mother Teresa's career: her rescue of thirty-seven children from a bomb-damaged hospital in West Beirut in August 1982.

The 1982 Lebanon War between Israel and the Palestine Liberation Organization began in June, and Beirut was largely in ruins. Some Lebanese children were trapped in the Dar al-Ajaza al-Islamia Mental Hospital, which had been damaged by bombs and artillery fire.

Mother Teresa had been trying to get to Beirut but could not fly in because the airport was destroyed. She learned she could take a "ferry boat" from Cyprus to Beirut, and the documentary crew went along with her. The "ferry boat" turned out to be a Palestinian gun-running boat.

As Mother Teresa led the camera crew aboard the boat, she carried a candle with her and said, "This is a candle to Our Lady of Peace. When we get to Beirut we are going to light this candle, and we will have peace."

As the boat was crossing the Mediterranean toward Lebanon, the documentary crew experienced a moment of panic: Mother Teresa had disappeared. They went searching for her—and found her below decks, cleaning the filthy toilet in the head.

After being set ashore, Mother Teresa and her entourage made their way to East Beirut, where the Missionaries of Charity operated the Spring School. The documentary crew captured a tense discussion between Mother Teresa, two priests, and a monsignor as they considered how to rescue the children from the bombed-out hospital in West Beirut.

"I feel the church should be there now," Mother Teresa said, referring to war-ravaged West Beirut. As she spoke, the microphones pick up the scream of artillery shells.

"If you wait a little bit," said one of the priests, "as soon as the heavy military activities are over, then it will be much more feasible. But if you go across by car to the other side, you might not be able to come back."

Mother Teresa dismissed his concerns about safety. "I think it's our duty," she said.

"Yes," the priest said, "it's our duty—but imagine if you go and you get stuck there."

Mother Teresa asked, "What if both sides stop fighting for a few hours?"

The priest responded that West Beirut was in chaos. A few weeks earlier, Palestinians had killed some Christian priests just for the sake of killing priests. And yet, the priest added, it was their job to risk their lives to save others.

"All for Jesus," Mother Teresa said. "We have to save one or two. We have to start.

You see, many years back, I picked up the first person off the street in Calcutta. If I didn't pick up that first person, I never would have picked up forty-two thousand in Calcutta. So I think we must go."

There was nothing more to be said.

Shortly after that discussion, Mother Teresa met with Philip Habib, President Reagan's special envoy to the Middle East. She told Mr. Habib she needed his help to cross over into West Beirut so that she could rescue the children.

Mr. Habib said, "Mother, you hear the shells?"

"Yes, I hear them."

"It is absolutely impossible for you to cross. We must have a cease-fire first."

Mother Teresa said, "Oh, but I have been praying to Our Lady and I have asked her to let us have a cease-fire tomorrow, the day before her Feast Day."

Ambassador Habib looked at Mother Teresa incredulously. "Mother, I am very glad you are on my side—that you are a woman of prayer. I believe in prayer and I believe that prayer is answered and I am a man of faith. But you are asking Our Lady to deal with Prime Minister Begin and with the PLO. Don't you think the time limit is a little short?"

With absolute confidence, Mother Teresa replied, "Oh, no, Mr. Habib, I am certain that we will have the cease-fire tomorrow."

"If we have the cease-fire," Ambassador Habib said, "I personally will make arrangements to see that you go to West Beirut tomorrow."

The next morning, Israel and the PLO agreed to a cease-fire. An awestruck Ambassador Habib kept his word and made arrangements for a Red Cross convoy to take Mother Teresa and her camera crew to the Dar al-Ajaza al-Islamia hospital in West Beirut.

The documentary camera crew recorded the amazing scene as Mother Teresa and the Red Cross personnel entered the hospital and located the Lebanese children. The children were all intellectually disabled. Some had cerebral palsy. Some appeared starved and skeletal. In the documentary, we see Mother Teresa embracing the children, lifting them up and holding them, cleaning them up and putting diapers on them (the youngest is at least seven years old).

One starved little boy, with arms like parchment stretched over bone, lies in a crib, his body quaking, his eyes wide with terror. Though his mental disability prevents him from understanding the world around him, he has spent days in this abandoned hospital, with the sound of artillery and exploding bombs and screaming jets all around. We see Mother Teresa bending over him, rubbing his chest, stroking his hair, raising him up on a pillow, looking into his eyes, smiling at him, telling him she loves him. He stops shivering, and the fear goes out of his face, and he looks peacefully into Mother Teresa's face.

Mother Teresa helped the Red Cross get the children out of the hospital and into the four Red Cross vehicles—thirty-seven children in all. They took the children to the Spring School in East Beirut, operated by the Missionaries of Charity. Mission accomplished.[10]

Without any thought for her own safety, Mother Teresa went into a war zone to rescue children. She prayed for a cease-fire and, like the Red Sea parting before Moses, the war clouds parted before this little Albanian nun. Mother Teresa went into West Beirut as a servant—*and she led.*

"I Will Smile at Your Hidden Face"

In April 1996, Mother Teresa fell and sustained a broken collar bone. A short time later she had heart surgery. It was clear that her heart was failing. On March 13, 1997, Mother Teresa stepped down from her position as head of the society she had founded. She passed away on September 5.

Mother Teresa had her share of critics and opponents. Authentic leaders always do.

Some critics claimed that Mother Teresa, as an outspoken opponent of abortion, should not have been awarded the Nobel Peace Prize. British atheist Barbara Smoker, then-president of the National Secular Society, complained that Mother Teresa used her Nobel acceptance as an opportunity "to spout anti-abortion propaganda," and that she denounced abortion as "the greatest evil of our time."[11]

But Smoker misquoted Mother Teresa, who actually called abortion "the greatest destroyer of peace today." Whatever your opinion on abortion, you have to agree that Mother Teresa, in her Nobel speech, advanced a thoughtful rationale for her claim, saying, "if a mother can kill her own child—what is left for me to kill you and you kill me—there is nothing between."[12]

Others (notably Christopher Hitchens) disparaged Mother Teresa for accepting donations from corrupt sources, such as the Duvalier family (which once ruled Haiti) or financier Charles Keating. Hitchens suggested that Mother Teresa should have returned Keating's donations to those who lost money on investments in his company. He reasoned that Keating's donations, which he made to the Missionaries of Charity long before the collapse of his financial enterprises, somehow constituted "stolen money."[13] Hitchens offered no evidence that Keating had "stolen" the donated funds. As for the Duvalier family, we could argue that Mother Teresa redeemed donations from corrupt dictators by using them to serve the poor.

A decade after her death, Mother Teresa's private journals and letters were published as *Mother Teresa: Come Be My Light*, edited by Brian Kolodiejchuk. These private writings reveal Mother Teresa's fifty-year struggle against doubt and depression. For example, in a 1959 letter to Father Lawrence Picachy, her Jesuit spiritual guide in Darjeeling, she wrote:

> *The darkness is so dark—and I am alone. —Unwanted, forsaken.*

—The loneliness of the heart that wants love is unbearable. —Where is my faith?—even deep down, right in, there is nothing but emptiness & darkness. —My God—how painful is this unknown pain. It pains without ceasing. —I have no faith. —I dare not to utter the words & thoughts that crowd in my heart—& make me suffer untold agony. So many unanswered questions live within me—I am afraid to uncover them—because of the blasphemy—If there be God,—please forgive me. —Trust that all will end in Heaven with Jesus.[14]

These words are painful to read—and such a contrast from the message she received from God in September 1946 on a train from Calcutta to Darjeeling. A decade after Jesus told her, "Come, be my light," she was struggling with spiritual darkness, feeling forsaken by God, bereft of faith.

Yet she seemed to cling to a perspective like that of the grieving father in the Gospel of Mark: "I do believe; help me overcome my unbelief!"[15] In that same 1959 letter, she commits herself to serving God to the end of her life, in spite of her doubts: "If this brings You glory, if You get a drop of joy from this—if souls are brought to You—if my suffering satiates Your Thirst—here I am Lord, with joy I accept all to the end of life—& I will smile at Your Hidden Face—always."[16]

The revelation of Mother Teresa's long struggle with doubt stunned many people. Her critics and detractors claimed she had "lost her faith." Some accused her of "hypocrisy," claiming to serve God after having lost her faith in God. But there is no hypocrisy here. Mother Teresa honestly expresses her struggle and her commitment to serving God in spite of her doubts. The Mother Teresa we meet in these writings is not an atheist, but a tormented believer steadfastly clinging to her faith. She struggles with her emotions, but her will is unshakable. Her commitment to serve God and others is steadfast.

Though she doubted her faith, she also doubted her doubts, clinging to faith. She continued serving God in spite of her feelings of emptiness, vowing, "I will smile at Your Hidden Face—always."

That's not hypocrisy. That's faith in the extreme.

Many saints have experienced similar crises of doubt. The sixteenth-century Spanish mystic St. John of the Cross expressed almost identical doubts in his collection of verses, *The Dark Night of the Soul*. Mother Teresa's own namesake, St. Thérèse of Lisieux, experienced decades of spiritual darkness and doubt. Even Jesus, in the depths of his suffering on the cross, cried out, "My God, my God, why have you forsaken me?"[17]

Most leaders and servants experience the dark emotion of doubt from time to time. Whatever Mother Teresa's doubts, she maintained her faith. She remained a faithful servant.

Mother Teresa's Leadership Lessons

The Seventh Side of Leadership is a serving heart. Mother Teresa teaches us that servanthood is not a means to an end. It's an end in itself. A leader with a serving heart doesn't serve others to get something in return. Servants expect nothing in return. Her life suggests a number of key leadership principles:

1. *A genuine servant is a shrewd strategist.* Mother Teresa was amazingly astute and street smart. One of the first things she did upon founding the Missionaries of Charity was to create a visual "brand"—the Indian-style habit—that would become recognizable the world over. She had excellent people skills and used them to persuade wealthy, powerful people to help her financially and politically.

Great servants use all the skills at their disposal to accomplish their servanthood goals. Mother Teresa charmed the rich and powerful into supporting the Missionaries of Charity, and countless poor people, sick people, and children benefited from her skills in networking, marketing, and persuasion.

2. *Effective servants think win-win.* When Mother Teresa needed a building to house the poor and sick, she went to the city leaders and cut a win-win deal with them. As a result of that bargain, Mother Teresa got the building she needed, and the city received help in solving its image problem. Great servants find ways to achieve their own goals while helping to solve the problems of others.

3. *Publicity is better than obscurity.* A leader with a serving heart welcomes fame and uses publicity to achieve even greater works of servanthood. Mother Teresa labored in obscurity for many years. In 1969, Malcolm Muggeridge brought Mother Teresa to the attention of the world. Mother Teresa parlayed that publicity into support for her ministries.

A serving leader remains committed to serving and uses fame only as a means to serve on a bigger scale. Mother Teresa never lost her humility, in spite of the fame and accolades she received. To her, fame was just another tool she used in serving God and others.

4. *Authentic servants think about others, not themselves.* When Mother Teresa was in Beirut, her only thought was how to get into West Beirut and rescue those children. When the priest kept telling her that it was not safe for her to go, she seemed not to hear. Arguments about her own safety didn't register. She cared only about getting those children to safety. That's the mind-set of the servant—and the mind-set of a leader.

5. *Authentic servants act on their faith, not their doubts.* As someone once said, "Never doubt in the darkness what God has shown you in the light." We may not be able to control emotions of doubt, but we can always control our actions. We can maintain our commitment to our faith, our principles, and our values, even when our faith seems weak. Faith is far more than a feeling. Faith is an act of obedience, an expression of the will.

Though Mother Teresa experienced doubt, she never forgot her experience of God in 1946, when she heard Jesus say, "Come, be my light." She answered that call—and she never looked back.

By blood, I am Albanian. By citizenship, an Indian.
By faith, I am a Catholic nun. As to my calling, I belong to the world.
As to my heart, I belong entirely to the Heart of Jesus.
MOTHER TERESA

21

ABRAHAM LINCOLN

The Great Emancipator

I freely acknowledge myself the servant of the people,
according to the bond of service. . . . I am responsible to them.
ABRAHAM LINCOLN

I became acquainted with legendary UCLA basketball coach John Wooden when he was in his nineties. I wrote several books about his philosophy of leadership and character building, and he graciously invited me into his home for many unforgettable conversations. Entering his home in Encino, California, was like stepping into a Hall of Fame. His hallway was lined with photos and memorabilia. The most prominent display was devoted to two people—Mother Teresa and Abraham Lincoln.

"They're my heroes," he told me. "I admire them both for their outstanding character traits—their courage and humility, and the way they selflessly served others. I can't think of two greater heroes to admire. Can you?"

I couldn't. I still can't. That's why I have devoted the last two chapters of this book to Coach John Wooden's two great heroes, Mother Teresa and Abraham Lincoln.

One of the earliest of the many stories told about Abraham Lincoln took place when he was just five years old—and it's a story about his serving heart.

Someone asked him what he knew about the Revolutionary War. Well, he didn't know much about the war, but he knew a little bit about soldiers. He said he'd been fishing one day and caught a little fish. While bringing the fish home, he said, he encountered a soldier in the road.

"I've always been told that we must be good to soldiers," young Abraham said, "so I gave him my fish."[1]

Even at age five, Lincoln exemplified the Seventh Side of Leadership: a serving heart.

CAPTAIN OF THE VOLUNTEERS

In 1859, before he ran for president, Abraham Lincoln wrote a short autobiography. Here is Lincoln's own account of his early life:

> I was born February 12, 1809, in Hardin County, Kentucky. My parents were both born in Virginia of undistinguished families. . . .

My mother, who died in my tenth year, was of a family of the name of Hanks. . . . My father. . .grew up literally without education. He removed from Kentucky to what is now Spencer County, Indiana, in my eighth year. We reached our new home about the same time the state came into the Union. It was a wild region with many bears and other wild animals still in the woods. There I grew up. . . .

When I came of age I did not know much. Still somehow, I could read, write, and cipher. . .but that was all. I have not been to school since. The little advance I now have upon this store of education I have picked up from time to time under the pressure of necessity.[2]

This is a humble story, told by a humble servant. He seems to suggest that his education ended when he learned to "read, write, and cipher." But that's when his *real* education began. He was a voracious reader from his boyhood to his final days. His education never ended because he was constantly reading throughout his life.

Raised in poverty, he possessed few books of his own. As journalist and historian Alexander McClure records, one of the few books Lincoln owned was one he made himself. It was a book listing a table of weights and measures that he used to learn his arithmetic (or "ciphering"). He borrowed a copy of the printed book, wrote out the information with pen and paper, then hand-stitched the binding himself.

As a youth, Lincoln tried his hand at poetry. On one page of his handmade book, he wrote:

> Abraham Lincoln,
> His Hand and Pen,
> He Will be Good,
> But God knows when.

When Abe was fourteen, his cousin from Kentucky, John Hanks, came to live with the Lincolns for a while. Hanks later described what his cousin Abe did every day after they finished their daily chores:

> When Lincoln and I returned to the house from work, he would go to the cupboard, snatch a piece of corn-bread, take down a book, sit down on a chair, cock his legs up as high as his head, and read.
>
> He and I worked barefooted, grubbed it, plowed, mowed, cradled together; plowed corn, gathered it, and shucked corn. Abe read constantly when he had an opportunity.[3]

One of Lincoln's best friends when he was a teenager was Joseph C. Richardson, who recalled that Lincoln was six feet tall at age sixteen, and "somewhat bony and raw, dark-skinned [and] he was quick and moved with energy. . . . He was exceedingly studious." Richardson recalled that Lincoln wrote a rhymed couplet in Richardson's school copybook, and those lines proved to be prophetic in Abraham Lincoln's own life:

Good boys who to their books apply
Will make great men by & by.[4]

Alexander McClure observed, "In all, Lincoln's 'schooling' did not amount to a year's time, but he was a constant student outside of the schoolhouse. He read all the books he could borrow, and it was his chief delight during the day to lie under the shade of some tree, or at night in front of an open fireplace, reading and studying. His favorite books were the Bible and Aesop's fables, which he kept always within reach and read time and again."[5]

In 1831, at age twenty-two, Lincoln struck out on his own and settled in the village of New Salem in Sangamon County, Illinois. There he worked at a series of jobs until the spring of 1832, when the Black Hawk War erupted. The Black Hawk War was a brief, small-scale conflict between a band of Native Americans led by Chief Black Hawk and a small United States force comprised of a few army soldiers and hundreds of poorly trained frontier militia men. Lincoln served in a volunteer militia during the Black Hawk War, and though his unit never saw combat, his fellow militia men elected him to be their leader. He later recalled, "I was elected a Captain of Volunteers—a success which gave me more pleasure than any I have had since."[6]

Lincoln's early leadership skills were rudimentary. On one occasion, Captain Lincoln led a squad of twenty militia men across a field. Ahead of them was a fence with a gate—but Lincoln couldn't remember the command for marching them through the gate. So, as his men approached the gate, he called, "Halt!" The militia men halted. "This company is dismissed for two minutes," Lincoln ordered, "and will fall in again on the other side of the gate."[7]

On one occasion during the Black Hawk War, an aging Native American warrior came into Lincoln's camp. Several of Lincoln's men seized the old man and roughed him up. Black Hawk's forces had recently slaughtered some settlers, including women and children, so tensions were high. The old warrior produced a sheet of paper guaranteeing safe conduct, signed by General Lewis Cass. But the militia men wanted vengeance, and they were ready to execute him.

Lincoln rushed into the midst of the men, placed himself in front of the old Native American, and saved the man from being executed. Lincoln's men were frustrated at first that he thwarted their vengeance—but they later admired him for his courage and sense of honor.[8]

The Black Hawk War lasted from May to August 1832, and ended with Chief Black Hawk's surrender. Lincoln returned from serving in the militia and made his first run for public office, campaigning for a seat in the Illinois state legislature. He lost, finishing eighth out of a field of thirteen candidates. Two years later, in 1834, he ran again and won—the first of four consecutive terms as state legislator. From the beginning, he was a vocal opponent of slavery.

MR. LINCOLN OF SPRINGFIELD

While serving in the Illinois state legislature, Lincoln studied law by reading books. Entirely self-taught, Lincoln was admitted to the bar in 1836. He moved to Springfield (shortly before it became the state capital) and began practicing law there. He had built a reputation as a tough adversary who was formidable in debate and cross-examination.

Alexander McClure relates a story told to him by an unnamed "lady of Springfield." It's a story about Abraham Lincoln's serving heart. "My first strong impression of Mr. Lincoln," the lady said, "was made by one of his kind deeds."

She was planning a journey by rail and had arranged for a carriage driver to pick her up, along with her heavy trunk. When the appointed time came, the carriage driver didn't show up. She began to panic, realizing she would miss the train. She stood by her front gate in her hat and gloves, sobbing.

Just then, the rising young Springfield lawyer, Abraham Lincoln, walked up and asked her why she was crying. The lady poured out her story.

"How big is the trunk?" Lincoln asked. "There's still time, if it isn't too big."

She led him to the trunk in her upstairs room.

"Dry your eyes," Lincoln said, "and come on quick!" He lifted the trunk, set it on his shoulders, and raced down the stairs, through the front yard, and into the street. He carried the trunk on his back all the way to the train station. The lady trotted after him as fast as she could, drying her tears as she went.

They reached the station just in time. "Mr. Lincoln put me on the train, kissed me good-bye, and told me to have a good time," the lady recalled. "It was just like him."[9]

Early in his law career in Springfield, Lincoln's law partner was Ward Lamon. A man named Scott came to them with a case involving his sister, who was mentally ill. The sister owned property and cash valued at about $10,000, which was managed by a conservator. A con man had become acquainted with her, learned she had money, and proposed marriage—but in order to get her money, he needed to go to court and have the conservator removed. The client, Mr. Scott, hired Lincoln and Lamon to prevent that from happening.

Lincoln quoted a fee of $250, which Mr. Scott thought was reasonable. He expected the trial to take some time. To everyone's surprise, the case was concluded within twenty minutes—Lincoln and Lamon won. Mr. Scott paid Mr. Lamon the entire $250 and was very satisfied.

But Abraham Lincoln was not satisfied. After Mr. Scott left the courtroom, Lincoln asked Mr. Lamon, "What did you charge that man?"

"I charged him $250," Lamon replied, "as we agreed."

"The service was not worth that sum," Lincoln said. "Give him back at least half."

They argued, and Lincoln prevailed. Grudgingly, Lamon tracked down Mr. Scott and returned half the fee.

Meanwhile, Judge David Davis had seen Lincoln and Lamon arguing. "Lincoln," the judge said, "I have been watching you and Lamon. You are impoverishing this bar with your puny fees, and other lawyers have reason to complain. You are now almost as poor as Lazarus, and if you don't charge more for your services, you will die as poor as Job's turkey!"

Lincoln's mind was made up. "That money," he said, "comes out of the pocket of a poor, demented girl. I would rather starve than swindle her in this manner."[10]

In Springfield Lincoln met Mary Todd, who came from a wealthy slaveholding family in Kentucky. They were married in Springfield on November 4, 1842. They had four sons, three of whom died before reaching adulthood. Mary Todd Lincoln suffered from migraines and clinical depression, and some historians speculate that she may have suffered from bipolar disorder.

A House Divided

Lincoln was elected to the House of Representatives in 1847. He served a single term then retired from politics to focus on his law practice. After leaving Washington, he said, he "practiced law more assiduously than ever before. . . . I was losing interest in politics, when the repeal of the Missouri Compromise aroused me again."[11]

The Missouri Compromise was passed in 1820 during the presidency of James Monroe. It prohibited the expansion of slavery into the new western territories. What Lincoln called "the repeal of the Missouri Compromise" was the Kansas-Nebraska Act of 1854, which permitted slaveholding in new territories west of the Mississippi River. Lincoln was so incensed by this betrayal that he came out of political retirement and decided to seek political office again. He joined the Republican Party, which was founded in 1854 specifically to oppose slavery.

Slavery deeply offended Lincoln's conscience. By joining the antislavery Republican Party, he hoped to liberate the slaves, put an end to the plantation system of the South, and collapse the economic power of the slave owners. In 1856, soldier and explorer John C. Frémont served as the Republican Party's first presidential candidate; Lincoln placed second in the balloting to become the party's vice presidential candidate. The Frémont-Lincoln ticket lost to Democrat James Buchanan.

In March 1857, the Supreme Court issued the infamous Dred Scott decision—the worst decision in Supreme Court history. Dred Scott, an African-American slave, had been taken to free states by his owners and had sued for his freedom under the laws of the nonslaveholding states. In his majority opinion, Chief Justice Roger B. Taney stated that African-Americans are not citizens under the Constitution and therefore have no rights. Taney thought his ruling would settle the slavery question once and for all. Instead, the 7–2 Dred Scott decision inflamed passions and made the Civil War practically inevitable.

The following year, Lincoln delivered his famous "House Divided" speech, inspired by Mark 3:25. He said, "A house divided against itself cannot stand. I believe this government cannot endure permanently half slave and half free. I do not expect the Union to be dissolved—I do not expect the house to fall—but I do expect it will cease to be divided. It will become all one thing, or all the other."[12]

Abraham Lincoln ran for the United States Senate in 1858. His opponent was Stephen A. Douglas—the proslavery scoundrel who authored the Kansas-Nebraska Act. The campaign of 1858 became famous for the Lincoln-Douglas Debates. Lincoln lost to Douglas. When a friend asked him how he felt about the loss, Lincoln replied, "Like the boy who stubbed his toe; I am too big to cry and too badly hurt to laugh."[13] Despite the loss, Lincoln gained name recognition and became a leader on the national stage.

In 1860, Lincoln ran for president—and won. He was inaugurated on March 4, 1861. On April 12, 1861, just five weeks into Lincoln's presidency, Confederate gun batteries opened fire on Fort Sumter in Charleston harbor.

The Civil War was on.

A SERVANT IN THE WHITE HOUSE

The intense pressures of being a wartime president seemed to bring forth the character traits of Abraham Lincoln—his honesty, humility, compassion, and fairness. Here are some stories from his White House years that reveal Lincoln's serving heart:

As a wartime president, Abraham Lincoln had great respect for his best generals—but they didn't all respect him. One of the most contemptuous of Lincoln's generals was George B. McClellan. In the early days of the war, Lincoln admired McClellan's ability to raise and train a well-organized Union army.

On several occasions, Lincoln went to McClellan's house to discuss war strategy. McClellan went out of his way to show contempt for President Lincoln, making Lincoln wait while he dealt with other matters. McClellan's disdainful treatment of the president was so obvious that even the newspapers began to comment on it.

Lincoln endured McClellan's mistreatment, saying, "I will hold McClellan's horse, if he will only bring us success."

(Ultimately, McClellan proved to be a disappointment in the field. Lincoln eventually removed him as general of the army of the Potomac, and McClellan ran unsuccessfully against Lincoln as a Democrat in the 1864 election.)

Lincoln's servant-like forbearance was legendary. During an inspection visit to Fort Stevens, which guarded the northern approach to Washington, DC, Lincoln was conducted by Captain Oliver Wendell Holmes Jr. (who would later be appointed to the Supreme Court by President Theodore Roosevelt).

Through a small gap in the fortification, Captain Holmes pointed out the location of the enemy. Lincoln, wearing his stovepipe hat, stood up for a better view. Instantly, gunfire erupted from the Confederate lines.

Captain Holmes grabbed the president and threw him down, shouting, "Get down, you fool!"

Lincoln picked himself up, brushed himself off, and continued the tour. Captain Holmes, meanwhile, fretted about the disciplinary action he had just earned.

At the end of his inspection, President Lincoln turned to his guide and said, "Captain Holmes, I'm glad to see that you know how to talk to a civilian."

And nothing else was said about the matter.[14]

On New Year's Day 1863, Secretary of State William H. Seward brought the carefully prepared document of the Emancipation Proclamation to the president for his signature. The proclamation conferred freedom on all slaves in the eleven states that were still in rebellion against the Union.

President Lincoln took his pen, dipped it in the ink, and poised it over the Proclamation. After a few seconds, he set the pen down. He tried again—but once again he set the pen down, leaving the document unsigned.

Lincoln looked up at Seward. "I have had so many visitors," he said, "and have shaken so many hands since nine o'clock this morning, that my right arm is almost paralyzed. If my name ever goes into history, it will be for signing this Proclamation, and my whole soul is in it. If my hand trembles when I sign, all who examine this document in years to come will say, 'Lincoln hesitated.'"

Finally, he took the pen up again, and with slow, deliberate strokes, he wrote, "Abraham Lincoln." Then he nodded to Seward and said, "That will do."

Abraham Lincoln personally visited encampments and hospitals to encourage the soldiers and comfort the wounded. In late 1864, the town of City Point, Virginia, served as the Union headquarters during the Siege of Petersburg. Dr. Jerome Walker was the administrator of the Union hospital at City Point, and he guided the president around the hospital wards occupied by Union soldiers. The president took time with each soldier, shaking hands and offering a word of thanks and encouragement.

Then they came to a ward filled with wounded Confederates. "Mr. President," Dr. Walker said, "there's no need to go in there. They're only rebels."

"You mean *Confederates*," Lincoln said. "I'd like to meet them."

Feeling chastened, Dr. Walker took the president in to meet the wounded

Confederates. Lincoln was as kind to the enemy soldiers as he had been to the Union soldiers. He shook their hands, asked them about their families, and treated them as if they were his very own men.

Dr. Walker later said he never again referred to Confederate soldiers as "rebels," and he never forgot President Lincoln's kindness to all the men in his hospital.[15]

As a leader with a serving heart, Lincoln had enormous sympathy and compassion for human failings. For example, his heart went out to a young army private named William Scott. After a long march, Private Scott had volunteered to stand watch on the picket, taking the place of a sick comrade.

But exhaustion overtook Private Scott, and he was caught sleeping on duty. Private Scott was court-martialed and sentenced to execution by firing squad. It was a harsh punishment, but the enemy was nearby, and Private Scott had placed his entire company in danger.

President Lincoln personally went to the army camp near Chain Bridge, on the Potomac River, and asked to see Private Scott. It was the day before the private's scheduled execution.

The moment the tent flaps parted and President Lincoln entered, Private Scott felt afraid. But as President Lincoln spoke to him, the young man's fears melted. Lincoln asked Private Scott about his family, his neighbors, his mother—and about the night he slept on duty. "A young man should always make his mother proud," Lincoln said, "and never cause her sorrow."

"Yes, sir," Private Scott said.

"My boy," Lincoln said, "look me in the face. I believe you when you tell me that you could not keep awake. I am going to trust you, and send you back to your regiment. But I have been put to a good deal of trouble on your account. I have had to come up here from Washington when I have got a great deal to do. How are you going to pay my bill?"

"I am grateful, Mr. Lincoln!" Private Scott said. "If there is some way to pay you, I will find it!"

The president said, "My boy, my bill is a very large one. There is only one way to pay this debt. If from this day William Scott does his duty as a soldier, then the debt be paid. Will you make that promise and try to keep it?"

Private Scott gave his word. Then he rejoined his comrades.

Sometime later, Private William Scott was seriously wounded in battle. He didn't know if he would survive or not. He asked his friends to get word to President Lincoln: Private William Scott remembered his promise and he tried to be a good soldier. He was grateful to President Lincoln for the chance to fall in battle like a soldier instead of dying in front of a firing squad.

Lincoln spared many young soldiers from the firing squad. His generals protested that these acts of executive clemency interfered with army discipline. But Lincoln looked at each case individually, and historians have concluded that his instincts were almost always right.

During one week, twenty-four deserters were sentenced to death, and their death warrants were sent to the president for his signature. Lincoln refused to sign them. A general met personally with President Lincoln and said, "Mr. President, unless these men are made an example of, the army itself is in danger. Mercy to the few is cruelty to the many."

"General," Lincoln said, "there are already too many weeping widows in the United States. Don't ask me to add to the number, for I won't do it."[16]

President Lincoln was also a servant to children. Whenever children came to the White House, Lincoln was delighted, and he always made them feel welcome.

During a Saturday afternoon reception at the White House, three young girls wandered in. They were shabbily dressed and looked completely out of place. They had probably walked into the White House out of curiosity. They attracted stares as they went from room to room.

President Lincoln noticed them and said, "Little girls, are you going to pass by me without shaking hands?"

Then he bent down to their level, shook each girl's hand, and chatted with each one. All who witnessed the incident were moved by his compassion.

On another occasion, a little girl accompanied her father to the White House for a visit with the president. The girl's father had warned her not to mention the president's appearance, because he was a very homely man. When she met the president, he picked her up, put her on his knee, and chatted with her in his cheerful way.

The girl turned to her father and said, "Oh, Pa! He isn't ugly at all! He's beautiful!"[17]

In November 1863, President Lincoln traveled by rail to Gettysburg, Pennsylvania, to dedicate the National Cemetery and deliver the Gettysburg Address. At one stop, Lincoln saw that someone had lifted a little girl to the open window of his railway car. The child held a small bunch of rosebuds in her hand. "Floweth for the Prethident," she lisped.

Lincoln leaned out the window and took the rosebuds then kissed the child and said, "You are a sweet little rosebud yourself. I hope your life will open into beauty like these flowers."

"DID STANTON SAY I WAS A FOOL?"

We glimpse the depth of Lincoln's serving heart in his difficult relationship with his secretary of war, Edwin Stanton. Lincoln and Stanton first became acquainted in 1857 when they served together on the same legal team. Stanton despised Lincoln, and referred to him as "a low, cunning clown," a "gorilla," and a person of "painful imbecility."

When Lincoln became president, he chose Simon Cameron as his secretary of war, but Cameron was forced to resign due to charges of corruption. Lincoln's secretary of the treasury, Salmon P. Chase, recommended Edwin Stanton for the job. Lincoln invited Stanton to the White House for a chat. Throughout their talk, Stanton was unaware that his visit was a job interview.

Near the end of the conversation, Lincoln said, "I called you here to offer you the portfolio of War." Stanton thought the president was joking.

Lincoln insisted he was serious. "The nation is in danger," he said. "I need the best counsellors around me. I have every confidence in your judgment."

Stanton accepted and went to work, reforming the War Department. Lincoln visited the War Office daily, conferring with Stanton, and gathering reports from the front.

For a long time, Stanton continued to be rude and abrasive toward Lincoln. President Lincoln, aware that Stanton had restored public faith in the War Department, endured Stanton's disrespect. He never doubted that he had chosen the right man as his secretary of war.

On one occasion, Congressman Lovejoy from Illinois (who was also an abolitionist minister) approached President Lincoln with some ideas regarding the war effort. Lincoln said, "Explain your ideas to the secretary of war," and sent him to Stanton's office.

Congressman Lovejoy met with Secretary Stanton and explained his ideas. Stanton was not impressed. "Did Lincoln tell you to come to me with these ideas?"

"He did, sir."

"Then he is a fool."

Lovejoy was startled. "Do you mean to say, sir, that the president is a fool?"

"Yes, sir, if he gave you such an order as that."

Congressman Lovejoy went back to the White House and related that conversation to the president. Lincoln asked, "Did Stanton say I was a fool?"

"He did, sir, and repeated it."

"Well," the president said, rising, "if Stanton said I was a fool, then I must be one, for he is nearly always right, and generally says what he means. I will slip over and see him."

Over time, Stanton softened in his opinion of President Lincoln, and the two men became friends. On November 8, 1864, Lincoln was re-elected in a landslide. He delivered his second inaugural address on March 4, 1865. A little more than a month later, on April 9, 1865, General Robert E. Lee surrendered his Army of Northern Virginia. Upon hearing the news of the surrender, the former adversaries, Lincoln and Stanton, embraced each other.

With hostilities ended, Secretary Stanton submitted his letter of resignation as secretary of war. The war was over, his work was done, and he felt it was his duty to resign.

President Lincoln, with tears in his eyes, ripped up the letter, put his arms around

Stanton, and said, "You have been a good friend and a faithful public servant. It is not for you to say when you are no longer needed."

"He Belongs to the Ages"

In early 1865, President Lincoln had a dream that disturbed him. In the dream, he entered the East Room of the White House and found it full of sobbing mourners. A catafalque bore the body of a dead man, decked out for his funeral. A pair of soldiers stood guard.

Lincoln asked one of the soldiers, "Who is dead in the White House?"

"The president," the soldier replied. "He was killed by an assassin."

Lincoln told his wife about the dream. She said, "I wish you hadn't told me."

"It was only a dream," he said. "Let's say no more about it."

On the afternoon of April 14, 1865, President Lincoln performed his last official acts as president—acts that flowed from a serving heart. He pardoned a Union soldier who was to be shot for desertion ("I think this boy can do us more good above ground than underground," he said). And he repatriated a Confederate prisoner who had taken the oath of allegiance, restoring him as a citizen of the United States.

That evening, Ford's Theater was packed. The president, Mrs. Lincoln, and two of their friends arrived a little after 8:30. The audience gave the president a standing ovation as he entered.

President Lincoln enjoyed the plays of Shakespeare but had little interest in this new play, "Our American Cousin." He went only as a favor to Mrs. Lincoln.

A little after ten, John Wilkes Booth entered the president's box, saw the president in his armchair, leaning on one hand, smiling and engaged in the play. Other members of the president's party were also intent on the play. Booth raised his derringer and pointed it behind the president's left ear. He fired one shot at point-blank range, mortally wounding President Lincoln.

One of the president's guests, Major Henry Rathbone, leaped up and grappled with Booth, but the assassin broke free, leaped over the railing, and made his escape.

Mrs. Lincoln saw that her husband was shot and cried, "His dream was prophetic!"

The wounded president was taken across the street to the Peterson House, where he lingered through the night in a coma. A grief-stricken Edwin Stanton was present throughout the vigil. At one point, he said, "There lies the most perfect ruler of men who ever lived."

President Lincoln died at 7:22 a.m. on April 15. A minister led in prayer; then Mr. Stanton said, "Now he belongs to the ages."

Lincoln's eldest son, Robert, was twenty-one when his father died. For days after Lincoln's death, Edwin Stanton would come to Robert's room every morning and sit with him. Stanton wouldn't say a word—he would just sit beside Robert and weep.[18]

Edwin Stanton had once been Abraham Lincoln's most bitter political enemy and cruelest critic. In the end, he mourned Lincoln as few others did. He had been won over by Abraham Lincoln's serving heart.

LEADERSHIP LESSONS FROM THE GREAT EMANCIPATOR

Starbucks CEO Howard Schultz said, "Lincoln's presidency is a big, well-lit classroom for business leaders seeking to build successful, enduring organizations. . . . [Lincoln] always looked upward and always called American citizens to a higher road and to a purpose bigger than themselves."[19] Here are some key leadership lessons we can draw from the life of the Great Emancipator, Abraham Lincoln:

1. *Great leaders must be lifelong learners.* Abraham Lincoln had one year of formal education. From school, he learned how to "read, write, and cipher." Everything he needed to know in order to be a fine lawyer and a great president, he learned from reading books. He was a student of history, military strategy, political science, law, literature, and mathematics (he taught himself trigonometry and surveying out of books). There's no limit to what you can achieve through a devotion to lifelong learning.

2. *Great leaders care about individuals.* From his earliest years to the final day of his life, Abraham Lincoln thought about others. As a five-year-old, he cared about a soldier he met on the road. As president, he cared about every soldier under his leadership.

Lincoln took time for individuals. He took time to encourage his soldiers, to comfort the wounded, to pardon the guilty, and to bless the children. That's what complete leaders do. They lead from a serving heart. Authentic leadership is servanthood. Leaders who don't understand how to serve do not understand how to lead.

3. *A serving leader answers the call.* Abraham Lincoln served a single term in the House of Representatives then retired from politics—or so he thought. He had planned to devote the rest of his career to the practice of law. But the repeal of the Missouri Compromise summoned him back to public service. Lincoln didn't need politics, but the nation needed Lincoln. He understood what was happening to his country. He had answered the call. Do you hear the call upon your life today? Have you answered the call?

4. *A leader with a serving heart looks beyond labels and sees people.* To Abraham Lincoln, Confederate soldiers were not "rebels;" they were Americans. His goal was to heal the divisions caused by the war, to erase distinctions between North and South, between black and white, and to make America one nation again. In his Second Inaugural Address a month before he was assassinated, Lincoln said, "With malice toward none, with charity for all, with firmness in the right as God gives us to see the right, let us strive on to finish the work we are in, to bind up the nation's wounds, to care for him who shall have borne the battle and for his

widow and his orphan, to do all which may achieve and cherish a just and lasting peace among ourselves and with all nations."

Lincoln dreamed of healing not just the North, but the South as well. What a tragedy that he was murdered before he could turn that vision into a reality.

5. *Serving leaders are more interested in restoration and redemption than in retribution.* Again and again, Abraham Lincoln looked for ways to redeem prisoners from their failures and restore them to active service. He never minimized the seriousness of a young soldier's dereliction. He held the young man accountable. Then he restored the young man to active duty.

Whenever you have to deal with a disciplinary issue, ask yourself, "What is the redemptive, restorative solution to this problem?"

6. *Serving leaders turn enemies into friends.* Lincoln could not have had a more stubborn, insulting, derisive critic than Edwin Stanton. To hear Stanton call Lincoln a "guerrilla" or a person of "painful imbecility," you would never imagine Stanton would one day eulogize Lincoln as "the most perfect ruler of men who ever lived."

Stanton didn't change his opinion of Lincoln overnight. Lincoln won him over by slow increments. But it began when Lincoln looked at Stanton in a new way and saw qualities in him he had never noticed before. Lincoln was willing to put up with Stanton's abrasive personality in order to win the war. And in the process of winning the war, Lincoln won a friend.

Who is the "Edwin Stanton" in your leadership life? What are you doing to win that person over as a friend?

Throughout this book, we have seen the Seven Sides of Leadership as they are exemplified in the lives of twenty-one great leaders. These seven facets of leadership are all learnable skills:

1. Vision
2. Communication
3. People Skills
4. Character
5. Competence
6. Boldness
7. A Serving Heart

If you lack any of these skills, you can acquire them. Once you possess all seven, you can't help but become an outstanding leader.

These twenty-one leaders have given us the pattern. Now it's our turn to make leadership history. The complete seven-sided leader is fully prepared to meet every leadership test, to conquer every leadership challenge.

And the leader who is complete will never be forgotten.

Don't kneel to me. That is not right. You must kneel to God only,
and thank Him for the liberty you will hereafter enjoy.
I am but God's humble instrument.
ABRAHAM LINCOLN (AFTER A FORMER SLAVE BOWED DOWN TO HIM, 1865)

Notes

Chapter 1

[1] Marvin Olasky, "No More Fantasyland," Townhall.com, October 16, 2001, http://townhall.com/columnists/marvinolasky/2001/10/16/no_more_fantasyland.

[2] Jim Clemmer, *The Leader's Digest: Timeless Principles for Team and Organization Success* (Kitchener, ON: TCG Press, 2003), 39.

[3] Disneyland Resort, "Buena Vista Street at Disney California Adventure Park Fact Sheet," DisneylandNews.com, July 31, 2014, http://disneylandnews.com/2014/07/31/buena-vista-street-at-disney-california-adventure-park-fact-sheet/.

[4] Grace Norwich, *I Am Walt Disney* (New York: Scholastic, 2014), 39.

[5] Brian Burnes, Dan Viets, and Robert W. Butler, *Walt Disney's Missouri: The Roots of a Creative Genius* (Kansas City, MO: Kansas City Star Books, 2002), 10–12.

[6] "Disneyland Long a Dream of Walt," *Long Beach Independent-Press-Telegram*, Friday, July 15, 1955, 46.

[7] Bob Aycock, "Walt Wednesdays: Dreaming Up Disneyland," MagicalDaddy.com, April 16, 2014, http://magicaldaddy.com/tag/griffith-park-merry-go-round/.

[8] William J. O'Neil, *Business Leaders & Success: 55 Top Business Leaders and How They Achieved Greatness* (New York: McGraw-Hill, 2004), 9.

[9] Gene N. Landrum, *Profiles of Power and Success: Fourteen Geniuses Who Broke the Rules* (New York: Prometheus, 1996), 352.

[10] Sam Land, "The Magic Kingdom: A Grand Entrance," SamLand's Disney Adventures, September 20, 2011, http://samlanddisney.blogspot.com/2011/09/magic-kingdom-grand-entrance_20.html.

[11] Bill Capodagli and Lynn Jackson, *The Disney Way, Revised Edition: Harnessing the Management Secrets of Disney in Your Company* (New York: McGraw-Hill, 2006), ix.

Chapter 2

[1] Charlayne Hunter-Gault, "Nelson Mandela, the Father," *The New Yorker*, May 3, 2013, http://www.newyorker.com/news/news-desk/nelson-mandela-the-father.

[2] Rita Bernard, ed., *The Cambridge Companion to Nelson Mandela* (New York: Cambridge University Press, 2014), 270.

[3] Nelson Mandela, *Long Walk to Freedom: The Autobiography of Nelson Mandela* (New York: Back Bay Books, 1995), 19.

[4] Ibid., 21.

[5] Ibid., 22.

[6] Ibid., 23.

[7] Ibid., 46.

[8] Ibid., 201.

[9] Ibid., 283.

[10] Edward J Perkins, *Mr. Ambassador: Warrior for Peace* (Norman: University of Oklahoma Press, 2006), 250.

[11] David Beresford, "Row Over 'Mother of the Nation' Winnie Mandela," *The Guardian*, January 27, 1989, http://www.theguardian.com/century/1980-1989/Story/0,,110268,00.html.

[12] Roque Planas, "Why Nelson Mandela Loved Fidel Castro," *Huffington Post*, December 6, 2013, http://www.huffingtonpost.com/2013/12/06/nelson-mandela-castro_n_4400212.html.

[13] Mike Cohen, Franz Wild, and Amogelang Mbatha, "Mandela Dies with Rainbow Nation Dream Still Work in Progress," Bloomberg News, December 5, 2013, http://www.bloomberg.com/news/2013-12-06/mandela-dies-with-rainbow-nation-dream-still-work-in-progress.html.

[14] John Carlin, *Playing the Enemy: Nelson Mandela and the Game That Made a Nation* (New York: Penguin, 2008), 188.

[15] Carmine Gallo, *10 Simple Secrets of the World's Greatest Business Communicators* (Naperville, IL: Sourcebooks, 2005), 46.

[16] Andrew Ross Sorkin, "How Mandela Shifted Views on Freedom of Markets," DealBook, *New York Times*, December 9, 2013, http://dealbook.nytimes.com/2013/12/09/how-mandela-shifted-views-on-freedom-of-markets/?_php=true&_type=blogs&_r=0.

Chapter 3

[1] Steve Jobs, "Steve Jobs Lost Interview 1990," YouTube.com, February 19, 2012, online video transcribed by the author, https://www.youtube.com/watch?v=2nMD6sjAe8I.

[2] Ibid., 97.

[3] Michael Moritz, *The Little Kingdom: The Private Story of Apple Computer* (New York: William Morrow, 1984), 101.

[4] Walter Isaacson, *Steve Jobs* (New York: Simon & Schuster, 2011), 53; cf. Scott Cohen, *Zap! The Rise and Fall of Atari* (New York: McGraw-Hill, 1984), 54–55, and Stephen Kent, *The Ultimate History of Video Games: From Pong to Pokemon and Beyond—The Story behind the Craze That Touched Our Lives and Changed the World* (New York: Three Rivers Press, 2001), Kindle ed. (unnumbered pages).

[5] Isaacson, *Steve Jobs*, 53–54.

[6] Sharon Begley, "Jobs's Unorthodox Treatment," TheDailyBeast.com, October 5, 2011, http://www.thedailybeast.com/articles/2011/10/05/steve-jobs-dies-his-unorthodox-treatment-for-neuroendocrine-cancer.html; Ramzi Amri, "Why did Steve Jobs Choose Not to Effectively Treat His Cancer?," Quora.com, October 13, 2011, http://www.quora.com/Why-did-Steve-Jobs-choose-not-to-effectively-treat-his-cancer; Dr. Kaayla T. Daniel, "iVegetarian: The High Fructose Diet of Steve Jobs," *Psychology Today*, January 19, 2012, http://www.psychologytoday.com/blog/naughty-nutrition/201201/ivegetarian-the-high-fructose-diet-steve-jobs.

[7] Alice G. Walton, "Steve Jobs' Cancer Treatment Regrets," *Forbes*, October 24, 2011, http://www.forbes.com/sites/alicegwalton/2011/10/24/steve-jobs-cancer-treatment-regrets/.

[8] Isaacson, *Steve Jobs*, 477.

[9] Ibid., 36.

[10] Ibid., 548–49.

[11] Ibid., 477, 487.

[12] Walton, "Steve Jobs' Cancer Treatment Regrets."

[13] Ibid.

[14] Brandon Griggs, "Apple Now Has More Cash Than the U.S. Government," CNN, July 29, 2011, http://www.cnn.com/2011/TECH/innovation/07/29/apple.cash.government/.

[15] Mona Simpson, "A Sister's Eulogy," *New York Times*, October 30, 2011, http://www.nytimes.com/2011/10/30/opinion/mona-simpsons-eulogy-for-steve-jobs.html?_r=0.

[16] Tate Linden, "Searching for Steve Jobs's 'Dent In The Universe,'" Stokefire.com, February 11, 2013, http://www.stokefire.com/2013/02/searching-for-steve-jobss-dent-in-the-universe/.

[17] Steve Jobs, "'You Got to Find What You Love,' Jobs Says," *Stanford Report*, June 14, 2005, http://news.stanford.edu/news/2005/june15/jobs-061505.html.

[18] Pat Williams, *How to Be Like Walt: Capturing the Disney Magic Every Day of Your Life* (Deerfield Beach, FL: HCI, 2004), 28.

[19] Randall Stross, "What Steve Jobs Learned in the Wilderness," *New York Times*, October 2, 2010, http://www.nytimes.com/2010/10/03/business/03digi.html?_r=0.

[20] Ibid.

[21] Ryan Tate, "What Everyone Is Too Polite to Say about Steve Jobs," Gawker.com, October 7, 2011, http://gawker.com/5847344/what-everyone-is-too-polite-to-say-about-steve-jobs.

[22] Malcolm Gladwell, "The Tweaker: The Real Genius of Steve Jobs," *New Yorker*, November 14, 2011, http://www.newyorker.com/magazine/2011/11/14/the-tweaker?currentPage=all.

[23] Adam Lashinsky, "How Apple Works: Inside the World's Biggest Startup," *Fortune*, May 9, 2011, http://fortune.com/2011/05/09/how-apple-works-inside-the-worlds-biggest-startup/.

[24] Dr. Relly Nadler, "Steve Jobs: Superman Syndrome, Low EQ, High IQ," PsychologyToday.com, November 16, 2011, http://www.psychologytoday.com/blog/leading-emotional-intelligence/201111/steve-jobs-superman-syndrome-low-eq-high-iq.

[25] Nadler, "Jobs: Guru and Goon."

[26] Betsy Morris, "Steve Jobs Speaks Out. . .On Apple's Focus," *CNN/Money*, March 7, 2008, http://archive.fortune.com/galleries/2008/fortune/0803/gallery.jobsqna.fortune/6.html.

Chapter 4

[1] "History's Most Inspiring Speaker? Guess Who," The Churchill Centre, September 2013, http://www.winstonchurchill.org/support/the-churchill-centre/publications/chartwell-bulletin/2013/63-sep/2503-inspiring-speaker-poll.

[2] President John F. Kennedy, "Declaration of Honorary Citizen of United States of America," April 9, 1963, The Churchill Centre, http://www.winstonchurchill.org/learn/speeches/speeches-of-winston-churchill/125-united-states-citizen.

[3] Gary Shapiro, "How Churchill Mobilized the English Language," *New York Sun*, June 12, 2012, http://www.nysun.com/new-york/how-churchill-mobilized-the-english-language/87862/.

[4] John Mather, MD, "Myth: Churchill's Speech Impediment Was Stuttering," The Churchill Centre, http://www.winstonchurchill.org/learn/myths/myths/he-stuttered.

[5] Harold Begbie, *The Mirrors of Downing Street* (New York: G. P. Putnam's Sons, 1921), http://www.gutenberg.org/files/15306/15306-h/15306-h.htm.

[6] Louis J. Alber and Charles J. Rolo, cited in Keith Sharp, "Winston Churchill, Stutterer," Utstat.UToronto.ca, November 30, 2012, http://www.utstat.utoronto.ca/sharp/Churchill.htm.

[7] Nicholas Soames, "Sweat and Tears Made Winston Churchill's Name," *Telegraph*, May 4, 2011, http://www.telegraph.co.uk/news/politics/av-referendum/8493345/Sweat-and-tears-made-Winston-Churchills-name.html.

[8] Winston Churchill, "The War Situation: House of Many Mansions," Broadcast, London, January 20, 1940, The Churchill Centre, http://www.winstonchurchill.org/learn/speeches/speeches-of-winston-churchill/98-the-war-situation-house-of-many-mansions.

[9] "Finest Hour: September 1940–1941," The Churchill Centre, http://www.winstonchurchill.org/learn/biography/timelines/finest-hour-september-1940-1941.

[10] Winston Churchill, "Blood, Toil, Tears and Sweat," First Speech as Prime Minister to House of Commons, May 13, 1940, The Churchill Centre, http://www.winstonchurchill.org/learn/speeches/speeches-of-winston-churchill/92-blood-toil-tears-and-sweat.

[11] Winston Churchill, "We Shall Fight on the Beaches," House of Commons, June 4, 1940, The Churchill Centre, http://www.winstonchurchill.org/learn/speeches/speeches-of-winston-churchill/128-we-shall-fight-on-the-beaches.

[12] Winston Churchill, "Their Finest Hour," House of Commons, June 18, 1940, The Churchill Centre, http://www.winstonchurchill.org/learn/speeches/speeches-of-winston-churchill/122-their-finest-hour.

[13] Winston Churchill, "Never Give In," Harrow School, October 29, 1941, The Churchill Centre, http://www.winstonchurchill.org/learn/speeches/speeches-of-winston-churchill/103-never-give-in.

[14] Winston Churchill, "This is Your Victory," Ministry of Health, London, May 8, 1945, The Churchill Centre, http://www.winstonchurchill.org/learn/speeches/speeches-of-winston-churchill/123-this-is-your-victory; compared and corrected against the BBC audio recording at http://www.archive.org/download/Winston_Churchill/1945-05-08_BBC_Winston_Churchill_VE_Day_Celebrations_Ministry_of_Health_Building.mp3.

[15] Clark Clifford, "Cold War—Episode Two: Iron Curtain," CNN Perspective Series, October 25, 2007, https://web.archive.org/web/20071025031206/http://www.cnn.com/SPECIALS/cold.war/episodes/02/interviews/clifford/.

[16] Winston Churchill, "The Sinews of Peace," Westminster College, Fulton, Missouri, March 5, 1946, The Churchill Centre, http://www.winstonchurchill.org/learn/speeches/speeches-of-winston-churchill/1946-1963-elder-statesman/120-the-sinews-of-peace.

[17] Shapiro, "How Churchill Mobilized the English Language."

[18] Ecclesiastes 6:11.

Chapter 5

[1] Martin Luther King Jr., "Chapter 1: Early Years," in *The Autobiography of Martin Luther King, Jr.*, The Martin Luther King, Jr. Research and Education Institute, http://mlk-kpp01.stanford.edu/index.php/kingpapers/article/chapter_1_early_years/.

[2] Alice Fleming, *Martin Luther King, Jr.: A Dream of Hope* (New York: Sterling, 2008), 9.

[3] Martin Luther King Jr., "Rediscovering Lost Values," Dexter Avenue Baptist Church, Montgomery, Alabama, November 4, 1956, Martin Luther King Jr. Online, http://www.mlkonline.net/christians.html.

[4] Martin Luther King Jr., "Loving Your Enemies," Dexter Avenue Baptist Church, Montgomery, Alabama, November 17, 1957, iPoet.com, http://www.ipoet.com/ARCHIVE/BEYOND/King-Jr/Loving-Your-Enemies.html.

[5] Martin Luther King Jr., "Eulogy for the Martyred Children," Birmingham, Alabama, September 18, 1963, Martin Luther King Jr. Research and Education Institute, http://mlk-kpp01.stanford.edu/index.php/kingpapers/article/eulogy_for_the_martyred_children/.

[6] Martin Luther King Jr., "How Long, Not Long" (aka "Our God Is Marching On),", Montgomery, Alabama, March 25, 1965, Martin Luther King Jr. Research and Education Institute, http://mlk-kpp01.stanford.edu/index.php/kingpapers/article/our_god_is_marching_on/.

[7] Martin Luther King Jr., "I've Been to the Mountaintop," Mason Temple (Church of God in Christ Headquarters), Memphis, Tennessee, April 3, 1968, AmericanRhetoric. com, http://www.americanrhetoric.com/speeches/mlkivebeentothemountaintop.htm (minor changes in punctuation made by the authors).

[8] Ed Pilkington, "40 Years after King's Death, Jackson Hails First Steps into Promised Land," *Guardian*, April 3, 2008, http://www.theguardian.com/world/2008/apr/03/usa.race.

[9] Tom Brokaw, *Boom! Voices of the Sixties—Personal Reflections on the '60s and Today* (New York: Random House, 2008), 15.

[10] Thomas Dexter Lynch and Peter L. Cruise, *Handbook of Organization Theory and Management: The Philosophical Approach* (Boca Raton, FL: Taylor & Francis, 2006), 596.

[11] 1 Corinthians 14:8.

Chapter 6
[1] WGBH, "American Experience: Reagan," Complete Program Transcript, PBS.org, http://www.pbs.org/wgbh/americanexperience/features/transcript/reagan-transcript/.

[2] George F. Will, foreword to *Rendezvous with Destiny: Ronald Reagan and the Campaign That Changed America*, by Craig Shirley (Wilmington, DE: ISI Books, 2009), xi–xii.

[3] Ronald Reagan, "We Will Be a City upon a Hill," First Conservative Political Action Conference, January 25, 1974, Reagan2020.us, http://reagan2020.us/speeches/City_Upon_A_Hill.asp.

[4] Ronald Reagan, "Address To Members of the British Parliament," June 8, 1982, Ronald Reagan's Major Speeches 1964–1989, Ronald Reagan Presidential Library & Museum, http://www.reagan.utexas.edu/archives/speeches/1982/60882a.htm.

[5] Ronald Reagan, "Remarks at the Annual Convention of the National Association of Evangelicals in Orlando, Florida," March 8, 1983, Ronald Reagan's Major Speeches 1964– 1989, Ronald Reagan Presidential Library & Museum, http://www.reagan.utexas.edu/archives/speeches/1983/30883b.htm.

[6] Serge Schmemann, "Soviet Says Reagan Has 'Pathological Hatred,'" *New York Times*, March 10, 1983, http://www.nytimes.com/1983/03/10/world/soviet-says-reagan-has-pathological-hatred.html.

[7] Lesley Stahl, *Reporting Live* (New York: Touchstone, 1999), 164.

[8] Paul Kengor, "Reagan's 'Evil Empire' Turns 30," *American Spectator*, March 8, 2013, http://spectator.org/articles/33780/reagans-evil-empire-turns-30.

[9] Ronald Reagan, "Address to the Nation on Defense and National Security," March 23, 1983, Ronald Reagan's Major Speeches 1964–1989, Ronald Reagan Presidential Library & Museum, http://www.reagan.utexas.edu/archives/speeches/1983/32383d.htm.

[10] Ben Bova, *Star Peace: Assured Survival* (New York: Tor, 1986), 157.

[11] "Ronald Reagan: Remarks at the Brandenburg Gate, 1987," Top Ten Greatest Speeches, *Time*, September 17, 2008, http://content.time.com/time/specials/packages/article/0,28804,1841228_1841749_1841743,00.html.

[12] Gardiner Morse, "How Presidents Persuade: A Conversation with David Gergen," *Harvard Business Review*, January 2003, http://hbr.org/2003/01/how-presidents-persuade/ar/1.

[13] James P. Farwell, *Persuasion and Power: The Art of Strategic Communication* (Washington, DC: Georgetown University Press, 2012), 122.

[14] Michael Reagan, *The New Reagan Revolution: How Ronald Reagan's Principles Can Restore America's Greatness Today* (New York: Saint Martin's, 2010), 303.

[15] Stephen F. Knott, quoted in Charles Dunn, ed., *The Enduring Reagan* (Lexington, KY: University Press of Kentucky, 2009), 90.

[16] WGBH, "American Experience: Jimmy Carter," Primary Resources: "Crisis of Confidence," PBS.org, http://www.pbs.org/wgbh/americanexperience/features/primary-resources/carter-crisis/.

[17] Warren G. Bennis, *On Becoming a Leader* (New York: Basic Books, 2009), 193.

[18] Colin Powell, quoted in Carmine Gallo, *10 Simple Secrets of the World's Greatest Business Communicators* (Naperville, IL: Sourcebooks, 2006), 35.

[19] Ken Khachigian, "What Made Reagan the Great Communicator," *Orange County Register*, February 4, 2011, updated August 21, 2013, http://www.ocregister.com/articles/reagan-287119-great-dollar.html.

[20] Ronald Reagan, *Speaking My Mind: Selected Speeches* (New York: Simon & Shuster, 1989), 14.

[21] Dinesh D'Souza, *Ronald Reagan: How an Ordinary Man Became an Extraordinary Leader* (New York: Simon & Shuster, 1999), 9.

[22] James Mann, *The Rebellion of Ronald Reagan* (New York: Viking, 2009), 164.

[23] Steven F. Hayward, *The Age of Reagan: The Conservative Counterrevolution*, 1980–1989 (New York: Crown Forum, 2009), 1–2.

[24] Ibid.

Chapter 7

[1] President George H. W. Bush, "Remarks on Presenting the Presidential Medal of Freedom to Samuel M. Walton in Bentonville, Arkansas," March 17, 1992, Public Papers—1992—March, George Bush Presidential Library and Museum, http://bushlibrary.tamu.edu/research/public_papers.php?id=4072&year=1992&month=3; the authors have made minor alterations to Mr. Bush's remarks for the sake of clarity.

[2] Jack Welch, quoted in Richard K. Vedder and Wendell Cox, *The Wal-Mart Revolution: How Big-box Stores Benefit Consumers, Workers, and the Economy* (Washington, DC, AEI Press, 2006), 50.

[3] Michael Bergdahl, *The 10 Rules of Sam Walton: Success Secrets for Remarkable Results* (Hoboken, NJ: Wiley, 2006), 109.

[4] Robert Slater, *How a New Generation of Leaders Turned Sam Walton's Legacy Into the World's #1 Company* (New York: Portfolio/Penguin, 2003), 7.

[5] Alexander E. M. Hess, "The Ten Largest Employers in America," *USA Today*, August 22, 2013, http://www.usatoday.com/story/money/business/2013/08/22/ten-largest-employers/2680249/.

[6] Sam Walton with John Huey, *Sam Walton: Made in America* (New York: Bantam, 1993), 19.

[7] Ibid.

[8] Ibid., 23.

[9] Ibid., 26.

[10] Ibid., 29.

[11] Ibid., 38–39.

[12] Ibid., 42, 46.

[13] Ibid., 107, 159.

[14] James Kouzes and Barry Posner, *The Truth about Leadership: The No-Fads, Heart of the Matter Facts You Need to Know* (San Francisco: Jossey-Bass, 2010), 137–38.

[15] Neil Snyder, James J. Dowd Jr., and Diane Morse Houghton , *Vision, Values, and Courage: Leadership for Quality Management* (New York: The Free Press, 1994), 56.

[16] Sam Walton, "Sam Walton in His Own Words," *Fortune*, June 29, 1992, http://archive.fortune.com/magazines/fortune/fortune_archive/1992/06/29/76578/index.htm.

[17] Walton with Huey, *Sam Walton: Made in America*, 267.

[18] Michael Armstrong, *How to be an Even Better Manager* (Philadelphia: Kogan Page, 2014), 287.

[19] Sam Walton, "10 Rules for Building a Business," Walmart.com, http://corporate.walmart.com/our-story/history/10-rules-for-building-a-business.

[20] Harold Meyerson, "In Wal-Mart's Image," *American Prospect*, August 14, 2009, http://prospect.org/article/wal-marts-image-0.

[21] Nelson Lichtenstein, *The Retail Revolution: How Wal-Mart Created a Brave New World of Business* (New York: Picador, 2010), 118–19.

[22] Walton with Huey, *Sam Walton: Made in America*, 162–63.

Chapter 8

[1] John Gunther, *Roosevelt in Retrospect: A Profile in History* (New York: Harper, 1950), 168.

[2] James MacGregor Burns, *Roosevelt: The Soldier of Freedom* (New York: Harcourt Brace Jovanovich, 1970), 16; John Gunther, *Roosevelt in Retrospect*, 178.

[3] Jean Edward Smith, *FDR* (New York: Random House, 2008), 29.

[4] David M. Oshinsky, *Polio: An American Story* (New York: Oxford University Press, 2005), 24–26.

[5] Frances Perkins, *The Roosevelt I Knew* (New York: Penguin, 2011), 29–30.

[6] Joseph E. Persico, *Franklin and Lucy: President Roosevelt, Mrs. Rutherfurd, and the Other Remarkable Women in His Life* (New York: Random House, 2008), 187.

[7] Paul F. Boller Jr., *Presidential Anecdotes* (New York: Oxford University Press, 1996), 259.

[8] Ibid., 258.

[9] Ibid., 261.

[10] Ibid., 259.

[11] Ibid., 269–70; Gil Troy, *Leading from the Center: Why Moderates Make the Best Presidents* (New York: Basic Books, 2008), 106–7.

[12] "Power / Influence / Authority," Learningful—The Art of Possibility, Learningful.ca, http://www.learningful.ca/power-influence-authority.php.

[13] Perkins, *The Roosevelt I Knew*, 369.

[14] Dale Carnegie, *How to Win Friends and Influence People* (New York: Simon & Shuster, 1998) 76–77; "E3 Spark Plugs Digs Hyde Park on Hudson—and Fab FDR Cars," E3 Spark Plugs News, December 10, 2012, http://www.e3sparkplugs.com/news/e3-spark-plugs-digs-hyde-park-on-hudson-and-fab-fdr-cars/.

[15] Will Swift, *The Roosevelts and the Royals: Franklin and Eleanor, the King and Queen of England, and the Friendship That Changed History* (Hoboken, NJ: Wiley, 2004), 140–41.

[16] Michael Fullilove, *Rendezvous with Destiny: How Franklin D. Roosevelt and Five Extraordinary Men Took America into the War and into the World* (New York: Penguin, 2013), 12–13.

[17] Robert Cross, *Shepherds of the Sea: Destroyer Escorts in World War II* (Annapolis: Naval Institute Press, 2010), 49.

[18] Boller Jr., *Presidential Anecdotes*, 262.

[19] Jonathan Yardley, "Review: *FDR* by Jean Edward Smith," *Washington Post*, May 27, 2007, http://www.washingtonpost.com/wp-dyn/content/article/2007/05/25/AR2007052500004.html.

[20] Perkins, *The Roosevelt I Knew*, 6.

Chapter 9

[1] Associated Press, "Pope John Paul II Forgave His Shooter on Way to Hospital," Associated Press, January 26, 2010, http://www.foxnews.com/story/2010/01/26/pope-john-paul-ii-forgave-his-shooter-on-way-to-hospital/.

[2] Randall J. Meissen, "A Mother's Hand Guided the Bullets: John Paul II, Forgiving a Would-Be-Assassin," Catholic.org, April 27, 2011, http://www.catholic.org/news/saints/story.php?id=41174.

[3] Ibid.

[4] Norman Davies, *Rising '44: The Battle for Warsaw* (New York: Viking, 2003), 253.

[5] George Weigel, *Witness to Hope: The Biography of Pope John Paul II* (New York: HarperCollins, 2001), 75.

[6] Ofer Aderet, "Edith Zierer, Holocaust Survivor Saved by Pope, Dies," Haaretz.com, January 16, 2014, http://www.haaretz.com/news/national/.premium-1.568993.

[7] Ted Harrison, *Tales of Three Popes: True Stories from the Lives of Francis, John Paul II, and John XXIII* (London: Darton, Longman, & Todd, 2014), 36.

[8] P. G. Maxwell-Stuart, *Chronicle of the Popes: The Reign-by-Reign Record of the Papacy from St. Peter to the Present* (London: Thames and Hudson, 1997), 233.

[9] Raymond Rolak, "John Paul II, the New Saint," *Polish News*, April 18, 2014, http://www.polishnews.com/newsy-news/wiadomoci-ze-wiata-news-from-around-the-world/5481-john-paul-ii,-the-new-saint; George Weigel, "Lessons of a Pontiff's Twilight," *Washington Post*, March 22, 2005, A17; John Thavis, "Pope John Paul II: A Light for the World," United States Conference of Catholic Bishops, Office of Media Relations, 2003, http://web.archive.org/web/20110623031352/http://www.usccb.org/comm/popejohnpaulii/biography.shtml.

[10] Richard Cavendish, "Election of John Paul II," History Today, October 2008, http://www.historytoday.com/richard-cavendish/election-john-paul-ii.

[11] Pope John Paul II, Apostolic Journey to Poland, "Holy Mass: Homily of His Holiness John Paul II," Victory Square, Warsaw, June 2, 1979, http://www.vatican.va/holy_father/john_paul_ii/homilies/1979/documents/hf_jp-ii_hom_19790602_polonia-varsavia_en.html.

[12] Peggy Noonan, "Make John Paul II a Saint," *Wall Street Journal*, April 30, 2011, http://online.wsj.com/news/articles/SB10001424052748704463804576291513299466454.

[13] Ibid.

[14] Ibid., 157–58.

Chapter 10

[1] James Thomas Flexner, *Washington: The Indispensable Man* (New York: Penguin, 1984), 110.

[2] Dr. Burton W. Folsom, "George Washington's Unimpeachable Character," Mackinac Center for Public Policy, February 1, 1999, http://www.mackinac.org/1652.

[3] Mark Alexander, "The Model for Presidential Character—George Washington," The Patriot Post, February 23, 2012, http://patriotpost.us/alexander/12704.

[4] Harold Kellock, *Parson Weems of the Cherry-Tree* (New York: The Century Co., 1928), 88.

[5] Michael D. McKinney, "George Washington's Rules of Civility & Decent Behavior in Company and Conversation," *Foundations* Online Magazine, http://www.foundationsmag.com/civility.html.

[6] Katherine Kersten, "George Washington's Character," Center of the American Experiment, March 6, 1996, http://www.americanexperiment.org/publications/commentaries/george-washingtons-character.

[7] "George Washington Biography," Biography.com, A&E Television Networks, 2014, http://www.biography.com/people/george-washington-9524786.

[8] David McCullough, "The Glorious Cause of America," assembly address at Brigham Young University, September 27, 2005, Speeches, http://speeches.byu.edu/reader/reader.php?id=10804.

[9] Troy O. Bickham, "Sympathizing with Sedition? George Washington, the British Press, and British Attitudes during the American War of Independence," *William and Mary Quarterly* (Omohundro Institute of Early American History and Culture), January 2002, 101.

[10] "George Washington Biography," Biography.com.

[11] The Claremont Institute, "Farewell Address 1796," Rediscovering George Washington, PBS.org, 2002, http://www.pbs.org/georgewashington/milestones/farewell_address_about.html.

[12] Thomas Sowell, "What Kind of 'Experience'?," Creators Syndicate, February 10, 2008, http://www.creators.com/conservative/thomas-sowell/what-kind-of-experience.html.

[13] Ann Rinaldi, appendix "Writings of George Washington about Slavery," in *Taking Liberty: The Story of Oney Judge, George Washington's Runaway Slave* (New York: Simon & Shuster, 2002), 260.

[14] Ibid.

[15] Stephen E. Ambrose, *To America: Personal Reflections of an Historian* (New York: Simon & Schuster, 2002), 1, 3, 13.

[16] Ibid., 10.

[17] John P. Kaminski, *The Great Virginia Triumvirate: George Washington, Thomas Jefferson, and James Madison* (Charlottesville, VA: University of Virginia Press, 2010), 78–79.

[18] Peter R. Henriques, *Realistic Visionary: A Portrait of George Washington* (Charlottesville, VA: University of Virginia Press, 2006), 187–88.

[19] Frank E. Grizzard, *George Washington: A Biographical Companion* (Santa Barbara, CA: ABC-CLIO, 2002), 74.

[20] Henriques, *Realistic Visionary*, 194.

[21] Ibid., 203.

Chapter 11

[1] Billy Graham, *Just As I Am: The Autobiography of Billy Graham* (Grand Rapids: Zondervan, 2007), 17.

[2] Ibid., 27.

[3] Ibid., 28–29.

[4] Ibid., 59.

[5] Ibid., 135.

[6] Ibid., 135–36.

[7] Ibid., 139.

[8] Ibid., xxii.

[9] Stanley High, *Billy Graham: The Personal Story of the Man, His Message, and His Mission* (New York: McGraw-Hill, 1956), 43.

[10] Billy Graham, *Just As I Am*, xxii.

[11] Merle Miller, *Plain Speaking: An Oral Biography of Harry S. Truman* (New York: Putnam, 1974), 363.

[12] Christian Broadcasting Network, "Billy Graham: Preacher to the Presidents," CBN. com, August 2007, http://www.cbn.com/entertainment/books/PreacherandPresidents.aspx; Nancy Gibbs and Michael Duffy, "Billy Graham: A Spiritual Gift to All," *Time*, May 31, 2007, http://content.time.com/time/nation/article/0,8599,1627139,00.html.

[13] Stephen P. Miller, *Billy Graham and the Rise of the Republican South* (Philadelphia: University of Pennsylvania Press, 2009), 30.

[14] Jeremy Gray, "Easter Sunday 1964, Billy Graham Brought Message of Hope to Integrated Audience at Birmingham's Legion Field," Blog.AL.com, March 20, 2014, http:// blog.al.com/spotnews/2014/03/easter_sunday_1964_billy_graha.html.

[15] Trevor Freeze, "Billy Graham, Nelson Mandela United by Apartheid Opposition," Billy Graham Evangelistic Association, December 6, 2013, http://billygraham.org/story/ billy-graham-nelson-mandela-united-by-apartheid-opposition/.

[16] Graham, *Just As I Am*, 128.

Chapter 12

[1] Patricia O'Toole, "The Speech That Saved Teddy Roosevelt's Life," *Smithsonian*, November 2012, http://www.smithsonianmag.com/history/the-speech-that-saved-teddy-roosevelts-life-83479091/?no-ist; Henry Blodget, "Here's the Famous Populist Speech Teddy Roosevelt Gave Right after Getting Shot," *Business Insider*, October 14, 2011, http://www. businessinsider.com/heres-the-famous-populist-speech-teddy-roosevelt-gave-right-after-getting-shot-2011-10; R. J. Brown, "Teddy Roosevelt Shot by Anarchist—Manuscript of Speech Saves His Life," HistoryBuff.com, February 15, 2007, http://www.historybuff.com/ library/refteddy.html.

[2] Joseph Bucklin Bishop, *Theodore Roosevelt and His Time—Shown in His Own Letters* (New York: Scribner, 1920), 1:3.

[3] Henry William Brands, *TR: The Last Romantic* (New York: Basic Books, 1997), 24.

[4] George Grant, *The Courage and Character of Theodore Roosevelt: A Hero among Leaders* (Nashville: Cumberland House, 2005), 94.

[5] Brands, *TR: The Last Romantic*, 31.

[6] Ibid., 80.

[7] Ibid., 162.

[8] National Park Service, "Roosevelt's bar fight," Theodore Roosevelt National Park, North Dakota, http://www.nps.gov/thro/historyculture/roosevelts-bar-fight.htm.

[9] Donald J. Davidson, ed., *The Wisdom of Theodore Roosevelt* (New York: Kensington: 2003), 11.

[10] James Arnt Aune and Martin J. Medhurst, *The Prospect of Presidential Rhetoric* (College Station: Texas A&M University Press, 2008), 141.

[11] Theodore Roosevelt, *Works: Presidential Addresses and State Papers, April 7, 1904, to May 9, 1905* (New York: Review of Reviews Co., 1910), 14.

[12] Howard G. Hendricks, *Values and Virtues: Classic Quotes, Awesome Thoughts and Humorous Sayings* (Garden City, NY: Doubleday, 1997), 70.

[13] Roosevelt, *Works*, 16–17.

[14] Bishop, *Theodore Roosevelt and His Time*, 2:391.

[15] Jacob A. Riis, *Theodore Roosevelt, the Citizen* (New York: Macmillan, 1918), 406.

[16] Davidson, *Wisdom of Theodore Roosevelt*, 48.

[17] WGBH, "American Experience: T.R.," Complete Program Transcript, PBS.org, http://www.pbs.org/wgbh/americanexperience/features/transcript/tr-transcript/.

[18] David Baldwin, *Royal Prayer: A Surprising History* (New York: Continuum International, 2009), 136.

Chapter 13

[1] University of Virginia, *Alumni Bulletin of the University of Virginia*, January 1922 (Charlottesville: University of Virginia Press, 1922), 377–78.

[2] Clifton Fadiman and André Bernard, *Bartlett's Book of Anecdotes* (New York: Little, Brown and Co., 2000), 317.

[3] Michael Nelson, ed., *The Presidency A-Z* (New York: Routledge, 1998), 225.

[4] Arthur M. Schlesinger Jr., "Rating the Presidents: Washington to Clinton," Frontline, PBS SoCal, October 12, 2004, http://www.pbs.org/wgbh/pages/frontline/shows/choice2004/leadership/schlesinger.html.

[5] George Will, "Jefferson Ranks as Top Person of Millennium," *Sumter [SC] Item*, December 16, 1990, 12A.

[6] Warren G. Bennis, *The Essential Bennis: Essays on Leadership* (San Francisco: Jossey-Bass, 2009), 229, 230.

[7] John C. Maxwell, *The 21 Indispensable Qualities of a Leader: Becoming the Person Others Will Want to Follow* (Nashville: Thomas Nelson, 1999), 30.

[8] Thomas Jefferson, *Jefferson Himself: The Personal Narrative of a Many-Sided American*, ed. Bernard Mayo (Charlottesville: University of Virginia Press, 1970), 5.

[9] Ibid.

[10] Ibid.

[11] Ibid., 6.

[12] Andrew Burstein, *The Inner Jefferson: Portrait of a Grieving Optimist* (Charlottesville: University of Virginia Press, 1996), 61–63.

[13] Thomas Jefferson, *Notes on the State of Virginia*, "Query XVIII: Manners,"

TeachingAmericanHistory.org, http://teachingamericanhistory.org/library/document/notes-on-the-state-of-virginia-query-xviii-manners/.

[14] Annette Gordon-Reed, *The Hemingses of Monticello: An American Family* (New York: W. W. Norton, 2008), 99–100; Jon Meacham, *Thomas Jefferson: The Art of Power* (New York: Random House, 2012), 49.

[15] PBS, "Interview: Andrew Burstein—Historian," Thomas Jefferson: A Film by Ken Burns, PBS.org, http://www.pbs.org/jefferson/archives/interviews/Burstein.htm.

[16] Elbert Hubbard with John Jacob Lentz, *Thomas Jefferson: A Little Journey* (East Aurora, NY: The Roycrofters, 1906), 101.

[17] Thomas Jefferson Encyclopedia, "Jefferson's Last Words," Monticello.org, http://www.monticello.org/site/research-and-collections/jeffersons-last-words.

[18] Thomas Jefferson Encyclopedia, "John Adams," Monticello.org, http://www.monticello.org/site/jefferson/john-adams.

[19] Proverbs 25:3 MSG.

Chapter 14

[1] Luisa Kroll, "The World's Billionaires," *Forbes*, March 5, 2008, http://www.forbes.com/2008/03/05/richest-people-billionaires-billionaires08-cx_lk_0305billie_land.html.

[2] James Wallace and Jim Erickson, *Hard Drive: Bill Gates and the Making of the Microsoft Empire* (New York: HarperCollins, 1992), 10–11.

[3] Ibid., 15–16.

[4] Ibid., 21.

[5] Anthony Fellow, *American Media History*, 2nd ed. (Boston: Wadsworth Cengage Learning, 2010), 376.

[6] Bill Gates, "Remarks by Bill Gates—Lakeside School," Bill & Melinda Gates Foundation, Pressroom Speeches, September 23, 2005, http://www.gatesfoundation.org/26 Ibid.

[7] Ibid.

[8] Wallace and Erickson, *Hard Drive*, 44–45.

[9] Paul Allen, *Idea Man: A Memoir by the Co-founder of Microsoft* (New York: Penguin, 2012), 72.

[10] Ibid., 6–9.

[11] Terry R. Bacon, *The Elements of Power: Lessons on Leadership and Influence* (New York: AMACOM, 2011), 27; Bill Gates, Paul Allen, Brent Schlender, and Henry Goldblatt, "Bill Gates & Paul Allen Talk—Check Out the Ultimate Buddy Act in Business History," *Fortune*, October 2, 1995, http://archive.fortune.com/magazines/fortune/fortune_archive/1995/10/02/206528/index.htm.

[12] Gates et al., "Bill Gates & Paul Allen Talk."

[13] Bill Gates, "Remarks by Bill Gates, Chairman and Chief Software Architect, Microsoft Corporation," University of Waterloo, Waterloo, ON, October 13, 2005, https://web.archive.org/web/20080406130809/http://www.microsoft.com/presspass/exec/billg/speeches/2005/10-13Waterloo.aspx.

[14] Paolo Boldi and Luisa Gargano, eds., *Fun with Algorithms: Fifth International Conference, Fun 2010, Ischia, Italy, June 2010 Proceedings* (Berlin, Germany: Springer, 2010), 369.

[15] Christos Papadimitriou, "People of ACM: Christos Papadimitriou," Association for

Computing Machinery, March 19, 2013, http://www.acm.org/membership/acm-bulletin-archive/march-19-2013-people-of-acm-christos-papadimitriou.

[16] John Naughton, "Idea Man: A Memoir by the Co-founder of Microsoft by Paul Allen—Review," *Guardian*, May 8, 2011, http://www.theguardian.com/technology/2011/may/08/paul-allen-idea-man-review.

[17] Ibid.

[18] Malcolm Gladwell, "The Tweaker: The Real Genius of Steve Jobs," *New Yorker*, November 14, 2011, http://www.newyorker.com/magazine/2011/11/14/the-tweaker?currentPage=all.

[19] Kevin Savetz, "Fred Thorlin: The Big Boss at Atari Program Exchange," Atari Archives, April 2000, http://www.atariarchives.org/APX/thorlininterview.php.

[20] Jeff Goodell, "Bill Gates: The Rolling Stone Interview," *Rolling Stone*, March 13, 2014, http://www.rollingstone.com/culture/news/bill-gates-the-rolling-stone-interview-20140313.

[21] Eleanor Goldberg, "Bill Gates to Stanford Grads: 'You Can Do Better At This Than I Did,'" *Huffington Post*, June 16, 2014, http://www.huffingtonpost.com/2014/06/16/bill-gates-stanford-speech_n_5500253.html.

[22] Charlie White, "10 Things You Didn't Know about Bill Gates," CNN.com, June 13, 2011, http://www.cnn.com/2011/TECH/innovation/06/13/personal.details.bill.gates.mashable/.

[23] Nicholas D. Kristof and Sheryl WuDunn, "The Women's Crusade," *New York Times*, August 17, 2009, http://www.nytimes.com/2009/08/23/magazine/23Women-t.html.

[24] Rachel Quigley "'None of It Bothers Me': Bill Gates Brushes off Criticism by Steve Jobs and Heaps Praise on His Late Competitor," *Daily Mail Online*, October 30, 2011, http://www.dailymail.co.uk/news/article-2055347/Bill-Gates-brushes-Steve-Jobs-criticism-praising-late-competitor.html.

[25] Ibid.

[26] Gladwell, "The Tweaker."

Chapter 15

[1] Stephen E. Ambrose, *Eisenhower: Soldier and President* (New York: Simon & Schuster, 1990), 16–17.

[2] Ibid., 16.

[3] Ambrose, *Eisenhower: Soldier and President*, 25; History Channel, "June 25, 1942: Eisenhower Takes Command," This Day in History, History.com, http://www.history.com/this-day-in-history/eisenhower-takes-command.

[4] Ambrose, *Eisenhower: Soldier and President*, 44.

[5] Stanley Weintraub, *15 Stars: Eisenhower, MacArthur, Marshall—Three Generals Who Saved the American Century* (New York: Free Press, 2007), xvi.

[6] Matthew F. Holland, *Eisenhower Between the Wars: The Making of a General and Statesman* (Westport, CT: Greenwood, 2001), 188.

[7] Weintraub, *15 Stars: Eisenhower, MacArthur, Marshall*, xii.

[8] John Wukovits, *Eisenhower: Lessons in Leadership* (New York: Palgrave Macmillan, 2006), 103.

[9] Ibid., 329.

[10] Richard Rhodes, *The Making of the Atomic Bomb: Twenty-Fifth Anniversary Edition* (New York: Simon & Shuster, 2012), 688.

[11] Steven P. Ambrose, *D-Day: June 6, 1944—The Climactic Battle of WWII* (New York: Simon & Shuster, 1994), 61.

[12] Ambrose, *Eisenhower: Soldier and President*, 54.

[13] Charles J. Pellerin, *How NASA Builds Teams: Mission Critical Soft Skills for Scientists, Engineers, and Project Teams* (Hoboken, NJ: Wiley, 2009), 77.

[14] Stephen E. Ambrose, *The Supreme Commander: The War Years of Dwight D. Eisenhower* (New York: Anchor, 1970), 322.

[15] John C. Maxwell, *The 360 Degree Leader: Developing Your Influence from Anywhere in the Organization* (Nashville: Thomas Nelson, 2011), 140.

[16] Ambrose, *D-Day: June 6, 1944*, 171.

[17] Dwight D. Eisenhower, Inaugural Address, Washington, DC, January 20, 1953, in "Quotes," Dwight D. Eisenhower Presidential Library, Museum, and Boyhood Home, Abilene Kansas, http://www.eisenhower.archives.gov/all_about_ike/quotes.html.

[18] Carlo D'Este, *Eisenhower: A Soldier's Life* (New York: Holt, 2002), 527.

Chapter 16

[1] Michael Janofsky, "Thousands Gather at the Capitol to Remember a Hero," *New York Times*, October 31, 2005, http://www.nytimes.com/2005/10/31/politics/31parks.html?_r=0.

[2] Rita Dove, "The Torchbearer—Rosa Parks," *Time*, June 14, 1999, http://content.time.com/time/magazine/article/0,9171,991252,00.html.

[3] Douglas Brinkley, *Rosa Parks: A Life* (New York: Putnam, 2000), 12–13.

[4] Rosa Parks with Gregory J. Reed, *Quiet Strength: The Faith, the Hope, and the Heart of a Woman Who Changed a Nation* (Grand Rapids: Zondervan, 1994), 54.

[5] Ibid., 42.

[6] Rosa Parks with Jim Haskins, *Rosa Parks: My Story* (New York: Puffin, 1992), 11.

[7] Ibid., 22–23.

[8] Brinkley, *Rosa Parks: A Life*, 24.

[9] Ibid., 24–25.

[10] Parks and Reed, *Quiet Strength*, 16.

[11] Parks and Haskins, *Rosa Parks: My Story*, 3–4.

[12] Jeanne Theoharis, *The Rebellious Life of Mrs. Rosa Parks* (Boston: Beacon Press, 2013), Kindle ed.

[13] Brinkley, *Rosa Parks: A Life*, 42–43.

[14] Ibid., 59; Jon Thurber, "James Blake, 89; Driver Had Rosa Parks Arrested," *Los Angeles Times*, March 26, 2002, http://articles.latimes.com/2002/mar/26/local/me-blake26.

[15] Parks and Reed, *Quiet Strength*, 23.

[16] Peter Dreier, "Rosa Parks: Angry, Not Tired," *Huffington Post, Blog*, April 5, 2013, http://www.huffingtonpost.com/peter-dreier/rosa-parks-civil-rights_b_2608964.html.

[17] Ibid.

[18] Martin Luther King Jr., *Birth of a New Age, December 1955–December 1956* "Integrated Bus Suggestions," vol. 3 of *The Papers of Martin Luther King Jr.*, ed. Clayborne Carson, Stewart Burns, Susan Carson, Dana Powell, and Peter Holloran (Berkeley: University of California Press, 1997), http://mlk-kpp01.stanford.edu/kingweb/publications/papers/

vol3/561219.001-Integrated_Bus_Suggestions.htm.

Chapter 17

[1] "Harry Truman the Piano Player," Harry S. Truman Library and Museum, http://www. trumanlibrary.org/kids/piano.htm.

[2] David Gergen, foreword to Warren G. Bennis and Robert J. Thomas, *Geeks and Geezers: How Era, Values, and Defining Moments Shape Leaders* (Boston: Harvard Business School Publishing, 2002), xxiii.

[3] Jonathan Daniels, *The Man of Independence* (Columbia: University of Missouri Press, 1998), 95–97.

[4] David Gergen, foreword to *Geeks and Geezers*, xxiv.

[5] Robert H. Ferrell, *Harry S. Truman: A Life* (Columbia: University of Missouri Press, 1994), 124.

[6] David McCullough, *Truman* (New York: Simon & Schuster, 1992), 436.

[7] Ibid., 430.

[8] David M. Kennedy and Thomas A. Bailey, *The American Spirit: U.S. History as Seen by Comtemporaries* (Boston: Wadsworth, 2010), 2:425.

[9] Alan Axelrod, *Profiles in Audacity: Great Decisions and How They Were Made* (New York: Sterling, 2006), 42.

[10] Ibid., 42–43.

[11] Harry S. Truman, *Mr. Citizen* (New York: Geis Associates, 1960), 263.

Chapter 18

[1] Margaret Thatcher, "The Brighton Bomb," excerpt from *The Downing Street Years* (1993), 379–83, Margaret Thatcher.org, http://www.margaretthatcher.org/speeches/displaydocument.asp?docid=109119.

[2] Paul Owen, "Margaret Thatcher: The Best Anecdotes," *Guardian*, April 9, 2013, http://www.theguardian.com/politics/blog/2013/apr/09/margaret-thatcher-the-best-15-anecdotes.

[3] John Blundell, *Margaret Thatcher: A Portrait of the Iron Lady* (New York: Algora, 2008), 30.

[4] David Runciman, "Rat-a-tat-a-tat-a-tat-a-tat," review of *Margaret Thatcher: The Authorised Biography* by Charles Moore, *London Review of Books*, June 6, 2013, http://www.lrb.co.uk/v35/n11/david-runciman/rat-a-tat-a-tat-a-tat-a-tat.

[5] John Blundell, ed., *Remembering Margaret Thatcher: Commemorations, Tributes and Assessments* (New York: Algora, 2013), 21.

[6] Margaret Thatcher, "Britain Awake," speech at Kensington Town Hall, Chelsea, January 19, 1976, Margaret Thatcher Foundation, http://www.margaretthatcher.org/speeches/displaydocument.asp?docid=102939.

[7] Charles Moore, "The Invincible Mrs. Thatcher," *Vanity Fair*, December 2011, http://www.vanityfair.com/politics/features/2011/12/margaret-thatcher-201112.

[8] Mike's America, "Margaret Thatcher Arrives at 10 Downing Street for the First Time as Prime Minister, May 4, 1979," YouTube.com, May 4, 2009, embedded video transcribed by the authors, http://www.youtube.com/watch?v=A23PQCndPYU.

[9] Gerry Holt and Nathan Williams, "Files Reveal Margaret Thatcher's Frugal Side," BBC

News, December 29, 2011, http://www.bbc.com/news/uk-16319101.

[10] Liz Kulze, "That Time Margaret Thatcher Spanked Christopher Hitchens," TheAtlantic.com, April 8, 2013, http://www.theatlantic.com/sexes/archive/2013/04/that-time-margaret-thatcher-spanked-christopher-hitchens/274779/.

[11] Charles Moore, "The Invincible Mrs. Thatcher," *Vanity Fair*, December 2011, http://www.vanityfair.com/politics/features/2011/12/margaret-thatcher-201112.

[12] Charles Moore, "The Invincible Mrs. Thatcher."

[13] Michael Reagan, *The New Reagan Revolution: How Ronald Reagan's Principles Can Restore America's Greatness Today* (New York: Saint Martin's, 2010), 71; Margaret Thatcher Foundation, "Reagan Library," http://www.margaretthatcher.org/archive/us-reagan.asp.

[14] Conor Burns "The Mention of Ronald Reagan's Name Brings an Immediate Smile to Lady Thatcher's Face," Centre for Policy Studies, July 4, 2011, http://www.cps.org.uk/blog/q/date/2011/07/04/the-mention-of-ronald-reagan-s-name-brings-an-immediate-smile-to-lady-thatcher-s-face/.

[15] James Baker, "The Margaret Thatcher I Knew: Twenty Personal Insights," *Guardian*, April 8, 2013, http://www.theguardian.com/politics/interactive/2013/apr/08/margaret-thatcher-i-knew.

[16] Sam Jones, "'Gee, Isn't She Marvelous': Politicians Share Thatcher Anecdotes," *Guardian*, April 10, 2013, http://www.theguardian.com/politics/2013/apr/10/politicians-thatcher-anecdotes; Blundell, ed., *Remembering Margaret Thatcher*, 32.

[17] Michael Forsyth, "Margaret Thatcher: She Never Stopped Serving Her Country," *Telegraph*, April 9, 2013, http://www.telegraph.co.uk/news/politics/margaret-thatcher/8523855/Margaret-Thatcher-She-never-stopped-serving-her-country.html.

[18] Bernard Ingham, "The Margaret Thatcher I Knew: Twenty Personal Insights," *Guardian*, April 8, 2013, http://www.theguardian.com/politics/interactive/2013/apr/08/margaret-thatcher-i-knew.

[19] Paddy Ashdown, "The Margaret Thatcher I Knew: Twenty Personal Insights," *Guardian*, April 8, 2013, http://www.theguardian.com/politics/interactive/2013/apr/08/margaret-thatcher-i-knew.

[20] Kenneth Clarke, "The Margaret Thatcher I Knew: Twenty Personal Insights," *Guardian*, April 8, 2013, http://www.theguardian.com/politics/interactive/2013/apr/08/margaret-thatcher-i-knew.

[21] Geoffrey Howe, "The Margaret Thatcher I Knew: Twenty Personal Insights," *Guardian*, April 8, 2013, http://www.theguardian.com/politics/interactive/2013/apr/08/margaret-thatcher-i-knew.

[22] Mikhail Gorbachev, "The Margaret Thatcher I Knew: Twenty Personal Insights," *Guardian*, April 8, 2013, http://www.theguardian.com/politics/interactive/2013/apr/08/margaret-thatcher-i-knew.

[23] WGBH, "Oral History: Margaret Thatcher," Frontline: The Gulf War, PBS.org, http://www.pbs.org/wgbh/pages/frontline/gulf/oral/thatcher/1.html.

[24] Lech Wałęsa, "The Margaret Thatcher I Knew: Twenty Personal Insights," *Guardian*, April 8, 2013, http://www.theguardian.com/politics/interactive/2013/apr/08/margaret-thatcher-i-knew.

[25] Clive James, "Thatcher Takes Command," originally published in the *Observer*, February 9, 1975, CliveJames.com, http://www.clivejames.com/books/visions/thatcher.

[26] Moore, "The Invincible Mrs. Thatcher."

Chapter 19

[1] M. K. Gandhi, *An Autobiography: The Story of My Experiments with Truth* (Boston: Beacon Press, 1993), 7.

[2] Ibid.

[3] Ibid., 8.

[4] George Orwell, *George Orwell: In Front of Your Nose, 1946–1950* (Jaffrey, NH: Nonpareil, 2000), 465.

[5] Gandhi, *An Autobiography*, 94.

[6] Ibid., 111.

[7] Ibid., 113–14.

[8] Ibid., 192–93.

[9] Emma Tarlo, *Clothing Matters: Dress and Identity in India* (Chicago: University of Chicago Press, 1996), 76–78.

[10] "Gandhi Invents Spinning Wheel," *Popular Science Monthly*, December 1931, 60.

[11] Stanley A. Wolpert, *Gandhi's Passion: The Life and Legacy of Mahatma Gandhi* (New York: Oxford University Press, 2002), 7–8.

[12] Orwell, *George Orwell: In Front of Your Nose*, 463.

Chapter 20

[1] Joyce Purnick, "Mother Teresa Gains Release of Three Prisoners," *New York Times*, December 25, 1985, http://www.nytimes.com/1985/12/25/nyregion/mother-teresa-gains-release-of-3-prisoners.html; Associated Press, "Mother Teresa Wants State to Release AIDS Prisoners," *New York Times*, January 3, 1986, http://www.nytimes.com/1986/01/03/nyregion/mother-teresa-wants-state-to-release-aids-prisoners.html; King Duncan, *The Amazing Law of Influence* (New York: Pelican, 2001), 193; Robert Palestini, *Feminist Theory and Educational Leadership: Much Ado about Something!* (Lanham, MD: Rowman & Littlefield, 2013), 119; Dale Carnegie, Stuart R. Levine, and Ross Klavan, *The Leader in You*, book excerpt, SimonAndSchuster.com, http://books.simonandschuster.com/Leader-in-You/Stuart-R-Levine/9780743549240/excerpt. Note: Some sources for this anecdote indicated that three prisoners were released; others said four prisoners. The *New York Times* listed three prisoners by name, so the authors believe three to be the accurate number.

[2] Mother Teresa, with Brian Kolodiejchuk, ed., *Mother Teresa: Come Be My Light* (New York: Doubleday Religion, 2007), 44–46.

[3] Joseph Langford, *Mother Teresa's Secret Fire: The Encounter That Changed Her Life, and How It Can Transform Your Own* (Huntington, IN: Our Sunday Visitor, 2008), 44.

[4] Palestini, *Feminist Theory and Educational Leadership*, 117.

[5] Duncan, *The Amazing Law of Influence*, 193.

[6] Kathryn Spink, *Mother Teresa: A Complete Authorized Biography* (New York: HarperCollins, 1997), 37.

[7] Palestini, *Feminist Theory and Educational Leadership*, 118–19.

[8] Spink, *Mother Teresa*, 55.

[9] Dwight Longenecker, "The Day I Met Mother Teresa," Patheos.com, September 5, 2007, http://www.patheos.com/blogs/standingonmyhead/2007/09/the-day-i-met-mother-teresa.html.

[10] Associated Press, "Hospital Is Visited by Mother Teresa," *New York Times*, August 15, 1982, http://www.nytimes.com/1982/08/15/world/hospital-is-visited-by-mother-teresa.html; Ann Rodgers, "Mother Teresa Revered for Putting Others First," *Pittsburgh Post-Gazette*, October 7, 2007, http://www.post-gazette.com/life/lifestyle/2007/10/07/Mother-Teresa-revered-for-putting-others-first/stories/200710070144; *Mother Teresa*, a documentary film by Petrie Productions, 1986, created by Ann Petrie, produced and directed by Jeanette Petrie and Ann Petrie, narration by Richard Attenborough.

[11] Barbara Smoker, "Mother Teresa—Sacred Cow," *Freethinker*, February 1980, https://web.archive.org/web/20140905221240/http://freethinker.co.uk/2014/07/18/mother-teresa-sacred-cow/.

[12] Mother Teresa, "Mother Teresa's Nobel Peace Prize Acceptance Speech," Oslo, Norway, Catholic Education Resource Center, December 11, 1979, http://www.catholiceducation.org/en/religion-and-philosophy/social-justice/mother-teresas-nobel-peace-prize-acceptance-speech.html.

[13] Christopher Hitchens, *The Missionary Position: Mother Teresa in Theory and Practice* (New York: Verso, 1995), 64–71.

[14] Mother Teresa, with Kolodiejchuk, ed., *Mother Teresa*, 187.

[15] Mark 9:24.

[16] Mother Teresa, with Kolodiejchuk, ed., *Mother Teresa*, 187–88.

[17] Matthew 27:46; Mark 15:34.

Chapter 21

[1] Alexander K. McClure, *Lincoln's Yarns and Stories* (Chicago & Philadelphia: John C. Winston Co., 1901), Project Gutenberg Edition, http://www.gutenberg.org/files/2517/2517-h/2517-h.htm (some dialogue paraphrased for the sake of clarity).

[2] Abraham Lincoln, "Short Autobiography—1859," The History Place, http://www.historyplace.com/lincoln/autobi-1.htm.

[3] McClure, *Lincoln's Yarns and Stories*.

[4] Douglas L. Wilson, and Rodney O. Davis, eds., "Joseph C. Richardson (William H. Herndon Interview)" in *Herndon's Informants: Letters, Interviews, and Statements about Abraham Lincoln* (Urbana: University of Illinois Press, 1998), http://lincoln.lib.niu.edu/cgi-bin/philologic/getobject.pl?c.6753:1.lincoln.

[5] McClure, *Lincoln's Yarns and Stories*.

[6] Lincoln, "Short Autobiography—1859."

[7] Clifton Fadiman and Andre Bernard, *Bartlett's Book of Anecdotes* (New York: Little, Brown and Co., 2000), 344.

[8] McClure, *Lincoln's Yarns and Stories*.

[9] Ibid.

[10] Ibid.

[11] Lincoln, "Short Autobiography—1859."

[12] Mario M. Cuomo and Harold Holzer, *Lincoln on Democracy* (New York: Fordham University Press,), 105–6.

[13] Fadiman and Bernard, *Bartlett's Book of Anecdotes*, 345.

[14] Ibid., 347.

[15] McClure, *Lincoln's Yarns and Stories.*

[16] Ibid.

[17] Ibid.

[18] Fadiman and Bernard, *Bartlett's Book of Anecdotes*, 349; McClure, *Lincoln's Yarns and Stories.*

[19] Nancy F. Koehn, "Lincoln's School of Management," *New York Times*, January 26, 2013, http://www.nytimes.com/2013/01/27/business/abraham-lincoln-as-management-guru.html?pagewanted=all&_r=0.

Acknowledgments

With deep appreciation I acknowledge the support and guidance of the following people who helped make this book possible:

Special thanks to Alex Martins, Dan DeVos, and Rich DeVos of the Orlando Magic.

Hats off to my associate Andrew Herdliska; my proofreader, Ken Hussar; and my ace typist, Fran Thomas.

Thanks also to my writing partner, Jim Denney, for his superb contributions in shaping this manuscript.

Hearty thanks also go to Annie Tipton, Paul Muckley, David G. Applin, and the entire Barbour team for their vision and insight, and for believing that we had something important to say in these pages.

And, finally, special thanks and appreciation go to my wife, Ruth, and to my wonderful and supportive family. They are truly the backbone of my life.

Contact

You can contact Pat Williams at:
Pat Williams
c/o Orlando Magic
8701 Maitland Summit Boulevard
Orlando, FL 32810
phone: 407-916-2404
pwilliams@orlandomagic.com

Visit Pat Williams's website at:
www.PatWilliamsMotivate.com

If you would like to set up a speaking engagement for Pat Williams, please call or write his assistant, Andrew Herdliska, at the above address, or call him at 407-916-2401. Requests can also be faxed to 407-916-2986 or e-mailed to aherdliska@orlandomagic.com.

We would love to hear from you. Please send your comments about this book to Pat Williams at the above address. Thank you.

Also available from
Pat Williams

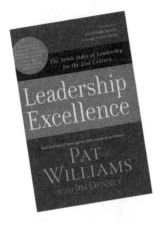

978-1-61626-727-8 (HB)
978-1-62029-783-4 (PB)

978-1-62416-130-8 (Flex)
978-1-63058-655-3 (PB)

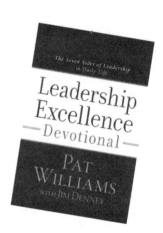

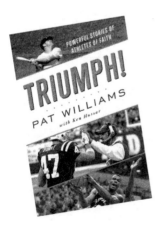

978-1-62836-970-0

Available wherever great books are sold